SAGE was founded in 1965 by Sara Miller McCune to support the dissemination of usable knowledge by publishing innovative and high-quality research and teaching content. Today, we publish over 900 journals, including those of more than 400 learned societies, more than 800 new books per year, and a growing range of library products including archives, data, case studies, reports, and video. SAGE remains majority-owned by our founder, and after Sara's lifetime will become owned by a charitable trust that secures our continued independence.

Los Angeles | London | New Delhi | Singapore | Washington DC | Melbourne

CYBER CRIMES
AGAINST WOMEN IN INDIA

CYBER CRIMES
AGAINST WOMEN IN INDIA

DEBARATI HALDER • K. JAISHANKAR

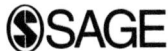

Los Angeles | London | New Delhi
Singapore | Washington DC | Melbourne

First published in 2017 by

SAGE Publications India Pvt Ltd
B1/I-1 Mohan Cooperative Industrial Area
Mathura Road, New Delhi 110 044, India
www.sagepub.in

SAGE Publications Inc
2455 Teller Road
Thousand Oaks, California 91320, USA

SAGE Publications Ltd
1 Oliver's Yard, 55 City Road
London EC1Y 1SP, United Kingdom

SAGE Publications Asia-Pacific Pte Ltd
3 Church Street
#10-04 Samsung Hub
Singapore 049483

Published by Vivek Mehra for SAGE Publications India Pvt. Ltd, typeset in 10/12 pts Minion Pro by Diligent Typesetter India Pvt Ltd, Delhi and printed at Chaman Enterprises, New Delhi.

Library of Congress Cataloging-in-Publication Data

Names: Halder, Debarati, author. | Jaishankar, K., author.
Title: Cyber crimes against women in India / Debarati Halder & K. Jaishankar.
Description: Thousand Oaks, California : SAGE, 2016. | Includes
    bibliographical references and index.
Identifiers: LCCN 2016023055| ISBN 9789385985775 (hardback : alk. paper) |
    ISBN 9789385985768 (epub) | ISBN 9789385985782 (ebook)
Subjects: LCSH: Computer crimes—India. | Women—Crimes against—India. |
    Internet and women—India.
Classification: LCC HV6773.3.I4 H35 2016 | DDC 362.88—dc23 LC record available
at https://lccn.loc.gov/2016023055

ISBN: 978-93-859-8577-5 (HB)

SAGE Team: Supriya Das, Guneet Kaur Gulati, Niharika Sah and Ritu Chopra

Dedicated to the women victims of
cyber crimes in India

Thank you for choosing a SAGE product!
If you have any comment, observation or feedback,
I would like to personally hear from you.
Please write to me at **contactceo@sagepub.in**

Vivek Mehra, Managing Director and CEO, SAGE India.

Bulk Sales

SAGE India offers special discounts
for purchase of books in bulk.
We also make available special imprints
and excerpts from our books on demand.

For orders and enquiries, write to us at

Marketing Department
SAGE Publications India Pvt Ltd
B1/I-1, Mohan Cooperative Industrial Area
Mathura Road, Post Bag 7
New Delhi 110044, India

E-mail us at **marketing@sagepub.in**

Get to know more about SAGE

Be invited to SAGE events, get on our mailing list.
Write today to **marketing@sagepub.in**

This book is also available as an e-book.

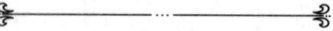

Contents

List of Abbreviations   ix
Foreword   xi
Preface   xiii
Acknowledgements   xvii

1. **Introduction**   1

2. **Freedom of Speech and Expression in the Cyber Space**   20

3. **Trolling and Gender Bullying**   43

4. **Online Grooming**   73

5. **Privacy Infringement**   89

6. **Online Sexual Offences**   115

7. **Right to be Forgotten: Liability of the Service Providers**   155

8. **Procedural Practices for Investigation, Prosecution, Arrest and Detention**   188

9. **Combating of the Offences**   228

Glossary   238
Annexure   241
Index   246
About the Authors   251

List of Abbreviations

BSNL	Bharat Sanchar Nigam Limited
CDA	Communication Decency Act, US
CrPC	Criminal Procedure Code, 1973
DCT	Digital Communication Technology
DMCA	Digital Millennium Copy Right Act, US
EU	European Union
HC	High Court
ICT	Internet Communication Technology
IPC	Indian Penal Code
IT Act	Information Technology Act
LGBT	Lesbian, Gay, Bisexual, Transgender
MMS	Multimedia Messaging Service
MPSNS	Multipurpose Social Networking Sites
No.	Number
POCSO Act	Protection of Children from Sexual Offences Act, 2012
SC	Supreme Court
SIM	Subscriber Identity Module
SMS	Short Message Service
SNWS	Social Networking Sites
UK	United Kingdom
UN	United Nations
USA	United States of America
V	Versus

Foreword

It is a great honour to write a foreword for this remarkable work by Debarati Halder and K. Jaishankar, and I take great pleasure indeed from being given the privilege to introduce this book to the readers. Although I have not met the authors in person, I had online interactions with them and have witnessed their continuous contributions to the field, and their immense energy channelled among other activities in editing and managing the first journal on *Cyber Criminology*. The authors have enlightened us over the past years with regard to various issues relating to cyber crimes. In one of their earlier studies, they have discussed the nature of some trends in internet-related crimes targeting women and children in India and have highlighted the need for policy guidelines regarding such crimes.

Their newest book, *Cyber Crime against Women in India*, which is a much needed and something of a more specialised and consolidated follow-up that in parts draws heavily on previous works, is a little treasure for scholars and policy makers interested in a synthesis of hot issues, not only related to crimes against women and cyber crime but also to the criminology emerging in the context of India. India is one of the fastest growing economies in the world and the biggest developer of information and communication technology (ICT). The country will most definitely receive increased attention in the future by the criminological enterprise. The contribution of Halder and Jaishankar to cyber crime studies is, therefore, extremely valuable and timely. Inadvertently, with their work, Halder and Jaishankar urge the international community of cyber crime studies to start paying more attention to the work that deals with the non-Anglo-American part of the globe and attempt a synthesis—empirical and theoretical—that can be extremely beneficial for the discipline.

The book, which is a multi-faceted contribution written with a simplicity and clarity that is for me a sign of the authors' scholarship, and is impeccably organised, consists of nine chapters including an introduction (Chapter 1). Chapter 2 discusses the freedom of speech and expression on the internet from the Indian perspective and a special reference is made to crimes against women. In Chapter 3, Halder and Jaishankar focus on cyber bullying and trolling targeting women in India, while Chapter 4 deals with online grooming. Chapter 5 looks into infringements of privacy in the cyberspace, while Chapter 6 deals with sexual offences on the Internet and 'fake avatars', 'the creation of obscene profiles of women in social media websites and adult sites [that] create false perception about the victim to the world wide audience' (p. 13). In Chapter 7, the authors focus on the responsibility of the internet and digital communication technology service providers, whereas in Chapter 8, they delve into the procedural practices for investigating and prosecuting internet crimes targeting women. The book ends with Chapter 9, in which several measures for dealing with cyber crimes against women from a legal and criminological point of view are put forward.

Needless to say, this rudimentary presentation of the chapters pays lip service to the richness of the book. Researchers of the cyber realm and the offences that take place in it and/or are facilitated by it will most certainly find this text a goldmine of information and examples (historical and contemporary), and will be delighted by the contents of *Cyber Crime against Women in India*, since a wide variety of issues are lucidly explored. Issues that—despite the often local and national prisms they are looked through—are resonant internationally. I am confident that Halder and Jaishankar's work will become an essential reading in comparative criminology.

Georgios A. Antonopoulos
Professor of Criminology
School of Social Sciences, Business & Law
Teesside University
United Kingdom

Preface

Even though the Constitution of India guarantees equal rights to men and women, women have been made second-grade citizens due to a patriarchal setup of the society. In our earlier research studies, we have found that, due to this peculiar social structure, often men vandalise women's profiles on the internet to destroy their marriage prospects. The present scenario is more alarming: Internet trolls take to social media websites and instant messaging services like WhatsApp to target women activists, journalists, celebrities, academicians, public intellectuals and so on to create 'hate wave' for their own sadistic purposes. Consider the cases of Kavita Krishnan, a noted women's right activist, or Meena Kandasamy, a rebellious feminist writer, or Sagarika Ghose, a noted journalist; all these women irrespective of their age and marital status had been viciously attacked on the Internet. Trolls had used filthy language to describe some of these women's sex appeal and their levels of capability to satisfy men, sexually. The situation is different from the Western societies, especially due to orthodox social norms (Consider S.509 of the Indian Penal Code which penalises any word, gesture, etc. that harms the modesty of women. Apparently the level of 'modesty of women' depends largely on the society, and the lead author in her capacity as a lawyer and managing director for their organisation, Centre for Cyber Victim Counselling, had come across several cases where victims have been blamed by the police officers when they had themselves shared their photographs on the internet which were 'objectionable' according to the policemen themselves). Apparently, some of the cases of Internet trolls still remain unsolved and this has created an encouraging example for many who wish to victimise women on the Internet or through digital telecommunication technologies.

Furthermore, it needs to be understood that traditional physical space crimes such as rape, sexual molestation, blackmailing, stalking and so on have gained new significance due to the development of information communication technology. There are incidences of rape and consequent storing of images of the rape scene in the mobile phone devices, extraction of money by threatening to publish photographs of intimate moments, grooming to subsequently use women for online porn markets, physical sexual exploitation of matured teen girl students by showing them sexually explicit images in mobile phones or in computer devices by the teachers. There are also hundreds of instances of crimes through digital telecommunication systems as well whereby women are repeatedly harassed by offending phone calls, SMSs and MMSs, instant messaging services and so on.

Furthermore, due to data swelling on the internet (even though the majority of such data may have been contributed by the private individuals themselves through social networking sites and various e-commerce sites), privacy in virtual world as well as in real life is literally shrinking. Women are indeed the most affected category in this regard. But is the category of 'victimized women' limited only to netizens? The answer is No. Matured teen girls, university students, housewives, working women, celebrities, writers, activists, transgender women and even tribal women like the Andaman Jarawa women, who have never come across modern telecommunication technology, have all been victimized in various modes in the Indian cyber space. There are also instances of preventing women from using digital communication technology and internet by village *khap panchayats*, and we feel that this must also be brought under the category of crimes against women in the digital era, especially, when women's right to access to the Internet or digital communication is curtailed due to unethical moral policing. Popular perceptions predict that women in India make most vulnerable targets on the Internet and digital communication technology due to their gender and the consumability of images of Indian women as porno materials. Also, the existing social norms play a major role in making women soft targets in the digital space. Considering the fact that their place in the patriarchal social structure of the country makes them more responsible for the good or bad reputation of the family, especially when the reputation of a woman as a 'modest woman of good character' often guarantees the good reputation of the whole family, many harassers target to vandalise women victim's profiles not only to destroy the woman's reputation but also to destroy the reputation of immediate family members, including father, brothers, sisters, husband and so on. But there are few cases of this nature which are actually registered and prosecuted in India. Social norms and orthodox values play a major role here. Women victims and their family members feel reluctant to report the crimes, especially due to fear of damage to their social reputation. Apart from this, there are various factual reasons for such less numbers of prosecutions and these may include, the lack of focused laws, the lack of proper infrastructure in the criminal justice machinery in India and above all, the absence of servers within the jurisdictions of India and clash of laws, especially between Indian laws and laws of countries which host the Internet companies. In India, the rate of cyber crime against women is ascending. The 2013 National Crime Records Bureau report for the very first time has published the numbers of cyber crime cases against women that were reported to the police; 1,203 cases involved obscene posts targeting women. One of the major reasons for such an ascending graph of the issue is the lack of proper understanding of the subject by the victims, the common people as well as the criminal justice machinery. This is evident from the pilot survey conducted by our Centre for Cyber Victim Counselling titled 'Use and Misuse of Internet by Semi-Urban and Rural Youth in India: A Baseline Survey Report' (2013), where it was shown that the understanding of privacy norms on the internet, understanding about conveying harassing communication, the lack of understanding of policy guidelines about photography in public places and the violation of privacy in physical spaces by sharing images of individuals captured in an unauthorised manner or without permission and so on are extremely low among the youth in semi-urban and rural places. It needs to be understood that India does not have any uniform law to regulate Internet or digital crimes targeting women. As such, there is always an imbalanced ratio of the growth rate of crimes and the conviction rate of criminals. As long as there is no uniform law, the police, prosecutors and the courts have to look into the existing laws which are scattered in traditional criminal laws such as Indian Penal Code (IPC), the Evidence Act or the recently developed laws such as the Information Technology (IT) Act and so on for providing justice to the victims. Furthermore, it has been noted by many researchers, court cases and police reports that many websites have their servers outside India and harassers take huge advantage of this. Even though the IT Act (2000, amended in 2008) extends its jurisdiction beyond the physical boundaries of India in cases where victimisation relates to any Indian citizen, the State of India or where the perpetrator is an Indian. There are hundreds of cases, especially involving crimes against women, where the harassers are never nabbed due to extra jurisdictional problems. Added with this, the anonymous nature of the Internet profiles also provides huge advantage to the harassers and stalkers at large.

Internet and digital communication technology have penetrated in urban and rural India, but the operation of cyber crime cells in police stations in many cities and urban areas have been very discouraging. Many non-metro cities, semi-urban and rural areas have no cyber crime cells, lack of efficient police force to deal with the online harassment of women and basic infrastructure to deal with Internet and digital crimes. The two later facts have made the whole criminal justice machinery including the police extremely reluctant to deal with cases of cyber crimes against women. It needs to be remembered that we don't have any uniform data privacy law like the European Union laws, or Canada; we neither have any consolidated perception of cyber civil rights as has been proposed by Professor Daniel Citron in the United States, especially for women who have been victimized by Internet and digital crimes and who may have suffered loss of job or social reputation due to this. Only a few provisions from traditional criminal laws and the IT Act as well as some other gender-related laws are now being used to deal with cyber crimes targeting women in India.

What is more disturbing is the reluctance of victims to report the crimes to the police or seek justice from the courts directly. We feel that this is largely because there is a gap of awareness regarding the present trends of cyber crimes against women, correct and focused laws in this regard and unaware police officials, lawyers and general public. This book aims to fill that gap. This book specifically discusses cyber crimes against women in India, various forms of the online crimes including hate speech, trolling and gender bullying, online grooming, infringement of privacy and sexual offences on the Internet. It also presents the preventive measures that the police and the judiciary and also the victims should adopt to combat the offences. Hence, it speaks about the liability of the websites and service providers, especially from the perspective of Right to forget from Indian and international perspectives, existing laws and legal procedures that should be adopted to combat the offences in India and general opinions of the authors regarding how to combat the offences through awareness and adopting social responsibility measures that may suit the Indian socio-legal structure.

Debarati Halder and
K. Jaishankar

Acknowledgements

At the outset, we thank several women in India who had been affected by various sorts of cyber crimes for their help and for permitting us to use their case studies to frame this book and also those who preferred to stay anonymous. This book would not have been possible without them. Next, we thank various police officials from different states in India who made us understand the technicalities of handling the cases and the challenges that the police departments have to face due to various reasons, including the jurisdictional issues. We also wish to thank transgender activist, Ms Kalki Subramaniam for her help in understanding the issues related to transgender women and cyber crimes in India. Further, we also sincerely thank Professors David Wexler, Vesna, Natti Ronel, and Mary Ann Franks for their support in preparing the framework for this book.

The uniqueness of this book lies in the recommendations for coping with the problems of cyber crimes, especially when women may not prefer to lodge complaints with the police or spend on lawyers for private suits. In this regard we wish to thank our friends and Secretaries of District Legal Services Authorities from Tamil Nadu, Kerala and West Bengal who provided us with valuable information regarding how free legal aid services may be made useful for issues relating to crimes against women in India, including cyber crimes.

We also wish to acknowledge the help of various social media websites, including Facebook, for rendering their support and letting us know about the newly developed mechanisms to cope with such problems.

Finally, we wish to thank our family members: D. J. Mriganayani, our daughter who has been the prime support for all our endeavours and Mrs Dipika Haldar, without her support this manuscript would not have been completed within the due date.

Debarati Halder and
K. Jaishankar

1

Introduction

The information and communication technology (ICT) is considered to be one of the greatest gifts of modern day development of technology and sciences. ICT finds its definition from various sources; however, a pertinent definition of ICT can be the following:

ICT (information and communication technology or technologies) is an umbrella term that includes any communication device or application, encompassing: radio, television, cellular phones, computer and network hardware and software, satellite system and so on, as well as the various services and applications associated with them, such as video conferencing and distance learning. (Rahman, 2008, p. 741)

In India, the term ICT finds a comprehensive definition in the 2012 National Policy on Information and Communication Technology in School Education, which defines the term as

all devices, tools, content, resources, forums, and services, digital and those that can be converted into or delivered through digital forms, which can be deployed for realising the goals of teaching learning, enhancing access to and reach of resources, building of capacities, as well as management of the educational system. These will not only include hardware devices connected to computers, and software applications, but also interactive digital content, internet and other satellite communication devices, radio and television services, web-based content repositories, interactive forums, learning management systems, and management information systems. These will also include processes for digitisation, deployment and management of content, development and deployment of platforms and processes for capacity development, and creation of forums for interaction and exchange.[1]

Even though this definition is focussed towards imparting education and training, grossly ICT may involve goals of growth in every aspect of social development.

As it can be understood from the earlier definitions, ICT involves two major types of communication technologies especially when seen from the perspective of modern day interactive communication system: these are internet communication technologies and digital communication technologies. The former may include tools and technologies to communicate, share information and so on via internet platforms including social media websites, commercial or government websites and web portals, blogs, internet and forums. The latter may include tools and technologies to exchange messages or communications, which are encrypted and decrypted in binary digit forms (bits), digital abstraction methodology and analog forms and related technologies, and this may include transaction of communication via email, sms, voice over internet protocol such as Skype, chat and instant messaging services such as WhatsApp. The two terms may seem to overlap because ICT may include digital communication technology as well. However, the hairline difference between the two terms lies in the tools and applications that make internet communication and digital communication technologies possible: The former is essentially through internet platforms, which may need a computer,[2]

---

[1] See National Policy on Information and Communication Technology (ICT) in School Education (2012), prepared by Department of School Education and Literacy, Ministry of Human Resource Development, Government of India. Available at http://mhrd.gov.in/sites/upload_files/mhrd/files/upload_document/revised_policy%20document%20ofICT.pdf (Accessed on 25 December 2014).

[2] According to S.2 (i) of the Information Technology Act, 2000 (amended in 2008), 'computer means any electronic, magnetic, optical, or other high speed data processing device or system which performs logical, arithmetic and memory functions by manipulations of electronic, magnetic or optical impulses and includes all input, output, processing, storage, computer software, or communication facilities which are connected or related to the computer in a computer system or computer network.'

computer networks,[3] computer resources[4] and so on, where servers[5] may be controlled by the internet service providers or intermediaries and may be physically present in the premises of the service provider company (especially in the cases of web-service providers and email-service providers) and clients or subscribers may include individuals or companies irrespective of the nationality of the service provider.

Digital communication technology (minus the internet communication technologies, which may include digital communication technologies) may include simple tools and applications especially for telecommunication, such as mobile phones and wireless telecommunication systems. Such technology or technologies may include services provided by telecommunication service operators who may be government undertakings or public sector companies and who may necessarily need to have license from the Central government for providing services, including basic and value added services, to various cities and telecom circles as per the government policies.[6] Such technologies may provide basic telecommunication services through satellite systems, which need to be approved by proper licensing authorities within the jurisdiction of India. ICT and

[3] S.2 (j) of the Information Technology Act, 2000 (amended in 2008) defines computer networks as 'the interconnection of one or more Computers or Computer systems or Communication device through—(i) the use of satellite, microwave, terrestrial line, wire, wireless or other communication media; and (ii) terminals or a complex consisting of two or more interconnected computers or communication device whether or not the interconnection is continuously maintained.'

[4] S.2 (k) of the Information Technology Act, 2000 (amended in 2008) defines 'Computer Resource' as 'computer, communication device, computer system, computer network, data, computer database or software'.

[5] Technically 'server' has been defined as 'a computer that provides data to other computers. It may serve data to systems on a local area network (LAN) or a wide area network (WAN) over the Internet.' (see http://www.techterms.com/definition/server). There can be many types of servers including web servers, mail server, file server etc. and each may run specific software for the particular purpose. C. Sebartin-Blanc has provided a simple method to understand the technical operation of server when it comes to client–server protocols: the server accepts the service request as proposed by the client, processes the service request and provides the result for the client (Sibertin-Blanc, 1993).

[6] See Annual Report, 2013–14 by Department of Telecommunications, Ministry of Communications & Information Technology, Government of India, New Delhi. Available at http://www.dot.gov.in/sites/default/files/AR%20 2013-14%20English%20%282%29_1.pdf (Accessed on 25 December 2014).

digital communication technology as a whole comprise an interactive cyber space, which has become part and parcel of the lives of Indian youth today.

Unlike the pre-1990s, communication via telecommunication medium became an easy option for one and all in India in the 2000s, with the introduction of cheap communication devices,[7] including mobile phones and affordable 'talking schemes' introduced by the telecommunication service providers such as Airtel, BSNL and so on. This made it easy for the common people to get connected through digital telecommunication technology, have access to internet (due to huge penetration of internet companies such as Yahoo, Google etc. in the Indian market for Indian consumers and also due to progressive government policies which included internet services as parts of telecommunication services) and availability of computers including desktop and laptop with connection to internet either at home or cyber cafes or workplace. Tablets, smart phones equipped with mobile operating systems such as android also made communication easy for students, employed and unemployed youth from all levels of economic background who have minimum level of computer knowledge and access to ICT.

Mobile phone and internet accessibility have spread all over the country and communication through ICT and digital communication technology has penetrated urban, semi urban and under-developed rural areas as well. The positive result has been extremely impressive: India now has 933.02 million telephone connections including 904.52 million wireless telephone connections;[8] and the number of broadband connections as of now has reached 60.87 million;[9] in almost all the 29 states and 7 union territories. The State and the UT governments have web-portals to display the administrative information, information about the criminal justice machinery, medical facilities, tourism, history and so on. The Central government has elaborate web-portals for various schemes including providing assistance to women and children, tribal people, people below the poverty line, educational web-portals for benefiting students, universities, schools and so on., There are web-portals about public transport, ticket booking system, grievance cells, civil supplies,

---

[7] S.2 (ha) of the Information Technology Act, 2000 (amended in 2008) defines 'Communication device as '...Cell Phones, Personal Digital Assistance (Sic), or combination of both or any other device used to communicate, send or transmit any text, video, audio, or image.'

[8] See supra @ 6.

[9] See supra @ 6.

citizenship and identity related information; all these have been made accessible by internet communication system including accessing these portals through the e-forms or the emails or even by toll free numbers, which have been possible due to advances in digital communication systems. While banking sectors had already availed the ICT to spread the internet among urban and semi-urban existing as well as possible customers, usage of ICT helped the banking sector to penetrate the rural market as well. Also, the private commercial enterprises have been tremendously benefited by the ICT and digital communication technologies through steep growth of the e-commerce prospective. Consider the steep growth of popularity of 'online mega store' Flipkart especially during the Deepavali festival in 2014 (Vijaykumar, 2014). While such online mega stores have paved the way for easy shopping for men and women in India, it has shown adverse results as well. OLX.com, another online shopping portal, came up in news in 2013 when someone had put up an advertisement for sale of a particular woman for ₹2000 (Gupta, 2013). OLX removed the advertisement within hours of notification, but this is one example as how women are treated as soft targets on the internet by predators.

The developments in the field of ICT have made internet a pool of resources. Consider the recent advertisement of Idea Cellular,[10] which shows a boy in his early twenties who wishes to study science and technology in some reputed university but due to his father's pressure he had to join the family bakery business. He uses 'Idea' network to 'get more idea' to be creative. He searches and researches the internet through and with the help of Idea internet and builds up a talking drone to help his father in product delivery. This advertisement is a reflection of the present day situation where people of all age groups take to the internet to look for innovative ideas, academic references and social bonding. Information communication technology was mainly designed for national defence security in its earlier days. Since ICT became commonly available for one and all, internet and digital telecommunication services started being used for communication, content and knowledge sharing. However, progress in science, especially information communication technology, has adverse effect as well.

Technology and human usage of technology may not always be for the positive development of the society. The foremost examples of misuse of

---

[10] See Idea Cellular (according to the company's website) is a 'pan India integrated GSM operator offering 2G and 3G services and has its own NLD and ILD operations and ISP license'. Available at http://www.ideacellular.com/aboutus/aboutidea

ICT are the various terrorist attacks and security disruptive plans plotted on the internet and executed via internet and digital telecommunication technologies and systems. Consider the 9/11 attacks in the US or 26/11 attacks in India by terrorist outfits where internet and digital communication technologies were used to identify the hotspots and execute the attacks. Money laundering, monetary scams and phishing attacks constitute the other category of crimes that resulted due to negative growth of ICT. Both of these, i.e., terrorist activities and monetary crimes, were considered as serious crimes in the internet era, which have potentials to clog the growth of the human race as a whole. The European Union Convention on Cybercrime, 2001 in Budapest, which can be said to be the first international convention to categorise issues related to cyber crime, took note of it and categorised these as criminal activities. These two criminal activities in the cyber space (which are also done in the physical space with the aid of the cyber space) are also recognised as crimes against the government and crimes against corporate. The EU convention recognised one more type of content-related internet activity that is harmful to individuals; paedophilic activities carried on through internet and digital communication technology like SMSs, MMSs, web based messaging services etc.; this is commonly termed as child pornography.[11] Based on this convention, many countries including India developed their own laws and policy guidelines to deal with internet and telecommunications and certain categories of crimes. With the last category of criminalisation, many researches evolved on victimisation of children on the internet globally as well as in India. However, there is still a lacuna in researches and laws regarding online victimisation of women and female children.

Background

Until 2011, there was no dedicated book or full length research on the issue of cyber crimes against women. In 2011, we had published a book titled *Cyber Crime and the Victimization of Women: Laws, Rights, and*

---

[11] See EU Convention on Cybercrime, available at http://conventions.coe.int/Treaty/en/Treaties/Html/185.htm & Additional Protocol to the Convention on Cybercrime, concerning the criminalisation of acts of a racist and xenophobic nature committed through computer systems, Strasbourg, 28 January 2003. Available at http://conventions.coe.int/Treaty/en/Treaties/Html/189.htm

Regulations in which we had elaborately discussed several typologies, motives and possible hubs of cyber crimes against women. In this book, laws towards prevention of cyber crimes against women in five countries including India were discussed. The book provided the first-ever definition of cyber crime against women, which is as follows: Cyber crimes are 'Crimes targeted against women with a motive to intentionally harm the victim, using modern telecommunication networks such as the internet (chat rooms, emails, notice boards and groups) and mobile phones (SMS/MMS)' (p. 15). However, the issue of internet crimes against women was gaining academic attention in the US through scholarly articles such as Citron's works 'Cyber Civil Rights' (2009a), and 'Law's Expressive Value in Combating Cyber Gender Harassment' (2009b), Bartow's 'Internet Defamation as Profit Center: The Monetization of Online Harassment' (2009), Kim's 'Website Proprietorship and Cyber Harassment' and so on. The recent book by Danielle Citron titled *Hate Crimes in Cyber Space* (2014) also speaks about internet crimes targeting women. However, even though these works have highlighted various issues of internet crimes targeting women, there is no book specifically discussing internet crimes and digital telecommunication crimes targeting women in India and laws related to this.

In our earlier researches, we had discussed about present trends on the internet crimes targeting women in India (Halder & Jaishankar, 2011a). We had also highlighted on the specific laws, legal lacuna and need for policy guidelines in regard to internet crimes targeting women and children (Halder, 2013; Halder & Jaishankar, 2009, 2011b, 2013, 2014a, 2014b). But we feel that there should be a more consolidated and voluminous work concentrating on the issue of internet and digital telecommunication crimes targeting women and children in India. By the term 'children' we intend to limit the scope of the book to only female children. Given the fact that such crime trends are growing in India and ICT is being used to victimise women in real life as well, and also that law is never static in this regard, we decided to write this book focussing on the issues from Indian perspective. It must also be understood that even though India is considered as one of the fastest growing market for information and communication technology as well as one of the biggest developer of information technologies, the social structure of the country is not the same as the West.

Even though the Constitution of India guarantees equal rights to men and women, women have been made second grade citizens due to the patriarchal setup of the society. In our earlier researches we have shown that due to this peculiar sociological structure, often many men take on vandalising women's profiles on the internet to destroy future marriage prospects of young women. The present scenario is more alarming: internet trolls take to social media websites and instant messaging services like WhatsApp to target women activists, journalists, celebrities, academicians and so on to create 'hate wave' for their own sadistic purposes. Consider the cases of Kavita Krishnan, a noted women's right activist, or Sagarika Ghosh, a noted journalist; all these women have been viciously attacked on the internet. Trolls have used filthy language to describe some of these women's sex appeal and their levels of capability to sexually satisfy men. The situation is different from the Western societies especially due to orthodox social norms and laws which support or defy such social norms.[12] Apparently most of such cases of internet trolls still remain unsolved and this has created an encouraging example for many who wish to victimise women on the internet or through digital telecommunication technologies.

Further, it needs to be understood that traditional physical space crimes such as rape, molestation, blackmailing and stalking have gained new significance due to the development of information and communication technology. There are incidences of rape and consequent storing of images of the rape scenes in the mobile phone devices, extraction of money by threatening to publish photographs of intimate moments, grooming to subsequently use the woman for online porn markets, physical sexual exploitation of matured teen girl students by showing them sexually explicit images in the mobile phone or in the computer devices by the teachers. There are also hundreds of instances of crimes through digital telecommunication systems whereby women are repeatedly harassed by offending phone calls, SMSs and MMSs and instant messaging services. Matured teen girls, university students, housewives, working women, celebrities, writers, activists, transgender women and even tribal women such as the Andaman Jarawas (Halder & Jaishankar, 2014a), who have never come across modern telecommunication

---

[12] Consider S.509 of the Indian Penal Code, which penalises any word, gesture etc. that harms the modesty of women. Apparently the level of 'modesty of women' depends largely on the society and the lead author in her capacity as a lawyer and managing director for the organisation Centre for Cyber Victim Counselling, had come across several cases where victims have been blamed by the police officers when they had themselves shared their photographs on the internet which were regarded 'objectionable' by the policemen themselves.

technology, have all been victimised in various modes in the cyber space in India. There are also instances of preventing women from using digital communication technology and internet by village khap panchayats (Halder, 2012) and we feel this must also be brought under the category of crimes against women in the digital era, especially when women's right to access to internet or digital communication is curtailed due to unethical moral policing.

Popular perceptions predict that women in India make most vulnerable targets on the internet and digital communication technology due to their gender and the consumability of images of Indian women as porno-materials. Further, existing social norms play a major role in making women soft targets in the digital space. Considering the fact that their place in the patriarchal social structure of the country makes them more responsible for the good or bad reputation of the family, especially when reputation of women as a 'modest woman of good character' often guarantees good reputation of the whole family, many harassers target to vandalise women victim's profiles to not only destroy the woman's reputation but also to destroy the reputation of immediate family members, including father, brothers, sisters and husband.

But there are few cases of such nature that are actually registered and prosecuted in India. Social norms and orthodox values play a major role here. Women victims and their family members feel reluctant to report the crimes especially due to fear of damage to social reputation. Added with this, there are various factual reasons for such less numbers of prosecutions, these may include lack of focussed laws, lack of proper infrastructure in the criminal justice machinery in India and above all, absence of servers within the jurisdictions of India and clash of laws especially between Indian laws and laws of countries which host the internet companies. In India, the rate of cyber crime against women is ascending. The 2013 National Crime Records Bureau report for the very first time published the number of cyber crime cases against women that were reported to the police. There were 1,203 cases involving obscene posts targeting women.[13] One of the major reasons for such ascending graph is lack of proper understanding of the subject by the victims, the common people as well as the criminal justice machinery. This is evident from the recent pilot survey conducted by Centre for Cyber Victim Counselling

---

[13] See Table 18.6: Incidence of Cyber Crimes Cases Registered During 2013 (IT Act 2000), National Crime Records, published by National Crime Records Bureau. URL: http://ncrb.nic.in/ (Accessed on 26 December 2014).

(Halder & Jaishankar, 2013), where it was shown that understanding of privacy norms on the internet, understanding about conveying harassing communication, lack of understanding of policy guidelines about photography in public places and violation of privacy in physical spaces by sharing images of individuals captured in unauthorised manner or without permission are extremely low among the youth in semi-urban and rural places (Halder & Jaishankar, 2013).

It needs to be understood that India does not have any uniform law to regulate internet or digital crimes targeting women. In this regard it becomes essential to discuss about cyber jurisprudence in India. In 2000, the Information Technology Act, 2000 (IT Act) was introduced in India to govern cyber-related issues and it came into force on 17th October 2000. However, the scope of this provision was limited to provide legal recognition to electronic commerce, e-filing of electronic records and creation and management of digital signature and amendment of Indian Penal Code, Indian Evidence Act, 1872, Banker's Book Evidence Act, 1891 and the Reserve Bank of India Act, 1934. Apart from this the IT Act had limited provisions for penalising certain types of offences including damage to computer systems, hacking, publication of obscene materials in the digital form and so on. This version of the IT Act had extra jurisdictional scope. Further, it also provided immunity to network service providers from third party liability in cases where offences had been committed without the provider's knowledge. To facilitate smooth performances of this Act, several Rules were also created. However, this version of the IT Act suffered multiple drawbacks including those related to governing cyber crimes against women (Halder & Jaishankar, 2008), cyber terrorism, identity theft related offences, corporate liability towards protection of data and so on. To rectify this, a new amended version of the IT Act was brought in, which was made functional from 2008. The latter (known as Information Technology Act, 2000 (amended in 2008; IT Act, 2008), was able to fill in the lacuna to a certain extent with the amended provisions as well as the newly inserted provisions and also the Rules, introduced in 2011. While this amended version of the IT Act is now being used to effectively implement and govern e-commerce related issues, cyber terrorism and related surveillance issues, issues related to civil damages for failure to protect private data by the corporates, and in certain cases sexually explicit and obscene contents and child porn materials; the Act has severely failed to provide any effective solution either for hate speech[14] or

---

[14] See Chapter 2 for detailed discussion on this.

for cyber crimes against women. After the brutal gang rape of 'Nirbhaya' in late 2012, the parliament did amend the Indian Penal Code to bring in a bunch of new penal provisions for crimes against women: some crucial issues including voyeurism and stalking including cyber stalking. But as such, still now, India does not have any consolidated focussed laws on governing cyber crimes against women. Similarly, the present IT Act also suffers from several drawbacks, which have made the concept of cyber jurisprudence still a half-baked legal philosophy.

As such, there is always an imbalanced ratio of growth rate of the crimes and conviction rate of the criminals. As long as there is no uniform law, the police, prosecutors and the courts have to look into the existing laws which are scattered in traditional criminal laws, such as the Indian Penal Code, the Evidence Act or the recently developed laws, such as the IT Act for providing justice to the victims. Further, it has been noted by many researchers, court cases and police reports that many websites have their servers outside India and harassers take huge advantage of this. Even though the IT Act extends its jurisdiction beyond the physical boundaries of India in cases where the victimisation relates to any Indian citizen, the State of India or where the perpetrator is an Indian, there are hundreds of cases especially involving crimes against women, where the harassers are never nabbed due to extra jurisdictional problems. Added with this, the anonymous nature of internet profiles also provides huge advantage to the harassers and stalkers at large.

Internet and digital communication technology have penetrated in urban and rural India, but the operation of cyber crime cells in the police stations in many cities and urban areas have been very discouraging. Many non-metro cities, semi-urban and rural areas have no cyber crime cells, they lack efficient police force to deal with online harassment of women and basic infrastructure to deal with internet and digital crimes. The two latter facts have made the whole criminal justice machinery including the police extremely reluctant to deal with cases of cyber crimes against women. It needs to be remembered that we do not have any uniform data privacy law like the European Union laws, or as in Canada; we neither have any consolidated perception of cyber civil rights as has been proposed by Danielle Citron in the US, especially for women who have been victimised by internet and digital crimes and who may have suffered loss of job or social reputation due to this. Only a few provisions from traditional criminal laws and the IT Act as well as some other gender-related laws are now being used to deal with cyber crimes targeting women in India. What is more disturbing is the reluctance of victims to report the crimes to the police or seek justice from the courts directly. We feel this is largely because there is a gap of awareness regarding the present trends of cyber crimes against women, correct and focused laws in this regard and unaware police officials, lawyers and general public. This book aims to fill that gap.

With the growth of crimes against women especially on the internet and through digital communication technology, the need for a book for comprehending the issue for the criminal justice officials has become essential. This book not only caters this need, but also would serve as a resource material for students of law, gender studies, criminology, sociology, psychology and information technology; the police officials, lawyers, judges and general public interested in knowing about cyber crime against women and related issues. The objectives of this book are manyfold: To present a holistic picture of cyber crime against women in India, to discuss about the laws that can be used to deal with the problems, including the Indian Penal Code, Criminal Procedure Code and the Indian Evidence Act along with specialised laws such as the Information Technology Act (2000 amended in 2008), Indecent Representation of Women (Prohibition) Act (1986), Protection of Children from Sexual Offences Act (2012), Sexual Harassment of Women at Workplace (Prevention, Prohibition and Redressal) Act (2013) and so on to know whether and how these provisions can be beneficial for the victims of internet and digital communication crimes against women in India, to find out the socio-cultural-criminological reasons for the growth of internet and digital crimes against women and finally to lay down a pathway for solution of the problem.

The book is divided into nine chapters including the introduction. The second chapter discusses about freedom of speech and expression on the internet from Indian perspective with special reference to crimes against women. The current debates about free internet argue that there should be no legal restrictions or minimum regulations in regard to speech on the internet. In India S.66A of the IT Act, 2000 (amended in 2008) has been used to regulate online speech on various occasions. Even though right to free speech as has been guaranteed by Article 19(1)(a) of the Constitution has been restricted on grounds as provided in Article 19(2) of the Constitution, the constitutionality of S.66A of the IT Act has been questioned due to its gross misuse by the police. However, it needs to be understood that such confusions regarding restrictions of freedom of expression and speech on the internet and growing support for free internet have given birth to huge expectations of being anonymous and inaccessible by the law and justice machinery. This in turn has encouraged many perpetrators to victimise their victims, especially women on the internet. Consider the cases of Sagarika Ghosh or Kavita Krishnan; they were humiliated, insulted and threatened by trolls especially because of the anonymous nature of the internet and the freedom to speak whatever they wished to. Also consider the case of Kalki Subramaniam, a transgender activist, actor and founder of Sahodari Foundation, an organisation working for transwomen, who was victimised on the internet, especially on Facebook when her images were posted as one who solicits sex; she was also harassed over mobile phone by men who wanted to build up emotional relationship with her. These women are the faces of hundreds of other women who have been targeted on the internet by perpetrators who feel internet and digital communication technology give them the power to express themselves, which may not be done in the physical world. Simultaneously there is a growing concern regarding second and third wave of feminism on the internet especially in the Indian social milieu. Several women have taken to internet to express their concern regarding women's freedom by posting selfies or images defying Indian orthodox dress code. While this may fall under the rights of expression as has been guaranteed by Article 19(1)(a) of the Constitution, this had been the major cause for their victimisation on the internet as well, as we have noted that many male users of internet may take such images of women as subjects to visual sexual gratification and may misuse such images, profiles and information of women not only on the internet but also in real life. Repeatedly the police as well as cyber crime experts have cautioned women and children to post information and images safeguarding their own safety first. Here arises the conflict between right to speech and expression and right to sexual fantasy. The second chapter deals with such issues in detail.

The third chapter discusses gender bullying and trolling, targeting women in India. Gender bullying again is no more limited in the physical space within the workplace or the institutions. Bullies targeting women have taken to internet and digital communication technology and this may destroy the reputation, job prospects and social life of not only the victim, but also her entire family. Both trolling and gender bullying have remained a much misunderstood subject by the academics and law-enforcement agencies in India. Constant debates about free speech in India and the constitutionality of S.66A of the IT Act have created extremely negative impact on the understanding of needs of 'good speech' on the internet and digital communication technology. What should be done in cases like these? What are the possible solutions? These are discussed in Chapter 3.

The fourth chapter explores online grooming. Researchers have shown that in crimes targeting women and children on the internet, online grooming plays a significant part in trapping the victim. Grooming is the first stage of establishing a vicious nexus towards committing cyber crimes. There are several factors which may motivate the perpetrator to trap and groom his victim; among these, the most important is the feeling of loneliness. In India with growing nuclear families and breaking of joint family systems, people are becoming more and more self-centred. Women may feel extremely lonely at different stages of their lives; for example, an older teenage girl may feel lonely when both the parents are working and she does not have proper communication with any other family members including her grandparents; a young woman may undergo severe stress and loneliness immediately after marriage if she is unemployed or due to post-natal depression, women in their mid-30s may also undergo such deserted feeling when their children find their peer in the schools and husbands spend time in their workplaces. Such women may take to internet to socialise with old friends or strangers (Saha & Srivastava, 2014). Online predators may take such women as their target. But apart from this one factor, there can be several other factors which may motivate grooming for ulterior purposes. Online grooming may also have different stages. In India online grooming is relatively an unknown factor. Chapter 4 will provide a definition of online grooming and discuss the methodology of grooming and the possible results of grooming and would find the legal solutions for this problem from the existing laws.

Chapter 5 addresses infringement of privacy in the cyber space. There can be different patterns of privacy infringement of women and girls in the cyber space, which includes but is not limited to hacking, stalking, voyeurism and so on. While the term hacking' finds no legal definition in the present laws in India, the issue has been addressed by laws under the term 'unauthorised access'. How are women affected by such activities and what are the legal prescriptions for this are dealt with in Chapter 5. Further, after the gruesome rape case of the young paramedic in Delhi in 2012, the government of India decided to amend the Indian Penal Code to include stricter punishment for sexual harassment for women. In this, the Verma Committee which drafted the amendments included provisions for stalking, as well as online stalking (Halder, 2014), and voyeurism for the first time. In many researches worldwide, cyber stalking has been considered as one of the worst types of harassment that can be meted out to women on the internet and through digital communication technology. In India, cyber stalking had not been recognised as an offence earlier. Hence, there was no clear perception of online stalking either with the police and lawyers, or with the general public (Halder & Jaishankar, 2010). Further, in what context voyeurism can become a serious threat to the privacy of women? What are the types of infringement to privacy targeting women and girls? This chapter broadly discusses these issues.

Chapter 6 deals with online sexual offences. We know that pornography and online obscenity are the most discussed topics when speaking about cyber crime against women in India.[15] It has also been seen in various media reports that pornography and obscenity are the most disturbing trends that are taken up by the harassers to victimise women.[16] Pornography and obscenity are the focal point of many legal debates, court rulings and academic debates when it comes to discussion about free speech on the internet, cyber safety for women and security of children on the internet. However, we argue that the concept of sexual offences on the internet is broader. The issue of sexual offences on the internet and digital communication technology may necessarily involve pornography and obscenity, but it needs to be broadly discussed what pornography is, what obscenity is from the Indian perspectives, why these two terms take the centre point in discussions regarding sexual offences on the internet, what are the other issues that are involved in the discussions on sexual offences and what the legal stand is in India regarding sexual offences on internet and digital communication technology. Further, Chapter 6 also deals with sexting. It may be noted that sexting as a behavioural issue among older teenagers has been researched in Western countries such as the US for quite some time. However, in India sexting has not received much attention from academic perspective or legal perspective even though it has been recognised as an alarming issue by a few scholars (Agustina & Gómez-Durán, 2012; Ahern, &

---

[15] This is evident from the 2013 NCRB reports published in Table 18.6: Incidence of Cyber Crimes Cases Registered During 2013 (IT Act 2000), National Crime Records, published by National Crime Records bureau of India. http://ncrb.nic.in/ Accessed on 26 December 2014.

[16] Also, it may be noted that there are many public interest litigations filed in India to ban porn websites, especially Janhit Manch and Ors. versus The Union of India, PIL NO. 155 OF 2009, decided on 3 March 2010 in the High Court of Bombay, whereby the Bombay High court ruled that there cannot be a blanket ban on porn websites.

Mechling, 2013; Döring, 2014; Halder & Jaishankar, 2014b; Jaishankar, 2009) and media reports.[17] Sexting may not be considered as crime if seen from the angle of voluntary contribution to one's own sexual fantasy feelings. But if seen from legal perspectives, especially in the present socio-legal background, sexting may attract several legal punishments. Why is it so? What is sexting? How does it adversely affect matured teens as well as adult women? Whether there are any legal provisions attached to it? Chapter six discusses all these.

Chapter 6 also deals with 'fake avatars' (Halder, 2013) on the internet. One of the most reported crimes on the internet is creation of obscene profiles of women in social media websites and adult sites. Such profiles create false perception about the victim to the worldwide audience. These are called 'fake avatars' (Halder, 2013). There are various types of 'fake avatars' which are created to victimise women and matured teenager girls. Even though there are provisions such as S.67and 67A of the IT Act, which are heavily depended upon when cases involving creation of fake avatars are reported, we need to know what the other laws are that can be and must be used for dealing with such problems. Chapter 6 therefore deals with such questions as why harassers create fake avatars? How does it impact on victims? What are the legal recourses for this problem? Related to sexting and sexual offences, it becomes necessary to discuss revenge pornography. In the US, revenge pornography has attracted many academic as well as legal debates and it is now being considered to be declared as a penal offence. In India, discussions on revenge porn from academic perspective have been very rare (Halder & Jaishankar, 2013). Majority of cases of interpersonal online victimisation of women including older teens in India have involved revenge porn. We still do not have any focussed laws on revenge porn; neither is there a sensitisation among the police officers and lawyers regarding this issue. Chapter 6 will also discuss about revenge porn and the socio-legal issues related to it.

While we need to understand the issues on human behaviour when discussing cyber crime against women, and such discussion may remain meaningless without discussions on legal remedies and legal lacuna, we also need to understand about the responsibility of the internet and

---

[17] The lead author had been interviewed by various news media on sexting. See Madhumitha Srinivasan (2013), Bully in Cyber Space, published in *The Hindu* on 18-10-2013. http://www.thehindu.com/todays-paper/tp-in-school/bully-in-cyber-space/article5245174.ece (Accessed on 29 December 2014).

digital communication technology service providers. It is true that most of the popular social media websites and email service provides are situated in jurisdictions outside India and may not have their servers within the jurisdictions of India. But does it make them free of their liability? Consider the legal debates on 'Right to forget' and its application on the internet companies which makes them liable to erase the past unwanted data about any individual. In India, such applications of Right to forget especially in cases of cyber crimes targeting women are now extremely necessary. But how far such right can be implemented? The Information Technology Rules and the Telecom Regulatory Authority regulations have created India's own guidelines and principles regarding internet service providers and the digital communication service providers. How far are these guidelines functional when it comes to international companies such as Google or Facebook? Are these internet giants less sensitive towards the victimisation of women than the adult entertainment sites? What are the liabilities of the digital communication service providers based in India? How they can be bind by other traditional criminal as well as civil laws in India? Chapter 7 will discuss these.

Chapter 8 looks into the issue of procedural practices for investigating and prosecuting the internet crimes targeting women. Even though for prosecuting cyber crimes, traditional criminal laws including Criminal Procedure Code, Indian Penal Code and Evidence Act must be followed along with rules and regulations from the specialised laws such as the IT Act, when it comes to women and older teenager girls, the laws take a different stance. This chapter broadly discusses these issues along with the lacunas which are debarring the criminal justice machinery from providing complete justice to the victims. It needs to be understood that policing cyber crimes against women in India suffers a great set back due to two main factors: (a) social orthodox mindset of the victims, which discourages victims from reporting or continuing with the case after initial reporting, and (b) some practical problems such as absence of mutual legal assistance treaties for dealing with cyber crimes targeting women and children, problems in accessing the IP address and profile details, message logs and so on especially when the server is situated outside the jurisdiction of India or when the accused is a foreign national. This chapter highlights these particular issues as well.

The book closes with Chapter 9 which serves as the concluding chapter. In this chapter several measures for combating cyber crimes against women and girls both from legal as well as socio-criminological-victimological aspects are proposed.

References

Agustina, J. R., & Gómez-Durán, E. L. (2012). Sexting: Research criteria of a globalized social phenomenon. *Archives of Sexual Behavior, 41*, 1325–1328.

Ahern, N., & Mechling, B. (2013). Sexting: Serious problems for youth. *Journal of Psychosocial Nursing and Mental Health Services, 51*(7), 22–30.

Bartow, A. (2009). Internet Defamation as Profit Center: The Monetization of Online Harassment. *Journal of Law and Gender, 32*, 384–428.

Citron, D. K. (2014). *Hate crimes in cyber space.* Harvard: Harvard University Press.

Citron, D. (2009a). Cyber Civil Rights. Research Paper No 2008-41. Social Science Research Network Electronic paper collection, SSRN, (21st May 2010) from http://ssrn.com/abstract=1271900

———. (2009b). Law's Expressive Value in Combating Cyber Gender Harassment, *Michigan Law Review, 108*, 373.

Döring, N. (2014). Consensual sexting among adolescents: Risk prevention through abstinence education or safer sexting? *Cyberpsychology: Journal of Psychosocial Research on Cyberspace, 8*(1). Available at http://www.cyberpsychology.eu/view.php?cisloclanku=2014031401&article=9 (Accessed on 15 August 2014).

Gupta, J. (2013). Woman on Sale for ₹2,000. [Ad on popular portal] *The Times of India* (published on 30 October 2013). Available at http://timesofindia.indiatimes.com/india/Ad-on-popular-portal-Woman-on-sale-for-Rs-2000/articleshow/24898237.cms (Accessed on 25 December 2014).

Halder, D. (2011). Information Technology Act and cyber terrorism: A critical review. In P. Madhava Soma Sundaram, & S. Umarhathab (Eds.), *Cyber Crime and Digital Disorder* (pp. 75–90). Tirunelveli, India: Publication Division, Manonmaniam Sundaranar University.

———. (2012). 'Gagging the right to digital communication for girls', 3rd December, 2012. Available at http://debaraticyberspace.blogspot.com (Accessed on 26 December 2014).

———. (2013). Examining the scope of Indecent Representation of Women (Prevention) Act, 1986, in the light of cyber victimization of women in India. *National Law School Journal, 11*, 188–218.

Halder, D., & Jaishankar, K. (2008) Cyber crimes against women in India: Problems, perspectives and solutions. *TMC Academy Journal, Singapore, 3*(1), 48–62.

———. (2009). Cyber socializing and victimization of women. *Temida—The Journal on Victimization, Human Rights and Gender, 12*(3), 5–26.

———. (2011a). Cyber gender harassment and secondary victimization: A comparative analysis of US, UK and India. *Victims and Offenders, 6*(4), 386–398.

———. (2011b). *Cyber crime and the victimization of women: Laws, rights, and regulations.* Hershey, PA: IGI Global.

Halder, D., & Jaishankar K. (2013). Revenge porn by teens in the United States and India: A socio-legal analysis. *International Annals of Criminology, 51*(1–2), 85–111.

———. (2014a). Online victimization of Andaman Jarawa tribal women: An analysis of the 'human safari' YouTube Videos (2012) and its effects. *British Journal of Criminology, 54*(4), 673–688.

———. (2014b). Teen sexting: A critical analysis on the criminalization vis-à-vis victimization conundrums. *The Virtual Forum Against Cybercrime (VFAC) Review, 1*(6), 26–43.

Jaishankar, K. (2009). Sexting: A new form of victimless crime. *International Journal of Cyber Criminology, 3*(1), 21–25.

Kim, N. S. (2009). Website Proprietorship and Online Harassment, *UTAH Law Review, 3*, 995–1059. (10 Feb 2011). Available at http://epubs.utah.edu/index.php/ulr/article/view/248/220.

Rahman, H. (2008). Interactive multimedia technologies for distance education in developing countries. In P., Margherita (Ed.), *Encyclopedia of Multimedia Technology and Networking*, Second Edition: Volume 3 Hershey, PA: IGI Global.

Saha, T., & Srivastava, A. (2014). Indian Women at Risk in the Cyber Space: A Conceptual Model of Reasons of Victimization. *International Journal of Cyber Criminology, 8*(1), 57–67.

Sibertin-Blanc, C. (1993). A client-server protocol for the composition of Petri nets, in Application and Theory of Petri Nets 1993: 14th International Conference Chicago, Illinois, USA, 21–25 June, 1993. Proceedings, Springer, pp. 377–396. DOI 10.1007/3-540-56863-8_57 (accessed on 26 December 2014).

Vijaykumar, S. (2014). Flip(ped)kart. *The Hindu* (published on October 7, 2014). Available at http://www.thehindu.com/business/Industry/flippedkart/article6476414.ece?homepage=true (Accessed on 25 December 2014).

2

Freedom of Speech and Expression in the Cyber Space

In the month of June 2000, the name of one Manish Kathuria flashed on almost all news channels, print media as well as on the internet. He was arrested for 'harassing' Ritu Kohli, a woman in her 30s.[1] The case presented a unique situation as both the police and the courts were utterly confused regarding the correct laws that could have been applied in this case. The case deserved attention for three specific reasons: (i) *The medium of harassment*: It included chat sessions in the website by Kathuria in the name of Kohli. It also included circulation of phone number of Kohli by Kathuria, whereby she started getting obscene calls. (ii) *Nature of victimisation*: For the first time in the history of Indian criminal justice machinery there was this case where the victim was not directly contacted by the harasser always, but she was being contacted by others at the instigation of the harasser through phone. Also, her digital identity, including email id and website login id were being used without authorisation. (iii) *The laws*: Even though the IT Act was introduced in the year 2000, in this specific case, no provisions of the said law were used at the time of registering the offence or in the later years. It is so because the IT Act did not recognise Kathuria's acts as offence. The case was however registered under S.509 IPC, which prescribes punishment for using any word, gesture and so on which harms the modesty of women. Often Kohli's case is referred as

[1] See for full details of the case in Staff reporter (2000). First cyber sex crime in Delhi, Published in *The Hindu* on 18-6-2000, Available at http://www.thehindu.com/thehindu/2000/06/18/stories/14182186.htm (Accessed on 12 March 2015).

India's first cyber stalking case.[2] But as it may be seen from the discussions in the later chapters of this book, Kohli's case was not particularly a case of cyber stalking only. It included some more elements: identity theft, creation of fake avatar and so on. In 2004, Ravi Raj, a student of IIT Kharagpur placed an MMS video for sale for ₹125. To quote from the judgement of the Baazee.com case, 'The electronic website baazee.com when visited had the following item description on its site: 'Item 27877408—DPS Girls having fun!!! full video + Baazee points'. The price was ₹125. Under the column 'seller's details' the name indicated was: 'alice elec' and location: 'Kharagpur'. The seller was shown as a member since 21 July 2004. Upon clicking on the item description, the listing read as: DPS Girls having fun!!! Do you want to see that video clip which has rocked the whole DELHI and now has become a hot point of discussion in the entire Nation? YES, Then what are you waiting for!!!! Just order for this product and it will be delivered to you within few hours. This video is of a girl of DPS RK PURAM which has been filmed by his boyfriend in very sexual explicit conditions. Please note: This video clip of around 2:30 Minutes and will be sent to you as an email attachment...' (para 3.3, Avinash Bajaj vs. State, 2008).[3] Within a few days of listing this video clipping, a few persons from different cities had purchased the item before it was notified to the authorities, who subsequently closed the advertisement. On receiving information of this MMS clipping being sold, Delhi police lodged a First Information Report (FIR) and started investigating. Simultaneously, a Delhi-based newspaper also published about the DPS girl's pornographic MMS being sold through the website. The police later arrested Ravi Raj and also Avinash Bajaj especially on S.292 IPC (punishment for sale of obscene books, publications and so on), 294 IPC (punishment for obscene acts and songs to the annoyance of others) and S.67 of the IT Act, 2000 (punishment for publishing obscene materials). Further investigation also found that the clipping was sent to Ravi Raj by one minor boy, who was later suspended from the school. However, there was no news regarding prosecution against this boy (Halder & Jaishankar, 2013, pp. 100–101).

---

[2] See for instance some study materials which are available in websites including http://www.nalsarpro.org/CL/Modules/Module4/CHAPTER_6.pdf.

[3] See Avnish Bajaj vs. State (N.C.T.) of Delhi. 2005 CompLJ364 (Del), 116(2005) DLT427, 2005(79) DRJ576. See for the full judgement of the case. Available at http://indiankanoon.org/doc/309722/ (Accessed on 20 March 2015).

In 2012, BBC journalist Gethin Chamberlin published a sensational news report about the circulation of videos of Andaman Jarawa women who were caught dancing at the instruction of the tourists, tour operators and the police. The videos became viral through social media, especially YouTube. Till today a search in the search engines with key words such as *Andaman jarawa dance, tribal dance, vulgar dance of Andaman* and so on may pull up videos of Andaman Jarawa women, who were caught shaking their bodies (women captured in the video were in their tribal attire and were half naked) on their own tribal songs. The clippings are not longer than five to eight minutes. But the clippings are still floating on the internet with sexist taglines and many posters have their posts in these videos, which have obscene, offensive and vulgar words to degrade the morals of these women (Halder & Jaishankar, 2014).

Kalki Subramaniam, a transgender activist and founder of Sahodari, an organisation working for transgender people, has experienced bullying and harassment by people in her social media profile because she refused to provide her personal phone number to men who wanted to have lewd sex chat with her.[4]

All these incidences have elements of offensive speech. Some of such offensive speeches are recognised by laws in India, some are not. Question is why these incidences attracted general public's as well as researcher's interests as internet crimes against women? Incidences similar to either or all of the four examples discussed here happen to hundreds of women and girls in India almost every day. Women in picnic or tourist spots, public bathing places, trial rooms in textile shops, hotels or even in court washrooms are captured by spy cameras or mobile phone cameras. Such voyeur images are spread across the internet, digital communication technology for sexual gratification of millions. Many of them are intentionally done to damage the reputation of women and these may be various forms of revenge porn (Halder, 2013). Such images irrespective of whether they are revenge porn materials or viral voyeur videos or rape videos, express numerous human emotions. Some are spread to create awareness ignoring the fact that such videos or spreading of the same may cause serious damage to the psychological state of the victim; some are spread to share the sexual pleasure one may get by visualising the pain, fear or in some cases the exposed private body parts of innocent victims; some videos or images are necessarily accompanied by texts to make it more 'enjoy-worthy'.

---

[4] In this regard the lead author interviewed Kalki in 2014 and the later confirmed that it was not once, but regularly she and her other transgender friends receive such harassing messages in their social media profiles.

Women are targeted by trolls, bullies, ex-lovers, ex-husbands, in-laws, agitated relatives, jealous colleagues with insulting, defamatory, derogatory and hate speeches on the internet. Even when women and girls are not connected to the worldwide web, they may be harassed and stalked by unnecessary phone calls and SMSs. This may further create a serious problem whereby women may be completely barred from using any sort of telecommunication services even to speak with their own parents, teachers, or to access any sort of information that may be available through digital communication services.[5] As such, we get to see two types of violation of rights of women and girls through the improper exercise of right to speech and expression on the internet. These are (i) violation of basic human rights including right to equality as has been guaranteed under Article 14 of the Constitution and right to live with dignity as is guaranteed under Article 21 of the Constitution; and (ii) violation of right to be informed. Ironically, while deciding the fate of S.66A in Shreya Singhal vs. Union of India, the Supreme Court emphasised upon right to information through free speech, but simultaneously a big lacuna was completely neglected. This lacuna was about victimisation of women on the internet and through the internet. Victimisation of this sort is carried out through the misuse of right to speech and expression on the internet.[6] Such misuse of rights and expressions on the internet can turn extremely dangerous for women especially because of the nature of the internet as a medium of information, which is different from traditional print media. In Shreya Singhal's case, the additional Solicitor General of India arguing for applying a 'relaxed standard of reasonableness of restriction', pointed out the following distinctive characteristics of the internet:

(1) Internet is without boundaries and has a global reach; it has a greater audience and the harassment, abuse etc. can be viewed by people sitting in different geographic locations.

---

[5] For more information see Halder, D. (2012). 'Gagging the right to digital communication for girls', 3rd December 2012. Available at http://debaraticyberspace.blogspot.com. (Accessed on 2 February 2015).

[6] It may be necessary to point out here that unlike the US First Amendment Guarantee, Article 19 (1)(A) guarantees right to speech and expression (Shreya Singhal vs. Union of India, Writ Petition (Criminal) NO.167 OF 2012. Available at http://supremecourtofindia.nic.in/FileServer/2015-03-24_1427183283.pdf (Accessed on 4 May 2015) and as such both the expressions may be interpreted separately as well as holistically when right to speech may need to be explained.

(2) Literate as well as illiterate people can access internet and the information spread through it since only one click is sufficient to download an objectionable content including text or audio-visual content; similarly, perpetrators need not spend huge amount of money to upload or post any abusive, inflammatory, damaging content. A simple portable smart device like a mobile phone or a laptop or a tablet can be used for this by the perpetrator sitting in any location using any anonymous identity. As such, internet is the better medium when compared to print or television medium to spread rumours and affecting trillions of people within shortest period without any check

(3) Pre-censorship is not possible for internet since each individual uploading or posting a content may become publisher, producer, printer, director and broadcaster.

(4) Internet has the potentiality to morph images, change voices etc. by way of advanced technology which may create serious social disorder;

(5) Internet provides wider opportunity to invade privacy of individuals and violate basic right to life, liberty and dignity as has been guaranteed under Article 21.

(6) On the internet unlike other mediums like newspaper, television etc., it is possible to remain anonymous and sexually harass, outrage the modesty of others or using filthy language especially to create social disorder;

(7) Internet helps the perpetrator to carry on his/her attacks anonymously. Anonymous nature of the perpetrator can be revealed only after thorough investigation, which must be carried out by the criminal justice machinery with the cooperation of the websites concerned in many cases.

(8) Using free speech and expression on the internet or the pattern of using the internet itself depends upon individualistic approach. There is a huge lacuna regarding check and balance and ethical norms in this regard.[7]

These observations are crucial when we discuss the reasons as why we should be considered about crimes against women and girls on the internet.

The courts in their various recent judgements have held that right to information is a crucial right to every citizen. But consider what sorts

---

[7] See pp. 29–31 in Shreya Singhal judgment. Available at http://supremecourtofindia.nic.in/FileServer/2015-03-24_1427183283.pdf (Accessed on 4 May 2015).

of information are imparted when a perpetrator creates a fake avatar (Halder, 2013)[8] of a woman or publishes offensive text messages in the form of bullying or trolling on the internet? Definitely all this information is not essential for many, but may prove dangerous for the victim. On the other hand, consider the second point by the Solicitor General: Because of the widespread information and myths about crimes against women and related social taboo, that many societies consider, is created due to the fault of the victim herself, many khap panchayats and families deny the right to information to the girls and women. Consider again the point mentioned by the Assistant Solicitor General of India in Singhal's case where he said '...internet is solely based upon individualistic approach of each individual without any check, balance or regulatory ethical norms for exercising freedom of speech and expression under Article 19[1] [A].' As it may be seen, right to speech and expression is considered without limit by many when it comes to targeting women on the internet. It is so because hardly anyone is aware as what constitutes offensive speech against women and girls on the internet and how it happens. After S.66A of the IT Act, 2000 (amended in 2008) was declared unconstitutional by the Supreme Court in Shreya Singhal vs. Union of India, we were asked by many stakeholders including journalists, researchers and police officers as how can the offensive speech be regulated on the internet especially when it is targeted against women.[9] Needless to say, there are many regulations to curtail speech for the benefit of the society. But still, there exists a lacuna in understanding why free exercise of right to speech and expression is not always welcome especially in relation to crimes against women and girls on the internet.

---

[8] See detailed discussion on this in Chapter 6.

[9] For example, numerous news reports were published on this very issue where the lead author was interviewed after S.66A was declared unconstitutional. For better understanding see news reports including Taneja, S. (2015). Cyber bullying: Nip it in the bud. Published in *Livemint E-Paper* on 26 May 2015. Available at http://www.livemint.com/Leisure/lpQCFqjgETbXachoWRxysO/Cyber-bullying-Nip-it-in-the-bud.html (Accessed on 2 July 2015); Chaudhuri, P. (2015). Cry, you nasty trolls. Published in *The Telegraph* on 26 April 2015. Available at http://www.telegraphindia.com/1150426/jsp/7days/story_16661.jsp (Accessed on 2 July 2015); Deccan Herald (2015). Cyber bullying rampant in India, legal vacuum persists. Published in *Deccan Herald* on 19 April 2015. Available at http://www.deccanherald.com/content/472554/cyber-bullying-rampant-india-legal.html (Accessed on 2 July 2015).

Offensive Speech and Expressions on the Internet Targeting Women

In India, right to speech and expression is not unlimited. Article 19 (1)(a) guaranteeing right to speech and expression has been expanded over the time by the courts in India within the meaning of the eight limitations that are specified in Article 19(2),[10] and the latest of such judgements is the Shreya Singhal case where the Supreme Court held that a vague law such as S.66A of the IT Act, 2000 (amended in 2008), which did not explain the grounds of restriction of speech, cannot stand in the way of exercising right to speech and expression especially in case of internet speech. As such, the courts specified the criteria by which speech and expression can be illegal. Speech and expression falling under these criteria can be offensive as well. But offensive speech may not always be illegal. One of the recent judgements of the US can be taken as an appropriate example in this regard: In Elonis vs United States,[11] the Supreme Court pronounced its decision in favour of Elonis, who was earlier convicted for posting violent messages on Facebook fantasizing killing of his estranged wife, who had a 'protection order' against Elonis. His posts (which may no more be found in Facebook) ran like these: 'There's one way to love ya, but a thousand way to kill ya'; 'fold up your protective order and put it in your pocket. Is it thick enough to stop a bullet?' He did not stop with his thoughts about harming his wife, he fantasised a school shooting and then targeting a female FBI agent also. As the judgement suggests, when Elonis's boss came to know about it, he was fired and the concerned boss alerted the FBI as well. May be because Elonis was targeting their own departmental staff in his 'fantasy', along with posting violent messages targeting schools, that they started monitoring the posts made by him and subsequently he was indicted under 18 USC S.875(c) (it says 'Whoever transmits in interstate or foreign commerce any communication containing any threat to kidnap any person or any threat to injure the person of another, shall be fined under this title or imprisoned not more than five years, or both'). After the Supreme Court judgement was

---

[10] These are (i) security of the State, (ii) friendly relation with foreign states, (iii) public order, (iv) decency (v) morality, (vi) speech in relation to contempt of court, (vii) defamation, (viii) incitement to an offence.

[11] Elonis vs United States, No. 13–983. Argued December 1, 2014—Decided June 1, 2015. Available at http://www.supremecourt.gov/opinions/14pdf/13-983_7l48.pdf (Accessed on 2 July 2015).

published on the internet, concerned stakeholders published their own thoughts and opinions about the same. While some felt that the judgement re-established the principles of free speech in regard to internet, some expressed concern regarding safety of women especially in domestic abuse cases. Precisely, the court felt that the posts of Elonis were his own thoughts and even though the posts apparently seemed like threat messages to his wife or that the messages exposed his desire for a school shoot or harming a female FBI agent, the government failed to prove that the speaker's (Elonis) 'subjective intent' was to execute the threats in real life. As Chemali and Frank (2015) on the issue pointed out, 'While the court did not go so far as to hold that a true threat turns on what the speaker intended to accomplish, the ruling suggests that the determination of what constitutes threat rests with the speaker and not his audience.[12]

Our attention is attracted to this particular judgement because Elonis was actually targeting women (his wife and the female FBI agent) and children (consider his post regarding school shoot out). In its detailed judgement, it may be seen that the court was convinced by the defence of Elonis whereby he stated that he was actually posting those messages in the style of rap lyrics; that his posts were not direct threats that were to be executed like what happened for many other cold blooded murders or attacks including that of the blogger Abhijit Roy, who was supposedly sent warning messages by radical extremists who finally killed him in Bangladesh.[13] It may be noted that this judgement came after Shreya Singhal's judgement which scrapped down S.66A, which became infamous as a speech curtailing law. In future, we may get to see many other Indian judgements such as Elonis, where courts may decide the illegality of the offensive speech on the basis of the effects of the same on the complainant, on the society at large and also the eight exceptions to Article 19(1)(a). Because like the US, in India also in order to be illegal, offensive speech needs to pass through several tests including contemporary community standard test, especially if it is deemed to be obscene. However, it may be assumed that unless courts give a thorough consideration on the condition of women complainants from Indian perspectives, the results of similar decisions may be devastating.

[12] See Chemali & Franks, Supreme Court may have online abuse easier, published on 3 June 2015. Available at http://time.com/3903908/supreme-court-elonis-free-speech/?xid=tcoshare (Accessed on 3 July 2015).

[13] This paragraph was earlier published in the blog of the lead author. To see the main write up see Halder, D. (2015), 'The Elonis decision: Why would Indian women feel bothered?' 6th June 2015, published in Available at http://debaraticyberspace.blogspot.com (Accessed on 2 July 2015).

It may be pointed out that there is no uniform definition of offensive speech in India. Halder (2015) termed offensive speech as 'bad talk' and explained it in the following way:

> Considering the huge volume of researches on hate speech, indecent speech etc., and the growing trends of online victimisation including cyber bullying, trolling, phishing, vishing, smishing, creation of 'fake avatar', cyber stalking, grooming, infringing privacy by leaking personal information etc., hacking by way of misleading communication etc., it may be seen that online communication or speech plays an important role in all these sorts of victimisation. Such speech may be termed as 'bad talk'. It may be explained through the graphical explanation in Figure 2.1.

> The term 'bad talk' therefore can be defined as talk or speech which generates harassment for the recipient; or which instigates people to get indulged in violent activities like mob violence which may lead to mass killing, religious or racial riots etc.; or which may actually aid terrorism. I call it 'bad talk' because such speech may generate negative emotional stimuli as it may happen when an individual experiences bad touch.[14]

Figure 2.1:
Nature of bad talk

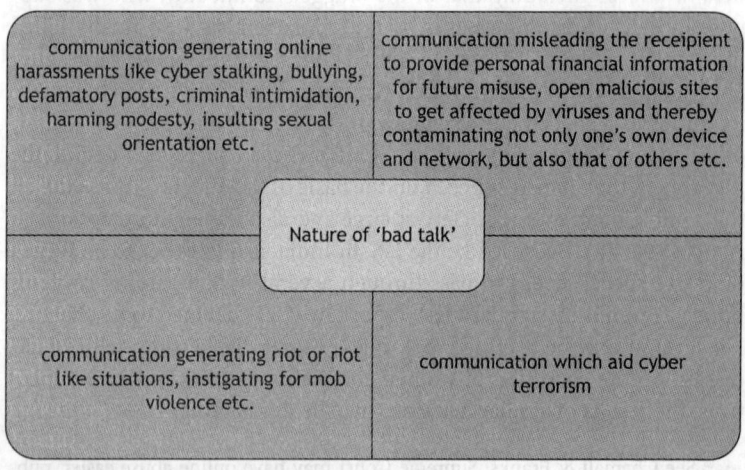

Source: Authors.

[14] Halder, D. (2015). A retrospective analysis of S.66A: Could S.66A of the Information Technology Act be reconsidered for regulating 'bad talk' in the internet? *Indian Student Law Review (ISLR)*, *1*(1), 98–128.

It may need to be mentioned that the term 'bad talk' can be used as synonymous to offensive speech as well, and as such the mentioned definition and characterisation of 'bad talk' can be applicable to define offensive speech as well.

Patterns of Offensive Speech against Women

Under the Indian laws, certain categories of interpersonal offensive speech and expression have been recognised as illegal. These have stemmed from the restricted speech category under Article 19(2) of the Constitution and some of these are gender specific while some are not; these are as follows:

(i)   *Obscene speech:* S.292 of the Indian Penal Code establishes the main guideline for terming a speech as obscene speech and expression if it is lascivious or appeals to the prurient interest or if its effect—or (where it comprises two or more distinct items) the effect of any one of its items—is, if taken as a whole, such as to tend to deprave and corrupt persons, who are likely, having regard to all relevant circumstances, to read, see or hear the matter contained or embodied in it. As such, obscene speech and expression has been recognised as illegal under various regulations including S.67 of the Information Technology Act.[15]

(ii) *Speech and expression which are sexually explicit in nature or sexually harassing in nature:* S.67A of the IT Act, 2000 (amended

---

[15] S.67A of the Information Technology Act, 2000 (amended in 2008) prescribes punishment for publishing or transmitting obscene material in electronic form. It says, 'Whoever publishes or transmits or causes to be published in the electronic form, any material which is lascivious or appeals to the prurient interest or if its effect is such as to tend to deprave and corrupt persons who are likely, having regard to all relevant circumstances, to read, see or hear the matter contained or embodied in it, shall be punished on first conviction with imprisonment of either description for a term which may extend to two three years and with fine which may extend to five lakh rupees and in the event of a second or subsequent conviction with imprisonment of either description for a term which may extend to five years and also with fine which may extend to ten lakh rupees.'

in 2008) regulates sexually explicit acts, speech and expression on the internet.[16] Even though there are few judgements to establish the nature of speech and expression which may fall in this category,[17] such sorts of speech and expression may be different than obscene speech and expression. It may need to be noted that while both the mentioned regulations are gender neutral; there are certain laws which made obscene and sexually explicit speech and offensive speech of sexually harassing nature gender specific. These may include Ss. 354A(1) of Indian Penal Code,[18] and again quite in the same line to this section, S.2(n) of the Sexual Harassment of Women at Workplace (Prevention, Prohibition and Redressal) Act (2013), wherein special sorts of speech and expression are categorised as sexually harassing, which may include making sexually coloured remarks, showing pornography to women, asking for sexual favours and so on,

---

[16] S.67A of the Information Technology Act, 2000 (amended in 2008) prescribes punishment for publishing or transmitting of material containing sexually explicit act, etc. in electronic form. It says, 'Whoever publishes or transmits or causes to be published or transmitted in the electronic form any material which contains sexually explicit act or conduct shall be punished on first conviction with imprisonment of either description for a term which may extend to five years and with fine which may extend to ten lakh rupees and in the event of second or subsequent conviction with imprisonment of either description for a term which may extend to seven years and also with fine which may extend to ten lakh rupees.' The exception: clause says 'This section and section 67 does not extend to any book, pamphlet, paper, writing, drawing, painting, representation or figure in electronic form- (i) the publication of which is proved to be justified as being for the public good on the ground that such book, pamphlet, paper, writing, drawing, painting, representation or figure is in the interest of science, literature, art, or learning or other objects of general concern; or (ii) which is kept or used bona fide for religious purposes.'

[17] See detailed discussions on this in later chapters.

[18] S.354A of the Indian Penal Code speaks about sexual harassment and punishment for the same. Subsection (1) lays down the acts or behaviour that shall constitute the offence of sexual harassment; these are: (i) physical contact and advances involving unwelcome and explicit sexual overtures, or, (ii) a demand or request for sexual favours, or (iii) making sexually coloured remarks, or (iv) forcibly showing pornography, or (v) any other unwelcome physical, verbal or non-verbal conduct of sexual nature.

s.354C of the Indian Penal Code,[19] which does not specifically indicate any offensive speech or expression, but indicts conduct of voyeurism and circulation, publication or production of the same on the internet or any other media and so on. It must also be noted that S.11 of the Protection of Children from Sexual Offences Act (2012)[20] has also prohibited any speech, expression or conduct targeted to children irrespective of gender, which may be sexual in nature.

(iii) *Speech and expression which are derogatory, demeaning and lowering the modesty*: Such sorts of offensive speech and

---

[19] S.354C of the Indian Penal Code prescribes punishment for voyeurism and states 'Whoever watches a woman engaging in a private act in circumstances where she would usually have the expectation of not being observed either by the perpetrator or by any person at the behest of the perpetrator shall be punished on first conviction with imprisonment of either description which shall not be less than one year, but may extend to three years and with fine, and be punished on a second or subsequent conviction with imprisonment for either description for a term which shall not be less than three years but may extend to seven years and also with fine.' Explanation 1: For the purpose of this section, "private act" includes an act of watching carried out in a place which, in the circumstances, would reasonably be expected to provide privacy and where the victim's genitals, posterior or breasts are exposed or covered only in underwear; or the victim is using a lavatory; or the victim is doing a sexual act that is not of a kind ordinarily done in public. Explanation 2: Where the victim consents to the capture of the images or any act, but not to their dissemination to third persons and where such image or act is disseminated, such dissemination shall be considered an offence under this section.

[20] S.11 of the POCSO Act speaks about sexual harassment and says 'Sexual harassment—A person is said to commit sexual harassment upon a child when such person with sexual intent, (i) utters any word or makes any sound, or makes any gesture or exhibits any object or part of body with the intention that such word or sound shall be heard, or such gesture or object or part of body shall be seen by the child; or (ii) makes a child exhibit his body or any part of his body so as it is seen by such person or any other person; or (iii) shows any object to a child in any form or media for pornographic purposes; or (iv) repeatedly or constantly follows or watches or contacts a child either directly or through electronic, digital or any other means; or (v) threatens to use, in any form of media, a real or fabricated depiction through electronic, film or digital or any other mode, of any part of the body of the child or the involvement of the child in a sexual act; or (vi) entices a child for pornographic purposes or gives gratification therefore. Explanation: Any question which involves 'sexual intent' shall be a question of fact.'

expression along with conduct are criminalised under S.509 IPC,[21] Ss.2 (c),[22] 3[23] and 4 of the Indecent Representation of Women (Prohibition) Act (1986).[24] It may be noted that these regulations are gender specific and are exclusively made to criminalise such sorts of speech and expression when targeted against women.

(iv) *Threatening, harassing and intimidating, misleading speech*: Indian Penal Code criminalises threatening and intimidating

---

[21] S.509 IPC (as amended in Criminal Law Amendment Act, 2013) states, 'Word, gesture or act intended to insult the modesty of a woman—Whoever, intending to insult the modesty of any woman, utters any word, makes any sound or gesture, or exhibits any object, intending that such word or sound shall be heard, or that such gesture or object shall be seen, by such woman, or intrudes upon the privacy of such woman, shall be punished with simple imprisonment for a term which may extend to three years, or with fine, or with both'.

[22] It says 'Indecent representation of women' means the depiction in any, in manner of the figure of a woman, her form or body or any part thereof in such a way as to have effect of being indecent, or derogatory to or denigrating, women, or is likely to deprave, corrupt or injure the public morality or morals.'

[23] It speaks about prohibition of advertisements containing indecent representation of women and says, 'No person shall publish, or cause to be published, or arrange or take part in the publication or exhibition of, any advertisements which contains indecent representation of women in any form'.

[24] It speaks about prohibition of publication or sending by post of books, pamphlets, etc., containing indecent representation of women and says, 'No person shall produce or cause to be produced, sell, let to hire, distribute, circulate or send by post any book, pamphlet, paper, slide, film, writing, drawing, painting, photograph, representation or figure which contains indecent representation of women in any form:
Provided that nothing in this section shall apply to (a) Any book, pamphlet, paper, slide, film, writing, drawing, painting, photograph, representation or figure,- (i) The publication of which is proved to be justified as being for the public good on the ground that such book, pamphlet, paper, slide film, writing, drawing, painting, photograph, representation or figure is in the interest of science, literature, art, or learning or other objects of general concern; or (ii) Which is kept or used bona-fide for religious purposes; (b) Any representation sculptured, engraved, painted or otherwise represented on or in, (i) Any ancient monument within the meaning of the Ancient Monument and Archaeological Sites and Remains Act, 1958 (24 of 1958); or (ii) Any temple, or any car used for the conveyance of idols, or kept or used for any religious purpose; (c) Any film in respect of which the provisions of Part-II of the Cinematograph Act, 1952 will be applicable'.

speech under Ss.503 (criminal intimidation),[25] 506 (punishment for criminal intimidation)[26] and 507 (criminal intimidation by anonymous communication).[27] These being gender neutral penal provisions, S.354D of the Indian Penal Code (stalking and punishment for stalking) criminalises speech and expression against women when such speech, expression and related conduct is carried out for stalking, including internet stalking. It may need to be understood that the scope of harassing and intimidating speech has been extended to cover several conducts including eve teasing as has been specified under several regional laws such as the Tamil Nadu Prohibition of Eve Teasing Act, 1988 etc., and also speech and expression which amount to mental torture under Protection of Women from Domestic Violence Act, 2005.[28] Misleading speech and expression on the

[25] S.503 IPC speaks about criminal intimidation and states 'Whoever threatens another with any injury to his person, reputation or property, or to the person or reputation of any one in whom that person is interested, with intent to cause alarm to that person, or to cause that person to do any act which he is not legally bound to do, or to omit to do any act which that person is legally entitled to do, as the means of avoiding the execution of such threat, commits criminal intimidation. Explanation: A threat to injure the reputation of any deceased person in whom the person threatened is interested, is within this section'.

[26] S.506 IPC says 'Whoever commits, the offence of criminal intimidation shall be punished with imprisonment of either description for a term which may extend to two years, or with fine, or with both.

If threat be to cause death or grievous hurt, etc. and if the threat be to cause death or grievous hurt, or to cause the destruction of any property by fire, or to cause an offence punishable with death or imprisonment for life, or with imprisonment for a term which may extend to seven years, or to impute, unchastity to a woman, shall be punished with imprisonment of either description for a term which may extend to seven years, or with fine, or with both'.

[27] S.507 IPC says 'Whoever commits the offence of criminal intimidation by an anonymous communication, or having taken precaution to conceal the name or abode of the person from whom the threat comes, shall be punished with imprisonment of either description for a term which may extend to two years, in addition to the punishment provided for the offence by the last preceding section'.

[28] See for example S.3 of the Act. S.3 of this Act provides definition of domestic violence. For the purposes of this Act, any act omission or commission or conduct of the respondent shall constitute domestic violence in case it, (a) harms or injures or endangers the health, safety, life, or well-being, whether mental or physical, of

other hand has been criminalised largely under Ss.416 of the Indian Penal Code (cheating by personation)[29] and also s.66D of the IT Act (punishment for cheating by personation by using computer resource).[30] These are gender neutral provisions and mostly used for financial crimes.

(v) *Defamatory speech and expression*: traditionally defamatory speech and expression has been criminalised by S.500 read with S.499 of the Indian Penal Code. The later provides a detailed definition of defamatory speech which is as follows:

> Whoever, by words either spoken or intended to be read, or by signs or by visible representations, makes or publishes any imputation concerning any person intending to harm, or knowing or having reason to believe that such imputation will harm, the reputation of such person, is said, except in the cases hereinafter expected, to defame that person.
>
> Explanation 1—It may amount to defamation to impute anything to a deceased person, if the imputation would harm the reputation

the aggrieved person or tends to do so and includes causing physical abuse, sexual abuse, verbal and emotional abuse and economic abuse; or (b) harasses, harms, injures or endangers the aggrieved person with a view to coerce her or any other person related to her to meet any unlawful demand for any dowry or other property or valuable security; or (c) has the effect of threatening the aggrieved person or any person related to her by any conduct mentioned in clause (a) or clause (b); or (d) otherwise injures or causes harm, whether physical or mental, to the aggrieved person. Explanation I (iii) further states 'verbal and emotional abuse' includes:

(a) insults, ridicule, humiliation, name calling and insults or ridicule especially with regard to not having a child or a male child; and (b) repeated threats to cause physical pain to any person in whom the aggrieved person is interested'.

[29] S.416 IPC states 'A person is said to 'cheat by personation' if he cheats by pretending to be some other person, or by knowingly substituting one person for another, or representing that he or any other person is a person other than he or such other person really is. Explanation: The offence is committed whether the individual personated is a real or imaginary person. Illustration: (a) A cheats by pretending to be a certain rich banker of the same name. A cheats by personation. (b) A cheats by pretending to be B, a person who is deceased. A cheats by personation.

[30] S.66D of the Information Technology Act, 2000 (amended in 2008) says, 'Whoever, by means of any communication device or computer resource cheats by personation, shall be punished with imprisonment of either description for a term which may extend to three years and shall also be liable to fine which may extend to one lakh rupees'.

of that person if living, and is intended to be hurtful to the feelings of his family or other near relatives.

Explanation 2—It may amount to defamation to make an imputation concerning a company or an association or collection of persons as such.

Explanation 3—An imputation in the form of an alternative or expressed ironically, may amount to defamation.

Explanation 4—No imputation is said to harm a person's reputation, unless that imputation directly or indirectly, in the estimation of others, lowers the moral or intellectual character of that person, or lowers the character of that person in respect of his caste or of his calling, or lowers the credit of that person, or causes it to be believed that the body of that person is in a loathsome state, or in a state generally considered as disgraceful.

The scope of this provision has been extended in many instances to cover almost all types of speeches and expressions that are discussed earlier.

Effects of Offensive Speech and Expression on the Internet on Women and Girls

As mentioned previously, we can see some forms of offensive speech which are illegal, the discussion may further show that offensive speech against women may be illegal as per the Indian laws only when such speech and expression falls in the previously discussed categories. In the context of internet, the concept of offensive speech and expression must be construed as inclusive of conducts as well. But we argue that the scope of offensive speech targeted at women is broader than that as has been shown in the above categorisation which includes illegal speech. Saying this, we emphasise upon the fact that while offensive speech largely depends upon receivers/viewer's own perception of feeling offended, it may not always attract speech censoring laws. Halder (2015) in her article on S.66A of the IT Act (2000 amended in 2008), compared such offensive speech with unwanted touch and observed as why such speech and expression may create an uncomfortable feeling with the recipient/viewer; she observed as follows:

Speech is the verbal expression of opinion just like how non-accidental touch may be perceived as an expression of interest.[31] Just like how touch may have positive and negative effects,[32] speech may have negative and positive effects as well. Right to speech and expression has been understood as quite synonymous to right to opine and right to provide as well as receive information.[33] But like all touches are not welcome, all forms of speech are neither welcome. It is on this very understanding that Article 19 of the International Covenant on Civil and Political Rights entrusted special duties and responsibilities while guaranteeing right to hold opinion and freedom of expression. These duties and responsibilities include rights or reputations of others and not hampering national security or breaching public order or exercising freedom of speech and expression which disturbs the established norms of public health and morals.[34] It may be necessary to mention that Article 29 of the Universal Declaration of Human Rights states about similar grounds of restrictions for any rights guaranteed therein. It says in paragraphs (2) and (3):

(2) 'In the exercise of his rights and freedoms, everyone shall be subject only to such limitations as are determined by law solely for the purpose of securing due recognition and respect for the rights and freedoms of others and of meeting the just requirements of morality, public order and the general welfare in a democratic society.

(3) These rights and freedoms may in no case be exercised contrary to the purposes and principles of the United Nations'.[35] The restrictions mentioned in Article 19(2) of the constitution of India are made on these grounds. It may be noted that after internet was made available for expressing personal views, right to speech and expression has received a tremendous level of understanding from the judiciary as well as the legislators from all over the world particularly basing on the grounds mentioned in Article 19 of the International Covenant on Civil and Political Rights.

---

[31] See Fisher.(1976). Hands touching hands: Affective and evaluative effects of an interpersonal touch, *Sociometry*, *39*(4), 416–421 Available at http://www.communicationcache.com/uploads/1/0/8/8/10887248/hands_touching_hands-_affective_and_evaluative_effects_of_an_interpersonal__touch.pdf. (Accessed on 10 April 2015).

[32] See ibid.

[33] See Sakal Papers (P) Ltd. & Ors. v. Union of India, [1962] 3 S.C.R. 842.

[34] See Article 19 of the International Covenant on Civil and Political Rights. Available at //treaties.un.org/doc/Publication/UNTS/Volume%20999/volume-999-I-14668-English.pdf (Accessed on 10 April 2015).

[35] See Article 29 of the Universal Declaration of Human Rights. Available at http://www.un.org/en/documents/udhr/ (Accessed on 10 April 2015).

Right to speech and expression on the internet from the Indian perspectives may be understood in the same meaning as had been interpreted by the Supreme Court as well as various High Court decisions for the fundamental right of speech and expression as has been guaranteed under Article 19(1)(A).[36] Thus, right to speech and expression on the internet extends to expressing one's own opinion through mail, messages or creating written contents by way of blogs, social networking updates creation of audio-visual contents or still images with or without written words and so on. Right to speech and expression on the internet also includes right to reply as had been held in *Manubhai Shah vs. Life Insurance Corp. of India*, [1992].[37] As such right to speech and expression therefore may also include right to reply to criticisms within the limits as has been enshrined in Article 19(2) of the Constitution. However, in India the censoring of right to speech in the cyber space appeared as early as 2000 with the introduction of the IT Act, 2000. One of the prime examples of such prohibited speech is publishing, transmitting or causing for publishing of any information which is obscene.[38]

It may further be noted that in India censoring of speech was already recognised prior to independence. According to S.5 of the Indian Telegraph Act, 1885, the government could exercise prohibitory power for censoring speech by way of interfering with conveying of messages by way of telegraph and taking possession of licensed telegraphs and intercepting the

---

[36] For better understanding see Sakal Papers (P) Ltd. & Ors. v. Union of India, [1962] 3 S.C.R. 842.

Romesh Thappar vs The State of Madras, 1950 AIR 124, 1950 SCR 594, which established that freedom of speech lay at the foundation of democracy; Bennett Coleman & Co. & Ors. v. Union of India & Ors.,[1973] 2 S.C.R. 757 at 829, which spoke about public criticism as the very base of democracy; S. Khushboo v. Kanniamal & Anr., (2010) 5, SCC 600, which spoke about the importance of freedom of speech and expression also implies to tolerance of unpopular views etc.

[37] Manubhai Shah v. Life Insurance Corp. of India, [1992] 3 SCC 637.

[38] S.67 of the erstwhile Information Technology Act, 2000 addressed in the publishing of obscene materials under the title 'Publishing of information which is obscene in electronic form '. It stated that: 'Whoever publishes or transmits or causes to be published in the electronic form, any material which is lascivious or appeals to the prurient interest or if its effect is such as to end to deprave and corrupt persons who are likely, having regard to all relevant circumstances, to read, see or hear the matter contained or embodied in it, shall be punished on first conviction with imprisonment of either description for a term which may extend to five years and with fine which may extend to one lakh rupees and in the event of a second or subsequent conviction with imprisonment of either description for a term which may extend to ten years and also with fine which may extend to two lakh rupees'.

messages. This provision was later amended in 1972. With the introduction of the amended Act in 2008, the scope of this particular provision was bifurcated into four groups, these include transmitting etc. of images of private parts by way of voyeurism (S.66E), publishing, transmitting, creation etc. of obscene materials (S.67), publishing, transmitting etc. of sexually explicit materials (S.67A) and publishing, creation, transmitting etc. of contents depicting children in sexually explicit act (S.67B). All of these may come within the meaning of decency, morality, defamation and public health as has been stated in Article 19(2) of the Constitution. Notably, no provision was framed to include or define other sorts of online speeches, which may fall out of the scope of protected speech, these may include hate speech, speech which mislead receiver to aid in financial crimes or identity theft cases, defamatory speech, extremely racial speech, speech that may instigate riot or aid in cyber terrorism issues, speech that may harm the modesty of women, speech that may insult or cause injury to the reputation of a person, threatening speech etc. Instead of properly defining or separately framing provisions for each of them, S.66A was framed to include all sorts of speeches that may raise several emotional situations which may be brought under the purview of law from time to time depending upon the situation. It was for this very reason that the court in Shreya Singhal's case termed S.66A as vague and unconstitutional.[39]

As can be understood from above, offensive speech can be devastating for women and girls. Let us refer to the definition of bad talk, which was framed by the lead author: When we speak about bad talk or offensive speech against women, we need to understand that such speech can be those speech and expression which generates harassment for the recipient or the viewer, which may create social crimes against women, which may create a negative stimuli in the mind of the recipient and which may have the potential to destroy or damage her reputation in the society. There are several speech and expression including conduct on the internet which may fall under this explanation; these may include gender bullying, trolling, speech and expression indented to infringe privacy of women and girls, stalking and speech and expression falling in the category of grooming and sexual offences. All of these categories of activities would be discussed in this book. However, this list should not be exhaustive, but inclusive. All of these may be offensive speech against women and girls including transgender women because they may generate different

---

[39] Halder, D. (2015). A retrospective analysis of S.66A: Could S.66A of the Information Technology Act be reconsidered for regulating 'bad talk' on the internet? *Indian Student Law Review (ISLR)*, *1*(1), 98–128.

kinds of negative effects in the minds of the women recipients, the viewers as well as the society at large once such speech becomes a publicly viewable content. However, it is unfortunate to note that not all of the offensive speech that are mentioned and that would be discussed in this book are illegal. Unfortunately the role of offensive speech and expression either as a text content or as a conduct may not always be considered worthy to be criminalised. This is because either the reporting authorities including the police are ignorant of the laws as well as technological measures in this regard or they treat such instances as trivial or the victims may feel extremely withdrawn to report it. This makes the issue extremely discriminatory for women.

Franks (2010) justified the types of online harassments that can be categorised as discriminatory in the following words:

It is only when the harassment in question is directed at a historically marginalized group in a way that reinforces their marginalization and undermines their equal participation in the benefits of society that harassment should be considered discrimination. There are, no doubt, some difficult questions about which groups should be considered marginalized, but settled discrimination law has recognized, at the very least, that racial minorities, religious minorities, the disabled, and women are among these groups. This does not mean that every time a woman or an African-American is harassed online it is a case of discrimination. But when, for example, a woman is attacked by name with unwelcome, graphically sexual or violent commentary that invokes and celebrates derogatory and objectifying sexist stereotypes, and results in significant interference with her ability to work, study, or take advantage of the resources and opportunities available to men, then that is discrimination and should be treated as such.... Why is it important to recognize that the harassment of marginalized groups on the basis of their identity as members of these groups is not simply a tort, or in some cases, a crime? Because both tort and criminal law are primarily aimed at individuals who are harmed as individuals, not as members of a group. When a woman is attacked on the basis of being a woman, it sends a message to women as a group: you do not belong here, you do not have the right to be here, you will not be regarded on the basis of your talents and abilities but rather on your sexuality, your appearance, your compliance with traditional gender roles. To interrupt the all-too-familiar process of unjust social segregation—whether it be along gender, racial, or religious lines—our legal response must express the condemnation of discrimination above and beyond any individual harm.

In India, unfortunately, women have been subjected as sexual minority group. So is the case of transgender women. As may be seen in the various chapters in this book, there are many instances where it can be seen that women are singled out to be victimised. Be it bullying or trolling or grooming, women, girls and transgender women are often targeted more than men. The speech and expression involved in it, the subsequent conduct that emanates from such offensive speech is always disturbing, if not illegal in the eyes of existing laws. Incidences of privacy infringement on the internet may always push women to an extremely dangerous position in the society. One single offensive speech about the woman or her private life may not only spoil her entire career as a professional woman, but it may also cause marital problems. We have come across cases where repeated unwanted missed calls by pranksters have made the woman face domestic violence. Instead of supporting her as a victim of cyber stalking, family members may consider her as committing infidelity; she may be prohibited from meeting her children or may also be denied any financial assistance from her husband or father. Consider again cases where fake avatars (Halder, 2013) are floated on the internet to take revenge for an old love affair. The revenge porn travels across jurisdiction, reveals the name and personal information of the victim and may make her as well as her family an outcaste from her own society. Such fake avatars may not affect men as much as it may affect women, because men unlike women would not be sexually objectified. We have also come across cases where flaming words in the form of trolling and gender bullying made the woman victim to attempt to commit suicide because she may have been denied any help by the websites concerned or even the police who considered it as trivial enough to take action against. Rather the victims may be blamed to participate in such victimisation even if they would not have really participated in it directly. Women victims are often discouraged from reporting because the police may ridicule them and make them feel more humiliated. Clearly, many women victims and their families as well, cannot stand dual victimisation because they feel scared, humiliated and insulted.

Men on the other hand may not be as affected as women by such offensive speech and expression on the internet. There are basically two reasons for this: (i) bullying or trolling or intimidating posts or phone calls may lead to defamation or infringement of privacy, but it may not create a social taboo on men as it may create on women in the Indian societies. Men can neither be easily targeted by way of sexual offences as has been discussed in later chapters in this book. It is because in Indian societies, traditionally men cannot be sexually objectified. (ii) Men generally have more financial as well as social independence to fight victimisation including cyber victimisation. Consider the case of *Ambikesh Mahapatra & another vs. State of West Bengal & others*,[40] where Mahapatra could afford to stand up against the arbitrary arrest for creating and publishing cartoon targeting the then Chief Minister Mamata Banerjee through a writ petition. On the contrary, consider the case of Shaheen Dhada, who was arrested for a Facebook post on the Mumbai strike on the occasion of the death of Shiv Sena supremo Bal Saheb Thackeray. She had to withdraw her post, was arrested and humiliated online as well as offline. She could not protest against the humiliation at first. She did not individually file any writ petition, but she got huge support from the public after leading newspapers and TV channels started publishing clippings showing her being arrested. Her face was covered by her dupatta. This was an instant reaction by her to save her own self from being targeted by possible trolls and sexual perpetrators who may vandalise her character on the internet, as well as to save herself from general media glare. Her action of trying to hide her face is no exception. Millions of other Indian women fear the same when they get to see offensive posts or hear about their own victimisation. Her arrest was criticised as an extreme abuse of law by none other than Justice Markendeya Katju, who had been a judge in the Supreme Court earlier. She was fortunate enough to quickly get a limelight for the wrong done to her by the criminal justice machinery. But not many women are as fortunate as her in getting support from their families as well as the public at large. It is because of such reasons that cyber crimes targeting women consisting offensive speech and expression become research worthy.

References

Franks, M. A. (23 February 2010). The banality of cyber discrimination, or, the eternal recurrence of September. *Denver Law Review Online*, 87, 5. Available at SSRN: http://ssrn.com/abstract=1569202. Accessed on 2 May 2015.

Halder, D. (2013). Examining the scope of Indecent Representation of Women (Prevention) Act, 1986, in the light of cyber victimization of women in India. *National Law School Journal*, 11, 188–218.

[40] Ambikesh Mahapatra & others vs. State of West Bengal & others, WP no.33241(W) of 2013. Available at http://indiankanoon.org/doc/38644431 (Accessed on 30 January 2016).

Halder, D., & Jaishankar, K. (June, 2011) *Cyber crime and the victimization of women: Laws, rights, and regulations.* Hershey, PA: IGI Global.

———. (2013). Revenge porn by teens in the United States and India: A socio-legal analysis. *International Annals of Criminology, 51*(1–2), 85–111.

———. (2014). Online victimization of Andaman Jarawa tribal women: An analysis of the 'human safari' YouTube videos (2012) and its effects. *British Journal of Criminology, 54*(4), 673–688.

3

Trolling and Gender Bullying

The two most under-researched issues in the arena of cyber crime against women in India are gender bullying and trolling on the internet. We know that online bullying has attracted much attention of researchers, especially in relation to school children, adolescent children and so on (Hinduja & Patchin, 2015; Jaishankar, 2009; Patchin & Hinduja, 2010). After the suicide of Megan Meier because of bullying by an imper-sonator who happened to be the mother of a girlfriend of Megan, the hard realities of internet including seriousness of cyber bullying and the dangers of playing with identity in the computer-mediated communications were realised by researchers, law makers as well as general internet users. Interestingly, Megan was not bullied by a child of her own age, but by a fictitious 'hot boy' created by an adult woman and who in turn, also encouraged some other child to send offensive messages to Megan through the account of the fictitious character.[1] Nonetheless, the adult bully knew which sorts of messages may hurt a child—such as Megan who already had a history of depression because of her looks,[2] and how to spread the fire among others. Even though suicide due to cyber bullying had been found as a common ultimate risk factor even when both the bully and his/her victim are children, it may be presumed that adults may be more dangerous bullies due to their maturity and exposure to the world as compared with children. Adults can actually cause hate crimes by bullying (Citron, 2014).

[1] As retrieved from Megan's Story. Available at http://www.meganmeierfoundation.org/megans-story.html (Accessed on 14 January 2015).

[2] Ibid.

Consider the case of Cathy Sierra or Anna Mayer, both of whom had been severely bullied on the internet and it grew into a massive hate attack on both of them (Citron, 2014). The primary target of the bullies in both the cases was to defame the two women and create a false impression about them. In India, adult bullying, especially gender bullying on the internet has received minimum highlight till now. But, gender bullying on the internet is becoming an issue of concern. As per the Baseline survey conducted by the Centre for Cyber Victim Counselling in 2010 (Halder & Jaishankar, 2010), it was found that among 60 adult women respondents from all over India, 33.3% had reported that they were bullied on the internet and 10% stated that they were not aware of the issue.

Since 2010, the computer-mediated communication system has developed rapidly if seen from the perspective of growth of social networking sites, mobile communication apps such as WhatsApp. The nature of gender bullying has also changed from simple messaging with annoying or insulting messages to accompanying texts with images including emoticons.[3] Gender bullying has become much easier with use of emoticons or smilies. In the latest survey conducted by the Centre for Cyber Victim Counselling on WhatsApp harassment in India (Halder & Jaishankar, 2015a), it was seen that 10.7% of the total 131 respondents (including 99 women and 32 men) from Kolkata, Delhi and Tirunelveli stated that they had received harassing, bullying messages on WhatsApp and 9.9% stated that they had received harassing emoticons. Gender bullying can happen in any forum, social networking sites, and mobile communication system or through emails. Gender bullying can also happen through simple SMSs as well. It is further interesting to note that gender bullying may also target transgender women in public forums or private chatrooms (Halder & Jaishankar, forthcoming).

Related to the issue of bullying, of late, the issue of trolling in the cyber space has also attracted the attention of researchers. Even though there are similarities between trolling and bullying if seen from the perspective of the method of execution and motive (some aspects only, which would be later discussed), trolling according to us may be more vicious, especially if targeted to women. Trolling also creates hate crimes (Citron, 2014) and can brutally destroy the reputation of women (Citron, 2014; Halder, 2013). Usually feminists, political parties, environmentalists, human

---

[3] Emoticons (emotion + icons) are the meta-communicative non-verbal representation of facial expressions of different moods of emotions of human beings.

rights activists and so on can be the key targets of trolls. Similarly, there are several types of trolls on the internet, including religion-defenders, art critics, critics of social issues, human rights trolls, free-speech defenders and private trolls who create messages for their own entertainment. In India, trolling in the computer-mediated communication has emerged as a new phenomenon which has the ability to create widespread ruckus in the civil society.

Consider the surfacing of trolls each time Justice Markandey Katju, posted comments in his Facebook or Twitter page on sensational issues, including the his post regarding gay relationship and marriage, parts of which read as follows:

> Nowadays there is a lot of talk of gay relationships and gay marriages. To my mind it is all humbug and nonsense. Will a gay relationship or gay marriage serve nature's requirement of continuing the species? No, it is only sex between a man and a woman which will give birth to a child, not sex between a man and a man, or between a woman and a woman.[4]

There were many troll posts on Facebook and Twitter after this comment and some of them expressed their anger publicly when Katju blocked them initially to prevent further insults and slanderous posts targeting him. But nonetheless, women and feminist pages are more susceptible to trolling than men. This is evident from the cases of three eminent women: Kavita Krishnan, an activist, Sagarika Ghosh and Barkha Dutt, noted journalists. All three were trolled for their comments regarding feminism, political situation and present social situation which pull down women respectively. Notably, no concrete order was passed by the courts or action was taken by the police in either of these cases which may create an example for prohibiting trolling which may harm women in the cyber space.

In India, gender bullying and trolling in the computer-mediated communication system targeting women are particularly important because of the orthodox patriarchal social mindset, and susceptibility of women to be attacked in the physical space due to gender bullying or trolling on the internet. We have often seen women being denied entry in the

[4] See *The News Minute* (2014). Justice Katju says LGBT relationships are humbug as that 'kind of sex' doesn't produce kids. Available at http://www.thenewsminute.com/socials/458 (Accessed on 12 January 2015).

so called marriage markets because of 'fake avatars' (Halder, 2013)[5] on Facebook or on the adult entertainment sites. There are instances of ridiculing the victim by her own family members, office colleagues and in-laws due to gender bullying in the computer-mediated communication system as well.[6] However trolling has comparatively less effect on general women users in India, but understanding the devastating nature of trolling and how it has already affected feminist ideologies and some notable women activists, it can be presumed that trolling needs better understanding from the perspective of online victimisation of women in India.

We need to understand that even though there are specific laws for preventing insulting words, gestures and so on targeted to women— as had been specified in S.509 of IPC, or in the workplace as has been specified in the Sexual Harassment of Women at Workplace (Prevention, Prohibition and Redressal) Act, 2013 or to children including matured teens as has been specified in Protection of Children from Sexual Offences Act, 2012—there are no specific legislation to regulate cyber bullying and trolling in India, especially cyber bullying and trolling targeting women. Even though the prohibitory regulations are scattered in different legislations, including the legislations mentioned earlier, in most cases, such legislations coupled with or without S.66A of the IT Act, 2000 (amended in 2008), may not prove fruitful due to various reasons. Resultant, gender bullying and online trolling targeting women may become permanent nuisance in Indian society. This chapter will explore on this vital issue from socio-legal aspects.

In this chapter, we aim to discuss about these two particular issues of gender bullying and trolling. First, we aim to build a profile of gender bullying targeting women and transwomen in India and also highlight the probable reasons for gender bullying and effects of the same on women in India. The issue of gender bullying is further taken forward through discussions on the methods and different virtual hubs. Second, we will

---

[5] Halder (2013) defines fake avatars as

a false representation of the victim which is created by the perpetrator through digital technology with or without the visual images of the victim and which carry verbal information about the victim which may or may not be fully true and it is created and floated on the internet to intentionally malign the character of the victim and to mislead the viewers about the victim's original identity.

[6] This is from the personal experience of the lead author as a cyber victim counsellor.

deal with trolling in the computer-mediated communication system with three case studies of Kavita Krishnan, Sagarika Ghosh and Barkha Dutt. We will try to provide answers to the following questions: Does trolling leave any deep and far reaching impact on women like gender bullying? Should women in India perceive trolling as a dangerous trend in the computer-mediated communication system? Last, we will discuss about existing legislations that can be used as anti-gender bullying and trolling laws in India in the context of online crimes against women.

Profile of Online Gender Bullying Targeting Women and Transwomen in India

Traditional bullying among children in India has existed since time immemorial. Consider the first few encounters of the Pandava and Kaurava children when Kunti comes back from exile with five young Pandavas after the death of her husband Pandu and his second wife Madri bullying incidences involving Duryodhona, the Kaurava prince and Bheema, the second brother of the Pandavas may showcase how new inclusion/s in the family or in schools may make the other children jealous (Jaishankar, 2009). Modern age researchers have seen bullying as an aggressive behavioural pattern (Coloroso, 2003) and negative action (Olweus, 1993), which may contain imbalance of power between the bully and his victim/s, intent to harm, threat to further aggression and terror (Coloroso, 2003). While majority of the researchers have agreed that such behaviour is and should be called 'bullying' when it involves children (when both the victim and the bully are under the age of 18, as well as when either of the victim or the bully is under the age of 18), but they have also argued that when it involves adults, it should be termed differently. For example, it can be called as 'eve teasing' when the bully is a man and his target is a woman, and the behaviour includes hurling sexual comments to the victim, making filthy gestures or trying to touch the victim in public places or institutions (Ramasubramaniam & Oliver, 2003), or verbal or non-verbal harassment or sexual harassment, which has been broadly defined as 'repetitive, unwelcome and inherently coercive acts' (Katz, Hannon & Whitten, 1996, p. 35) and 'where most harassed people are women' (MacKinnon, 1979, p. 193), or in some severe cases, domestic violence, when the harsh remarks hurled to either of the spouse becomes extremely insulting, derogatory and abusive. But we argue that all these mentioned behaviours are various sorts of bullying if the linguistic effect of the term bullying is seen from all the given definitions, and therefore bullying happens to adults as well. Cyber space is no different. On the internet and digital communication technology, women and transwomen are more prone to be bullied. However, cyber bullying has been termed as cyber harassment by many researchers including Citron (2014). According to Citron (2014) 'cyber harassment involves threats of violence, privacy invasions, reputation-harming lies, calls for strangers to physically harm victims, and technological attacks. Victims' in-boxes are inundated with threatening e-mails' (Citron, 2014, p. 4). Now consider some landmark definitions of cyber bullying: according to Parry Aftab,

Cyber bullying is any cyber-communication or publication posted or sent by a minor online, by instant messenger, e-mail, website, diary site, online profile, interactive game, handheld device, cell phone or other interactive device that is intended to frighten, embarrass, harass or otherwise target another minor.[7]

The definition in its later part further states that, 'If there aren't minors on both sides of the communication, it is considered cyber harassment, not cyber bullying.'[8] Shariff and Hoff (2007) stated that, 'Cyber bullying is an insidious and covert variation of verbal and written bullying. It is conveyed by adolescents and teens through electronic media such as cell-phones, websites, web-cams, chat rooms, and email.' According to Hinduja and Patchin (2014), cyber bullying is 'wilful and repeated harm inflicted through the use of computers, cell phones, and other electronic devices'. Willard (2007), however, perceived cyber bullying as a broader term, which has seven different forms including flaming, harassment, denigration, impersonation, outrage and trickery and exclusion and cyber stalking. Almost all the researchers mentioned here have agreed that cyber bullying essentially involves a 'power game' where the bully feels more powerful and attacks the victims who may have low self-esteem mostly because he/she wants to show off his/her superiority, and it differs from traditional bullying due to the medium of communication, that is, internet and digital communication technology (Fegenbush & Olivier, 2009). All these definitions may confirm that cyber bullying

---

[7] Available at http://www9.toysrus.com/assets/uploads/fact_sheets/A_Parents_Guide_to_Cyberbullying.pdf (Accessed on 7 September 2016).
[8] Ibid.

is an underlying term of online harassment if the same (online harassment) is seen from a narrower perspective of hurling insulting, derogatory remarks through digital communication technology for establishing dominance. Cyber bullying therefore happens to adults as well. In that context, the definition of cyber bullying was broadened from an Indian perspective by Jaishankar (2009) as

> abuse/harassment by teasing or insulting victims' body shape, intellect, family back ground, dress sense, mother tongue, place of origin, attitude, race, caste, class, name calling, using modern telecommunication networks such as mobile phones (SMS/MMS) and Internet (chat rooms, emails, notice boards and groups).

Online gender bullying is a feminist perception of cyber bullying targeting adults. On the internet women are targeted by bullies as much as young teenagers are targeted by bullies. Consider the case of 'Anna Mayer', who was initially bullied in the blog posts for defending her friend's blog post about sexual fantasy (Citron, 2014, p. 2). However, the bullying aggravated and it turned out to be a large-scale hate campaign against Mayer (Citron, 2014). From our experiences as counsellor for cyber crime victims and researchers, we have come across wide range of cases from different parts of India where women have been bullied in the group forums, chat sessions, Facebook profiles and pages, emails and mobile apps such as WhatsApp and SMS. Consider the case of this young woman 'Ujala'[9] who had been bullied on WhatsApp. She was doing exceptionally well in her managerial job. In a board meeting when she successfully finished her presentation, she received a filthy message in her office 'group chat' on WhatsApp,[10] describing her with double meaning words

---

[9] Name of the victim has been intentionally changed to provide her privacy and anonymity.

[10] On WhatsApp, one can create a 'group chat' to add people to chat in a closed group. One can create group chat for family, colleagues, friends and so on. The creator of the group chat can him/herself become the admin and can add people from his/her contacts. The admin can make other participants as admin. One participant in such group chats can withdraw him/herself from the group, but cannot join or re-join without the admin adding him/her again. Similarly, a participant can see the messages of a blocked contact in the group chat if the blocked contact is also a participant in the same group and that contact may also receive the messages posted by the participant who may have otherwise blocked the contact. (See https://www.whatsapp.com/faq/en/general/21073373).

in regional languages as well as in English with sexual connotations. She posted a strong reply to the bully and the bully in reply posted further insulting (not sexual) remarks. In her interview with the lead author, she said that she did not take the matter to the superior officers as her other colleagues advised her that this should be considered as normal behaviour of male colleagues who see women as weak competitors, and as an Indian woman, she must accept to adjust with such 'sex jokes' by men and keep quite. She informed the lead author that she eventually left the group.

It needs to be noted that the above category of verbal communication has been termed as 'sexual harassment' in relation to harassment of women in workplace in India as per S.2(n) (iii) and (v) in Sexual Harassment of Women at Workplace (Prevention, Prohibition and Redressal) Act (2013).[11] However, the law does not mention anything about continuous or repeated bullying behaviour, which constitutes such kinds of communicative harassment. It further needs to be remembered that this law does not limit the gender of the perpetrator to men. There is no provision to categorise as who can be the harasser (e.g., men, women, persons from LGBT community). Hence, it can be assumed that women can be bullied by women as well in the workplace and it may also be categorised as sexual harassment if the bullying communication includes any one or all of the characteristics as mentioned in S.2(n). Also, it is not necessary that online gender bullying can take place only in workplace or it may contain only sexual connotation, even though in our experience we have seen that in India working women are mostly attacked in their emails, private chat sessions or official group chats by colleagues or superior officers and such messages do have sexual connotations. Women are picked out for bullying in the social networking sites such as Facebook and Twitter in blog posts, in mobile communication apps and so on, on trivial issues (Halder & Jaishankar, 2011, pp. 26–27) including their

---

[11] S.2(n) of the Sexual Harassment of Women at Workplace (Prevention, Prohibition and Redressal) Act, 2013 states that,

> [S]exual harassment includes any one or more of the following unwelcome acts or behaviour (whether directly or by implication) namely:
> (i)   physical contacts or advances or,
> (ii) a demand or request for sexual favours, or
> (iii) making sexually coloured remarks, or
> (iv) showing pornography, or
> (v)   any other unwelcome physical, verbal or non-verbal conduct of sexual nature.

cooking skills, dressing sense, child rearing, defending single woman status and even their political ideologies.

In some cases, bullying may involve hurling abusive, sexually tinted, derogatory remarks targeted to the victim. In most cases, gender bullying may occur in private sessions such as private chat sessions, private groups or group chats, private exchange of emails, SMSs and so on. Consider this case of another single woman in her early 30s who was bullied by her peer in her Facebook chat session. Let us name her 'Sneha'.[12] In the interview with the lead author she stated that bullying started when she excused herself from supporting the peer due to her prior commitments. She continuously received annoying and insulting bullying messages in her inbox from the enraged bully who falsely charged her for compromising accounts. Prime examples of gender bullying can be the cases of female teachers who are bullied by their male students (children as well as adults). Consider the case of this woman faculty who contacted us as a victim of bullying by her student through private chats. She was ridiculed by the bully who told her that women cannot teach specific subjects and she, as a female faculty, does not possess the intellect to teach male students.[13]

It may also be noted that gender bullying does not necessarily happen between men as the bully and women as the victim. Women may also be the bully targeting other women. Consider the case of Pooja Bedi, a socialite and actress in Mumbai. As the news media reported, Bedi's seventeen-year-old daughter got involved in bullying with another girl of the same age who belonged to a renowned family of the Bollywood film industry. The two girls had a history of bullying relationship and finally the bullying took place in social networking sites. Bedi's daughter allegedly bullied the other girl (as per the media reports), and the mother of the other girl sent irate texts to Bedi's daughter. The two mothers got involved in a verbal duel, defending their daughters as well as themselves, which resulted in a complaint being lodged against Bedi. The news reports stated that Bedi herself also lodged a counter complaint on cyber bullying and harassment against the mother and the daughter.[14] Interestingly, the provisions that were used in this case were S.11 of the POCSO Act—which

---

[12] Name of the victim has been changed to provide her privacy and anonymity.

[13] The victim permitted us to use her case for the purpose of this book and prefers to remain anonymous.

[14] See Sayed, N. (December 19, 2014). Pooja Bedi booked under POCSO Act, Published in *The Times of India*. Available at http://timesofindia.indiatimes.com/entertainment/hindi/bollywood/news/Pooja-Bedi-booked-under-POCSO-Act/articleshow/45570074.cms (Accessed on 29 January 14).

expands the concept of sexual harassment of a child by including various offensive behaviours, including uttering any word or gesture, or showing of any body part with the intention that such sounds should be heard or such things should be seen by the child, making the child exhibiting his body parts to be seen by him/her or others, showing the child contents of pornography, enticing the child for pornographic purposes, stalking (physically or through cyber way) and so on—and S.12 which prescribes punishment for the same and Ss.500 (punishment for defamation), 506 (criminal intimidation), and 509 (words, gesture etc. uttered to insult the modesty of women) of IPC.

Online gender bullying may also include transwomen as victims (Halder & Jaishankar, forthcoming; Priebe & Svedin, 2012). In such cases the bullying may necessarily involve abusive sexual taunts. Consider the case of Kalki Subramaniam, a transgender activist and founder of Sahodari, an organisation for transgender people in Tamil Nadu. In her interview with the lead author, Kalki informed how she was bullied by unknown people in her profile page as well as in her chat on Facebook. She stated that her account is publicly accessible and her updates and photo albums are open for public. In one of her photos with fellow transgender women, she received comments from strangers asking her whether she is available for sex and what her price per hour is. But this is not the only occasion that she was bullied. In another account, a stranger asked for her phone number on her Facebook page. This person got angry when she did not respond and bullied her on her profile page. In both the occasions, she reported the comments to Facebook, and blocked the individual from contacting her again. She opined 'transgender women are prone to get bullied online like any other women and such comments may be more humiliating due to their gender identity' (Halder & Jaishankar, forthcoming).

Cyber bullying including online gender bullying need not always occur by conveying of angry, insult, teasing and verbal arguments through internet and digital communication technology. As has been stated in the opening paragraph, emoticons have become substitutes for linguistic expressions in many bullying occasions. Even though emoticons were not used for bullying in any of the cases mentioned earlier, as the latest survey of Centre for Cyber Victim Counselling shows (Halder & Jaishankar, 2015a), gender bullying may become extremely annoying if emoticons including angry mood, disgusting mood, kissing lips, hugging signs, slapping signs, winking signs and so on are used as part of bullying communication.

It must be understood that, in India, no legal provision has so far defined the concept of cyber bullying, let alone the online gender bullying. It may be noted that S.66A (b) of the IT Act, 2000 (amended in 2008) categorises a communication as offensive when it says,

> Any person who sends by means of computer resource or a communication device... any information which he knows to be false, but for the purpose of causing annoyance, inconvenience, danger, obstruction, insult, injury, criminal intimidation, enmity, hatred, or ill will, persistently makes by making use of such computer resource or a communication device.

Even though this particular provision as a whole is presently being targeted as unconstitutional due to over breadth of the same and gross misuse of it by police as well as moral policing group,[15] the provision to a certain extent touches the concept of cyber bullying as has been conceptualised by other scholars discussed earlier. But the mentioned cases and the related legal provisions may provide a better understanding as how cyber bullying, especially gender bullying, can be and should be perceived in Indian context. For this, it may be interesting to note the combination of the provisions which are generally used by the police for booking such offences.[16]

Whereas in one hand, abusive words tinted with sexual colour may attract provisions such as S.67 of the IT Act, which prescribes punishment for transmitting obscene material in electronic form, or S.67A of the IT Act, which prescribes punishment for transmitting sexually explicit materials in the electronic form, (especially when images are also included in the bullying), and also provisions dealing with sexual harassment as per the (in case of adults when the bullying has taken place in the workplace environment) Sexual Harassment of Women at Workplace (Prevention, Prohibition and Redressal) Act (2013); in case of children-bullying with sexual connotations, it can also be categorised as sexual harassment as per the Protection of Children from Sexual Offences Act (2012). Further, if the bullying texts contain sexted images or revenge porn images, S.67B of the IT Act (prescribes punishment for publishing, producing etc. of content depicting children in sexually explicit act through electronic form) may also be attracted. At the same time, there are other provisions from the traditional penal code

---

[15] Broad discussions on this have been carried out in Chapter 2.

[16] This is from the personal experience of the lead author as a lawyer as well as counsellor for cyber crime victims.

which can also stand guard for prohibiting such abusive words. This may include the following provisions:

(i) S.499 of the IPC which defines defamation and states,

> Whoever, by words either spoken or intended to be read, or by signs or by visible representations, makes or publishes any imputation concerning any person intending to harm, or knowing or having reason to believe that such imputation will harm, the reputation of such person, is said, except in the cases hereinafter expected, to defame that person.[17]

It may further be noted that S.501 of the IPC expands the scope of S.499 to written words. It states that 'Whoever prints or engraves any matter, knowing or having good reason to believe that such matter is defamatory of any person, shall be punished with simple imprisonment for a term which may extend to two years, or with fine, or with both.'

(ii) S.503 of the IPC defines criminal intimidation by stating,

> Whoever threatens another with any injury to his person, reputation or property, or to the person or reputation of any one in whom that person is interested, with intent to cause alarm to that person, or to cause that person to do any act which he is not legally bound to do, or to omit to do any act which that person is legally entitled to do, as the means of avoiding the execution of such threat, commits criminal intimidation.

---

[17] Explanation 1 to S.499 provides that:

It may amount to defamation to impute anything to a deceased person, if the imputation would harm the reputation of that person if living, and is intended to be hurtful to the feelings of his family or other near relatives. Explanation 2 provides that: It may amount to defamation to make an imputation concerning a company or an association or collection of persons as such. Explanation 3 provides that: An imputation in the form of an alternative or expressed ironically, may amount to defamation. Explanation 4 provides that: No imputation is said to harm a person's reputation, unless that imputation directly or indirectly, in the estimation of others, lowers the moral or intellectual character of that person, or lowers the character of that person in respect of his caste or of his calling, or lowers the credit of that person, or causes it to be believed that the body of that person is in a loathsome state, or in a state generally considered as disgraceful.

(iii) Section 509 of the IPC states that whoever, intending to insult the modesty of any woman, utters any word, makes any sound or gesture, or exhibits any object, intending that such word or sound shall be heard, or that such gesture or object shall be seen, by such woman, or intrudes upon the privacy of such woman, shall be punished with simple imprisonment for a term which may extend to one year, or with fine, or with both.

However, there are also instances where the bully would have decided to make it bigger by defaming the victim publicly and take the incidence to public forums or World Wide Web. In such cases, the bullying behaviour necessarily shapes into defamation or harassment depending upon the motive of the offensive behaviour, the pattern and the gravity of the injury[18] caused to the person of the victim. We argue that cyber bullying can be the base of interpersonal conflicts such as defamation, harassment including sexual harassment and threatening if the victim and the perpetrator had engaged in ego-power game. This is especially so if cyber bullying is seen from the perception of usage of a type of language. Willard (2003, p. 66) defined cyber bullying as a language that is 'defamatory, constitutes bullying, harassment or discrimination, discloses personal information or contains offensive, vulgar or derogatory comments.'

Online gender bullying in that sense may involve ego power game targeting women and sexual minority group including the transwomen through hurling of harsh, annoying, insulting, threatening sexually taunting verbal as well as written words, images, emoticons and so on, through ICT including emails, chats, social networking profiles, SMSs, mobile voice communication technology and message communication technology. However, we do not comprehend other traits of offensive behaviour including online grooming, cyber stalking, revenge porn, victimisation by creation of fake avatar (Halder, 2013) and so on, as interchangeable terms with the term 'online gender bullying', even though all these traits may or may not involve cyber bullying. This term may be used interchangeably with the term 'cyber bullying women' and it may overlap with the concept of online harassment. But online harassment again, is not online gender bullying only. The term online harassment must be taken

---

[18] It must be noted that S.44 of the IPC expands the legal meaning of the term 'injury' to cover character assassination of the victim as well. It says. 'The word "injury" denotes any harm whatever illegally caused to any person, in body, mind, reputation or property.'

in a broader sense to include many other offensive behaviours including cyber bullying or online gender bullying.

It may further be noted that Aftab (in Sutton 2011)[19] has classified four types of bullies in respect to cyber bullying among children, that is, the *vengeful angels*, who are 'righting the wrongs' and who may had been victims of cyber bullying themselves and now retaliating; the *power hungry* and *revenge nerds*, who may like to show off their authority through cyber bullying and who may 'take one on one' to express aggressiveness, the *mean girls* who may be females bullying other females; these four classification of bullies may exist among adult bullies as well. While many researchers have agreed that women are bullied (both offline as well as online) more than men (Aftab, 2008; Baughman, Dearing, Giammarco & Vernon, 2012; Shariff, 2008; Wimmer, 2009), we agree with Aftab (2008) and Wimmer (2009) in observing that women may be vicious cyber bullies targeting other women. As Wimmer (2009) has pointed out, women may bully either as simple 'bitching' or to spread rumour and gossip about the victim or out of professional jealousy. However, as may be seen from the case of Bedi, women may even bully for defending their children or other family members. Similarly, women may in rare cases bully transwomen as well. In saying this, we want to establish the fact that women may also be bullies in gender bullying.

Causes, Effects and Challenges

The causes and methods of adult cyber bullying may be similar to cyber bullying by adolescents (Baughman et al., 2012). Online gender bullying is no different. However, from the cases that we got to deal on cyber bullying and the review of literature on cyber bullying, we could ascertain two prime factors involving technological and socio-legal psychological aspects that may cause cyber gender bullying especially in the Indian context. These are as follows:

1. Internet as a medium of communication gives the privilege to remain anonymous (Citron, 2014). It gives a broader chance to hide one's subdued personality and camouflage in a powerful authoritative profile. While this has been accepted as a prime

[19] As per Aftab, as published in her interview with etcjournal.com

factor for empowering children (adolescent and teens) for bullying other children and adults (especially teachers) (Shariff, 2008), adults may also take this opportunity not only for cyber bullying peers, but also for many other offensive behaviour including grooming and child pornography (Jaishankar, 2009). With the advent of ICT, the availability of platforms for communication has also increased. As such, a user can create profile either with his/her name and information or with anonymous identity. The verification of the email id profiles or social networking site profiles may be connected with the associated email id or the phone number of the user; but again, in India both the verification procedures may result in poor security verification as there can be identity misrepresentation in producing a true identity for obtaining a SIM card for a mobile phone number in many rural as well as urban pockets in India.[20] Similarly, when one user becomes good friends with other/s online, the online relationship may not help her to understand how reliable the virtual friend may be (Jaishankar, 2009). The exchange of information and communication may make the other user feel superior and may obviously lead to ego clashes when the user on the other end may try to establish her point or showcase something which hurts the superior ego of the bully. In case of real life acquaintances who may have met on the internet or got reconnected through digital communication technology after a long time, the expectation of 'being the same old person' may not match if any one of the acquaintances have changed from a sweet natured, subdued personality to a rude and rough personality due to experiences in life. Internet thus provides a veil not only on the identity but also on the personality. Empowered by such a platform, a bully feels motivated to express his mind in the manner which may not be filtered or blocked by the service providers. Even though researches have been made to use particular methods to detect offensive textual content which have sexual predation (Parapar, Losada & Barreiro, 2014) or bullying words in social networking sites such as Twitter with the help of hashtag (Calvin, Bellmore,

---

[20] This information is obtained by the lead author from the one day national consultation on ways and means to safeguard women from cyber crimes in India, held by National Commission for Women at New Delhi on 23 July 2014, where the lead author was invited as a resource person and the Chief Rapporteur.

Xu & Zhu, 2015), none can be completely successful in intercepting and deleting the bullying words especially when it is a conversation between adults, and due to the broadening scope of the freedom of speech as per the First Amendment Guarantee of the US Constitution, which regulate the free speech and content policy in all the US-based web companies including Facebook, Google, Twitter and so on. This has further become a complicated task for anti-bullying or anti-sexual content software creators, especially due to the huge imbalance between excessive inflow of offensive language in regional languages and lesser presence of people or software to detect regional language bullying words.

2. While internet may provide a wider platform and mechanism for bullying, the socio-psychological factors must also be noted. Bullying in adulthood is often seen to be correlated with bullying habits in childhood (Baughman et al., 2012). From the literature review on cyber bullying it can be seen that cyber bullying may be caused due to peculiar psychological traits in individuals. It may include narcissism and resultant aggressiveness for manipulation (Baughman et al., 2012). The bully may refuse to take his victim as his equal when he finds out the victim is submissive, depressed, lower in designation or inferior due to her physical appearance or educational standards or her inability to express herself as boldly as the bully himself. In many cases we have seen that the bully may find these out from the online information contributed by the victim herself, or from his real life experiences of getting acquainted with the victim. It is for this reason that the concept of cyber bullying may be overlapped with the concept of cyber stalking, which may necessarily mean monitoring the victim for causing harm by repeated communication. But again, let us keep the two terms in different compartments for the sake of better understanding of each of the terms. The bully may take the trait of bullying as 'power game' (Shariff, 2008) to establish his dominance over the victim and this can best be executed by hurling intentional insulting, taunting, abusive languages with or without images and emoticons. The aggressiveness of the bully is satisfied when the victim emotionally breaks down and fails to defend herself. The other prime factor for motivating cyber bullying is the social value system in different cultures (Sun et al., 2005). In India caste and class bullying has remained an old socio-cultural phenomenon for a long time and

this may have affected the bullying pattern on the internet as well. Many social networking sites provide users to showcase their ethnicity or religious belief. Indian youth had carried out their identification or support to their caste lines in the social networking sites (Boyd, 2007). Further, the orthodox patriarchal social structure may have influenced bullying inferior gender including women and transwomen by men. This has also affected the cyber bullying pattern among Indian adults. The 'power game'(Shariff, 2008) in online gender bullying may necessarily include machismo to show off how women are inferior to men or are unable to equate themselves with men either socially or intellectually or in physical strength. However, as mentioned earlier, women bullies may also play the power game in cyber bullying other women especially to establish dominance, to defend their children and other family members or for defending their own actions, which may had been perceived as 'wrong' by the victim either in the real life or in the cyber space.

The primary effects of online gender bullying may not differ very much from those as has been found out in cases of cyber bullying among children. The victim may nonetheless feel traumatised, suicidal and may suffer from withdrawal symptoms in extreme cases. It may be noted that presently due to enormous web-literatures on online safety tips, many users may have become aware of the dangers involved in ICT including cyber bullying. But it does not guarantee that all probable victims (especially women) can cope with the atrocities including online gender bullying, especially if they are new to the internet communication technology. In certain cases the victims may even take to irrational coping mechanism such as revert bullying or relying on hacking mechanisms, expecting that this would stop the harassment once and for all (Halder & Jaishankar, 2015b). But this may create new problems for the victims and may pave the new ways for the bullies to come back with even more bigger plans to harass the victims.

It needs to be understood that even though the legal provisions like those we have mentioned earlier, may provide remedies for online gender bullying, in most cases the bullying victim does not report the cases. As we gathered from the victims and the literature reviews, in India women are taught from their childhood not to report bullying incidences and get adjusted to the bullying habits of men and older and stronger women in the household. This culture is prevalent in cases of adult online gender bullying as well. Even though the laws mentioned here can be used for regulating online gender bullying, it may be noted that there are some other specific laws which prevents bullying or name calling on the basis of caste or race including the Scheduled Castes and the Scheduled Tribes (Prevention of Atrocities) Amendment Bill, 2014, which amended the Scheduled Castes and Tribes (Prevention of Atrocities) Act, 1989 and prohibits name calling by caste etc. or writing or publishing anything to promote enmity (S.3u) or intentionally using any word, gesture of sexual nature to insult a woman of scheduled caste or tribe (S.3w(ii)). Proposals have also been made for introducing S.509A to IPC which would make any insulting word, gesture and so on intentionally made to humiliate members of any particular race, an offensive behaviour (Jain, 2015). But in reality, there are hardly any laws which are used for regulating online gender bullying. Along with the reluctant victims, there are unaware criminal justice machinery including the police and the lawyers who may ask the women to either close their accounts or ignore the bully (Halder & Jaishankar, 2011) and thereby cause secondary traumatisation.

Gender bullying may essentially target transwomen on social networking sites, emails, chat sessions and through digital telephone communication systems including mobile communication app. The primary factor for online bullying of the transwomen is their sexual orientation (NCTE, 2011) and their self-esteem, as well as their unwillingness to let men enjoy ridiculing their sexual orientation (Halder & Jaishankar, forthcoming). Consider again Kalki's case, when some men wanted to contact her for sexual gratification and she ignored their repeated messages for phone number. She was bullied in the message box as well as in her profile page. In general, such bullying may necessarily involve words which remind the transwomen about their past 'men-ship' and inability to satisfy women as males or words depicting harsh realities to remind them that they are neither 'full women' to give expected satisfaction to men. The legal factors for humiliating the transwomen in the cyber space through online bullying must also not be ignored. It is unfortunate to note that traditional Indian social mindset considers people belonging to LGBT community as a community to be humiliated. Transgender women are worst victims of such mindset whereby they are not only considered as substandard sexual partners, but also botheration for the society. This has motivated the society as a whole to socially ostracising them, bully them and treat them in an inhuman manner even when they approach the law and justice machinery for establishing their rights. This is more so because the present form of S.377 IPC[21] also provides a hostile legal outlook to the LGBT community. As the civil society members became aware of the fact that even the law does not support the transgender women, they have been targeted in a vicious way in the cyber space as well.

Ironically, the transgender women may not get any solace from criminal justice machinery for such online bullying victimisation in real life as well, because, in such cases, the police may further extend the scope of S.377 IPC to pull them out of their virtual homes and abuse them for being an 'illegal entity' surviving upon US laws to express their opinions. This can particularly happen because even though the Delhi High Court judgment on Naz foundation[22] recognised the rights of the LGBT people, the Supreme Court did not agree with the judgement. As has been highlighted by Baxi (2013), a particular part of the judgement of Naz foundation attracts our attention in this regard; the Supreme Court stated, '...Section 377 IPC does not criminalise a particular people, identity or orientation. It merely identifies certain acts which if committed would constitute an offence. Such a prohibition regulates sexual conduct regardless of gender identity and orientation.'[23] Many of the transgender women use their profiles for socialising and it may include sending direct messages through timeline updates as well as implied messages for searching partners through photographs. As has been pointed out by NALSA judgement later,[24] such ways of expression fall under the arena of Article 19(1)(a) and these may necessarily include 'prohibited conducts' in the broadest sense, if the Naz foundation judgement of the Supreme

---

[21] S.377 of the IPC states that

> Whoever voluntarily has carnal intercourse against the order of nature with any man, woman or animal, shall be punished with imprisonment for life, or with imprisonment of either description for a term which may extend to ten years, and shall also be liable to fine. The explanation attached to this section explains that penetration is sufficient to constitute the carnal intercourse necessary to the offence described in this section.

[22] Suresh Kumar Koushal and others v. Naz Foundation and others, Civil Appeal no. 10972 of 2013, decided by the Hon'ble Supreme Court on 11 December 2013.

[23] Baxi, P. (16 December 2013). Suresh Koushal v. Naz Foundation: Pratiksha Baxi. Available at http://kafila.org/2013/12/16/suresh-koushal-v-naz-foundation-pratiksha-baxi. (Accessed on 5 July 2016).

[24] National legal services authority v. Union of India Writ Petition (Civil) no. 400 of 2012 with Writ petition (Civil) no. 604 of 2013.

Court is interpreted in the broadest way to include speech and expression of the transgender women. We anticipate that the judicial misunderstandings that had happened in the case of Naz foundation judgement by the Supreme Court may further motivate the criminal justice administration as well as the moral policing groups to harass the sexual minority community for their virtual presence.

Trolling Targeting Women in India

Profiling of Trolling and Trolls

Compared to cyber bullying, trolling is a new phenomenon in India. Trolling may differ from the concept of cyber bullying on a hair line difference: One prime difference lies in the fact that trolls may not be directly or indirectly affected by the speech or action of their victims (Halder, 2013). They troll because mostly they want to divert the focus of the 'publication' (including the status update, comment or textual expression of the victim or the discussion following the status message or comment of the main commentator in public forum) and attract the attention of the readers towards their own vicious thoughts about the victim. Trolling is 'a game about identity deception' (Donath, 1999, p. 45) which may necessarily involve impolite language by the trolls (Hardaker, 2010) targeting his/their victim/s. The 'troll posts' are essentially 'provocative posting intended to produce a large volume of frivolous responses' (Herring et al., 2002). Herring et al. (2002) further opined that trolling may take place mostly in online groups, which may consist of marginalised people such as the LGBT section or religious or linguistic minority groups and especially women's groups or groups which are essential feminist in nature. This is mainly because men may become provoked by their resentment because of the exclusionary nature of such feminist groups (Hall, 1996; Herring et al., 2002). But not to forget that Herring et al. had this research in 2002, and now the pattern of computer mediated communication has seen a change due to the huge growth of social networking sites where women can enjoy their right to express their own opinion without being dependant on any particular news group.

Women can speak their minds through their own profiles on Facebook or Twitter and they may get virtual supports for their thoughts through the 'likes' and comments, re-tweets 'sharing' with positive note. In these cases, women update their status messages not to communicate with a particular person or a group of persons, but their status messages become mini-monologue in 140 characters in case of Twitter, and in case of Facebook, such monologue may run for a few paragraphs. They have the liberty to show the world the extract of their literary work, their write-ups in news media and so on through hyper-links, which may take the readers to the work published by her. Present day trolls no longer limit their trolling activities in the news-groups as Herring et al. (2002) had shown. They also take the liberty to express their unhappiness regarding their victim either through their own profiles or posting their comments in the comment section in the victim's status message. Present day trolling can be defined as 'an extreme usage of freedom of speech which is exercised to disrupt the community discussions in social networking sites and which is done to deliberately insult ideologies such as feminism, secularism etc.; of the topic starter or the supporters of the topic starter' (Halder, 2013). However, trolling in the feminist groups still exist. With the growth of mobile apps for communication such as WhatsApp, trolls have further found out avenues to continue their troll posts in feminist groups as well as their own groups where they may continue trolling targeting their chosen victims. Trolling becomes more (sadistically) enjoyable for the trolls due to the rapid circulation of the troll posts through digitised cartoons along with the message among other non-participant users of troll groups on WhatsApp. By this, they are able to spread their troll posts to those who may not use social networking sites.

However, now women users have become more aware of the privacy settings and also the host sites of such groups may provide more opportunity to manage the posts; such trolling may be controlled before it can attract voluminous 'frivolous posts'. Consider the case of activist Kavita Krishnan, who was attacked by trolls on Rediff.in. In 2013, when she was invited to speak on violence against women on Rediff on a live chat, she received tweets from a Twitter handle 'rapist' who first asked her to consider telling women to dress properly so that they are not targeted by rapists, and then the tweet handle returned with a direct threat which stated, 'Kavita tell me where I should come and rape you with a condom.' She told the media that while it was a live chat, the tweets from 'rapist' appeared in block letters attracting the attention of other viewers and this forced to her log off from the chat abruptly.[25] Similarly, in 2016,

[25] For more information on this case, see Sahay, P. (26 April 2013). Trolls threaten activist with rape during chat. *DNA*. Available at http://www.dnaindia.com/india/report-troll-threatens-activist-with-rape-during-chat-1827134 (Accessed on 10 February 2015).

she was further attacked on Facebook, where she was asked to join the commentator for demonstrating free sex. As the media reports suggests, she however, filed a police complaint in this regard under provisions for sexual harassment.[26]

Trolls are more active now on Twitter and Facebook since they may get to know the trending news in the social networking sites by data mining with the use of hashtags (#), which brings up the important metadata contributed by the users who would like to publicise their updates.

Consider again the case of Sagarika Ghosh, a senior woman journalist, who has worked with news channels such as CNN-IBN. Trolls targeted her on Twitter especially after her news reporting on particular political situations and political views on sensitive issues like Kashmir, and her views on pseudo-secularism followed by the particular political parties went viral due to excessive cross-postings by the news channels as well as by herself. Her name started trending on Twitter and trolls started their troll posts hash-tagging her name describing her as a biased journalist who showed too much solidarity to the Congress party. Sagarika made her own statements in her tweet profile and within hours some trolls turned from 'simple jokers' on the internet playing with Sagarika's name, to vicious trolls who started posting hate messages including death threats and rape threats to her as well as her school-going daughter. The hate messages 'successfully' affected Sagarika, who decided to take her daughter in her own car to the school because she was afraid that some of these trolls may really harm her daughter as they stated that they were aware of the routes by which Sagarika and her family travel. Trolls, in this case as well, were able to attract the news channels not only because Sagarika is a celebrated journalist, but also because of their extremely 'anti-liberal' attitude towards successful women achievers, especially noted writers, journalists, film personalities and so on.[27]

Similarly, consider the case of Barkha Dutt, a veteran woman journalist, who was targeted by the trolls heavily when she published her book *This Unquiet Land: Stories from India's Fault Lines*. Barkha was already targeted by the trolls earlier for her journalism, which, according to many

[26] Shankar, A. (May 26, 2016). Delhi Women's rights activist files sexual harassment complaint against former journalist. Available at https://in.news.yahoo.com/delhi-women-rights-activist-files-044600695.html on (Accessed on 3 June 2016).

[27] The authors of this book were interviewed by BBC on Sagarika Ghosh's Twitter troll abuse case.

of her trolls, apparently seemed to have given a negative impact about India. But with the publication of her book, where she had shared about her childhood sexual abuses, her experiences at Kargil War and so on, she was further attacked by trolls, who called her names, and even asked whether she was married and if yes, for how many times?[28]

As can be seen from the mentioned cases, three specific natures of trolling (as defined by Donath, 1999; Halder, 2013; Herring et al., 2002) can be found in both these cases: (a) trolls were successful in diverting the attention of the readers in the World Wide Web from the actual news item or write-up or literary work of the women authors. (b) Huge attention flowed towards what the trolls were discussing about the women and how they were ridiculed through impolite, insulting and abusive languages. (c) The troll posts subsequently provoked more frivolous responses from the readers who may not be trolls themselves, but who came to condemn the trolling, or who may be supporting the women in question. Unlike gender bullying, trolling in these cases did not necessarily involve repeated exchange of abusive communication with the victim herself, but involved multiple readers, who may have stopped after posting one or two comments to the troll posts and who may never have been messaged back by the trolls themselves.

Causes, Effects and Challenges

Unlike gender bullying, trolling may not be caused due to existing interpersonal enmity between the troll and his victim. As has been mentioned in many literatures on trolling, the trolls use the spare time to amuse themselves (Herring et al., 2002) by data mining about the serious issues and disrupting the same by suddenly exploding with their own views about the particular person who has created the news content or the write-up as had happened with Barkha and Sagarika. Such data mining may be done by following the trending news, viral posts or following celebrities including men and women, whose posts or status updates may instantly attract huge attention. The trolls use the 'liberal and libertarian views' (Herring et al., 2002) about usage of internet in regard to express

[28] See for more Ramani, P. (April 23, 2016). Why everybody loves to hate Barkha Dutt. Available at http://www.livemint.com/Leisure/C3zY1Y1ycBJYDNRmNPCmHK/ Why-everybody-loves-to-hate-Barkha-Dutt.html (Accessed on 24 April 2016).

their opinion in the broadest meaning of freedom of speech and expression as has been guaranteed by the First Amendment of the US Constitution and which is the guiding principle of the US-based social networking sites. Similar to online bullying, anonymous nature of the profiles further gives the trolls the 'power' to appear, disrupt the conversation and disappear, and perhaps to reappear through some other avatar. Further, there is a legal gap in India to deal with trolling in the cyber space.

Consider the ever expanding notion of freedom of speech in India. Depending upon the ethnic socio-cultural background, Article 19(2) of the Constitution added some specific grounds which may block or chill the freedom of speech and expression in India in real as well as in the virtual space. These grounds include disrupting the national integrity and security of the country, friendly relation with other states, incitement to the offence, contempt of court and harming the morality and decency of people in India. But courts in India have refused to chill the right to speech in many landmark judgements and thereby India has a 'celebrated right' for press freedom as well.[29] Basing on the grounds mentioned in Article 19(2) S.66A of the IT Act, 2000 (amended in 2008) was created which prohibits conveying of grossly offensive, menacing information and/or misleading information and/or information which the sender knows to be false but for the purpose of causing a series of negative psychological and social impacts including annoyance, inconvenience, danger, obstruction, insult, injury, criminal intimidation, enmity, hatred or ill will through electronic and digital communication services. But as has been mentioned earlier, the law is controversial due to misuse of the same as well as over breadth of the same.

Consider the recent case, where the court allowed an agitated couple to retain their Facebook post regarding how they were allegedly abused by a traffic police officer in Bangalore and quashing the FIR against them filed by the police officer.[30] Since trolling may essentially involve extremely liberal usage of freedom of speech, there are possibilities that courts in India may not chill the right to troll as long as it is limited to expressing one's

---

[29] For example, see Indian Express v. Union of India (1985). 1 SCC 641, or Romesh Thapar v. State of Madras, AIR 1950 SC 124.

[30] See Manik Taneja v. State of Karnatka, 2015 SCC On Line SC 51, 20-01-2015. Also see Chaudhuri, A. (22 January 2015). Babu bashing no crime, SC says. *The Times of India*. Available at http://timesofindia.indiatimes.com/tech/social/Online-babu-bashing-no-crime-SC-says/articleshow/45973495.cms (Accessed on 23 January 2015).

own opinion regarding a particular literary work or film or news reporting and does not violate personal rights such as harm against modesty,
decency and so on. But challenges begin when a troll creates troll posts
attacking the person of the writer or the journalist or the celebrity achiever
and especially if they are women, as it had been in the case of Barkha and
Sagarika. As we have mentioned earlier, the laws for harming the modesty of women and/or criminal intimidation and defamation along with
Ss.66A and 67 or 67A of the IT Act may be applied in such cases if the
posts carry not only impolite and abusive words, but also graphic images
depicting the women in an obscene manner. It may further be noted that
trolling may neither be dealt with under Sexual Harassment of Women at
Workplace (Prevention, Prohibition and Redressal) Act, 2013, if the troll
is not related to the victim through workplace.

The question which we have faced from many news channels as well
as many other researchers and students in these two cases is why Indian
women are being targeted over and over again on Twitter and Facebook
and now on WhatsApp by trolls? Our answer is much similar to what
Herring et al. (2002) provided: Male trolls may attack women (especially celebrity personalities) because they feel sidelined in the discussions about feminism and women's security issues. Moreover, in India the
society being patriarchal, many men still cannot accept women achievers
as persons who should get highlight of the media or the general people
shunning their male counterparts. They question about women's level of
understanding of the social, political and religious issues. Internet gave
them power to do so without actually fearing about facing the person in
real life and been blown away by her thoughtful defences. Added with
it, the vast audience and attention a troll can get, boosts the moral confidence and ego. However, it would be wrong to say that men are not
attacked by trolls. Trolling on Justice Katju may be a good example here;
he is trolled by male as well as female alike for his specific posts on
Twitter and Facebook. It may further be necessary to mention that there
can be women trolls as well who may be small in number, but they do
exist in closed groups or specific communities.[31] However, we have noted
that such trolls are either removed by the moderators or they are counter
attacked by the other members of the group and they (the female trolls)
generally withdraw or in some extreme cases, may turn into habitual
revenge seeker bullies.

---

[31] This is from the personal experience of the lead author in her designation as
counsellor for cyber crime victims.

The impact of trolling women may be devastating especially in Indian society. Majority of male trolls enjoy the impact to get sadistic pleasure and for this sort of gratification, they may come back again and again to troll other women. Consider the case of Sagarika; one troll threatened her to kill, others threatened to harm her daughter. For Barkha, trolls attacked her in filthy words relating to her work and personal life.[32] Trolls may threaten women to stop accessing internet and carry on regular blogging or regular work through ICT as women may fear about their social reputation, security and reputation of their children and extended family members. Once the simple trolling turns into massive 'hate wave' (Citron, 2014), it may become impossible for the women to sustain the daily virtual harassment not only from the troll himself, but from multiple sources. While in the US, women may be able to fight back the hate crimes by effective criminal justice mechanism (Citron, 2014), in India, it may be impossible for the victim to even convince the police about the occurrence of the offence and initiate criminal procedures. The police could not help her much in the trolling case effectively even if the troll posts are still visible on her Twitter page. One of the main reasons for such pathetic situation is the inherent nature of trolling, which may look similar to cyber stalking, but in reality, is different from cyber stalking. In the latter case, the stalker may continuously monitor the victim by digital surveillance with full knowledge that such digital monitoring can cause harm to the victim. He may try to harass the victim by repeated unwanted approach, which may include trolling, bullying, sending threatening mails/messages, invading into the digital privacy of the victim and so on. In trolling, the trolls may not get involved to intentionally cause harm to the victim. Also, unlike cyber stalking, they may suddenly stop posting their own opinions once they are satisfied with themselves and start feeling uninterested in the victim. The same has been observed by us

[32] The provisions of sub-section (1) shall not apply if: (a) the intermediary has conspired or abetted or aided or induced whether by threats or promise or otherwise in the commission of the unlawful act (ITAA 2008) [and] (b) upon receiving actual knowledge, or on being notified by the appropriate Government or its agency that any information, data or communication link residing in or connected to a computer resource controlled by the intermediary is being used to commit the unlawful act, the intermediary fails to expeditiously remove or disable access to that material on that resource without vitiating the evidence in any manner. Explanation: For the purpose of this section, the expression 'third party information' means any information dealt with by an intermediary in his capacity as an intermediary.

in Sagarika's case as well. Trolling has not stopped, but it has definitely decreased for Sagarika for the particular issue on which they attacked her. As such, she has taken the whole episode as a regular harassment that may have to be faced by any other working Indian women, and for which one cannot nag for justice. However, it must also be mentioned that in certain cases, police and criminal justice machinery in India may become handicapped when the social networking site refuses to cooperate and abide by the laws of the land, especially S.79(3) of the IT Act (which prescribes exemption of liability in certain cases for the intermediaries), or S.13 of the IT (procedure and safeguards for interception, monitoring and decryption of information) Rules, 2009 (which speaks about liabilities of the intermediary to provide facilities and so on).[33]

The authors feel that the greatest challenge that lies for Indian criminal justice machinery, civil law jurisprudence as well as cyber jurisprudence is to bring a fitting regulation for regulating bullying and trolling, including gender bullying. A proper framing of S.66A of the IT Act, 2000 (amended in 2008) shredding the ambiguity about the meaning and scope of the existing words and including the definitions of the terms cyber bullying and trolling must be considered (Halder, 2015). Cyber bullying and trolling may not be as devastating as creation of fake avatars or criminal defamation. But the viral nature of bullying and trolling may prove devastating if the same pulls up issues like revenge porn (Halder, 2015, pp. 116–117). Further, S.66A in its amended form may prove beneficial only if it changes from a retributive law to restorative law whereby the offences should be non-cognisable (especially because it should not be misused by politicians or fanatics who may influence the criminal justice machinery, especially the police) and bailable, and the sentencing may include public apology and undoing the harm by removing the bullying/trolling contents (Halder, 2015, pp. 116–117). It must simultaneously include provisions for compensation as well (Halder, 2015, pp. 116–117). If these observations are considered by the lawmakers, not only the issues of cyber bullying and trolling can be managed efficiently but also the perpetrators including the juvenile offenders may be brought under the scopes of restorative and therapeutic effects of the law (Halder, 2015, pp. 116–117).

However, the recent endeavour by Ministry of Women and Child Development along with the Home Ministry to make trolling targeting women a punishable offence must be noted in this regard. As the

---

[33] This had been informed by one of the police officials who prefer to remain anonymous.

ministries have planned, a scheme named Cyber Crime Prevention against Women and Children will be formed under the Nirbhaya fund (a fund created by the government to support endeavours regarding safety of women and children) and the portal, thus formed, would be assisting women victims of cyber harassment including trolling.[34] It is expected that this proposal would be beneficial for women victims of trolling.

References

Baughman, H. M., Dearing, S., Giammarco, E., & Vernon, P. A. (2012). Relationships between bullying behaviours and the dark triad: A study with adults. *Personality and Individual Differences, 52*(2), 571–575.

Baxi, P. (2013). Suresh Koushal v. Naz Foundation: Pratiksha Baxi. Available at http://kafila.org/2013/12/16/suresh-koushal-v-naz-foundation-pratiksha-baxi (Accessed on 11 February 2016).

Boyd, D. (December 3, 2007). Why youth (heart) social network sites: The role of networked publics in teenage social Life. In: D. Buckingham (ed.), *Youth, identity, and digital media*. The John D. and Catherine T. MacArthur Foundation series on digital media and learning (pp. 119–142). Cambridge, MA: The MIT Press.

Calvin, A. J., Bellmore, A., Xu, J. M., & Zhu, X. (2015). #bully: Uses of hashtags in posts about bullying on Twitter. *Journal of School Violence, 14*(1), 133–153.

Citron, D. K. (2014). *Hate crimes in cyber space*. Harvard: Harvard University Press.

Coloroso, B. (2003). *The bully, the bullied, and the bystander*. New York, New York: Harper Collins.

Donath, J. S. (1999). Identity and deception in the virtual community. In M. A. Smith and P. Kollock (eds), *Communities in cyberspace* (pp. 29–59). London: Routledge.

Fegenbush, B., & Olivier, D. (2009). 'Cyberbullying: A Literature Review'. In Annual Meeting of the Louisiana Education Research Association [online], p. 8. Available at http://ullresearch.pbworks.com/f/Fegenbush_Cyberbullying_LERAConferencePaper.pdf (Accessed on 11 January 2016).

Halder, D. (2013). Examining the scope of Indecent Representation of Women (Prevention) Act, 1986 in the light of cyber victimisation of women in India. *National Law School Journal*, 11, 188–218.

[34] For more on this, see Madhukatulya. A (19 May 2016). Maneka Gandhi to work on a portal with Home Ministry to punish online trolls. Available at http://www.dnaindia.com/india/report-now-a-portal-to-deal-with-online-abuse-of-women-2213801 (Accessed on 19 May 2016).

Halder, D. (2015). A retrospective analysis of S.66a: Could S.66a of the information technology act be reconsidered for regulating 'bad talk' in the internet? *Indian Student Law Review (ISLR), 3*, 91–118.

Halder, D., & Jaishankar, K. (2010). Cyber victimization in India: A baseline survey report. Tirunelveli, India: Centre for Cyber Victim Counselling. Available at http://www.cybervictims.org/CCVCresearchreport2010.pdf (Accessed on 11 January 2016).

———. (2011). Cyber crime and the victimization of women: Laws, rights, and regulations. Hershey, PA, USA: IGI Global.

———. (2015a). Harassment via WhatsApp in urban and rural India: A baseline survey report. Tirunelveli, India: Centre for Cyber Victim Counselling. Available at http://www.cybervictims.org/CCVCresearchreport2015.pdf (Accessed on 11 February 2016).

———. (2015b). Irrational coping theory and positive criminology: A frame work to protect victims of cyber crime. In N. Ronel and D. Segev (eds), *Positive criminology* (pp. 276–291). Abingdon, Oxon: Routledge.

———. (forthcoming). Bullying the bullied: A critical examination of the effect of the supreme court verdict on S.377 on the transgendered women in the cyberspace (Unpublished).

Hall, K. (1996). Cyber feminism. In S. C. Herring (ed.), *Computer-mediated communication: Linguistic, social and cross-cultural perspectives* (pp. 147–170). Amsterdam: John Benjamins.

Hardaker, C. (2010). Trolling in asynchronous computer-mediated communication: From user discussions to academic definitions. *Journal of Politeness Research, 6*(2), 215–242.

Herring, S. C., Job-Sluder, K., Scheckler, R., & Barab, S. (2002). Searching for safety online: Managing trolling in a feminist forum. *The Information Society, 18*(5), 371–384. Available at http://www-bcf.usc.edu/~fulk/620overview_files/Herring.pdf (Accessed 26 July 2016).

Hinduja, S., & Patchin, J. W. (2015). *Bullying beyond the schoolyard: Preventing and responding to cyberbullying.* Thousand Oaks, CA: SAGE Publications.

Jain, B. (January 2, 2015). Calling NE people 'chinki' will land you in jail. *Times of India.* Available at http://timesofindia.indiatimes.com/india/Calling-NE-people-chinki-will-land-you-in-jail/articleshow/45732987.cms (Accessed on 10 February 2015).

Jaishankar, K. (2009). *Cyber bullying: Profile and policy guidelines.* Tirunelveli, India: Department of Criminology and Criminal Justice, Manonmaniam Sundaranar University.

Katz, R. C., Hannon, R., & Whitten, L. (1996). Effects of gender and situation on the perception of sexual harassment. *Sex Roles, 34*(1), 35–42.

MacKinnon, C. (1979). *Sexual harassment of working women: A case of sex discrimination.* New Haven: Yale University Press.

National Centre for Transgender Equality (NCTE). (2011). Peer violence and bullying against transgender and gender nonconforming youth. Available at

http://www.transequality.org/PDFs/US%20Civ%20Rts%20Commn%20
NCTE%20statement%205%206%2011.pdf (Accessed on 9 February 2015).

Olweus, D. (1993). *Bullying at school: What we know and what we can do.*
Cambridge, MA: Blackwell Publishers, Inc.

Parapar, J., Losada, D. E., & Barreiro, I. A. (2014). Combining psycholinguistic
content based and chat based features to detect predation in chatrooms.
Journal of Universal Computer Science, 20(2), 213–239.

Patchin, J. W., & Hinduja, S. (2010). Cyberbullying and self-esteem. *Journal of
School Health, 80*(12), 614–621.

Patchin, J. W. (2014). What is cyber bullying? Available at http://cyberbullying.
us/what-is-cyberbullying (Accessed on 9 February 2015).

Priebe, G., & Svedin, C. G. (2012). Online or off-line victimisation and psychological wellbeing: A comparison of sexual-minority and heterosexual
youth. *European Child and Adolescent Psychiatry, 21*(10), 569–582.

Ramasubramaniam, S., & Oliver, M. B., (2003). Portrayals of sexual violence in
popular Hindi films, 1997–99. *Sex Roles, 48*(7/8), 327–336.

Shariff, S. (2008). Cyber-bullying: Issues and solutions for the school, the class-
room, and the home. Abington, Oxfordshire, UK: Routledge (Taylor &
Francis Group).

Shariff, S., & Hoff, D. L. (2007). Cyber bullying: Clarifying legal boundaries
for School supervision in cyber-space. *International Journal of Cyber
Criminology, 1*(1), 76–118.

Sun, P., Unger, J. B., Palmer, P. H., Gallaher, P., Chou, C. P., Baezconde-Garbanati,
L., Sussman, S., & Johnson, C. A. (2005). Internet accessibility and usage
among urban adolescents in Southern California: Implications for web-
based health research. *Cyberpsychology & Behavior, 8*(5), 441–453.

Sutton, B. (2011). Cyber bullying: An interview with Parry Aftab. Available at
https://etcjournal.com/2011/02/17/7299/ (Accessed on 20 May 2016).

Willard, N. (2007). *Cyberbullying and cyberthreats: Responding to the challenge of
online social aggression, threats, and distress.* Champaign, IL: Research Press.

Wimmer, S. (2009). Views on gender differences in bullying in relation to language
and gender-role Socialisation. Griffith Working Papers in Pragmatics and
Intercultural Communication, 2(1), 18–26. Available at https://www.griffith.
edu.au/__data/assets/pdf_file/0011/145289/2.-Wimmer---Gender-differ-
ences-in-bullying.pdf (Accessed on 12 February 2016).

4

Online Grooming

Grooming may mean preparing someone for a particular work, profile or future education. But in this digital era, the meaning and scope of grooming have expanded to include offensive activities which directly or indirectly aid in criminal activities targeting women and girls on the internet. In majority of cases relating to cyber crime against women, online grooming may form an essential part. Consider cases of phishing, sextortion, cyber stalking or creation of paedophilia; almost all the victims may say that they had met their perpetrators on the internet and these perpetrators motivated them to contribute in such victimisation. These online 'motivators' may play dangerous roles to create more harm to the victims. They groom the victims to contribute to the victimisation which may be designed by them (the groomers). They may create their own network involving many other groomers to allure innocent netizens. Groomers use different methodologies to find, groom and do the act which may create the offence. Often when reporting crimes, women victims may omit to mention about the groomers' role, but may directly speak about the harassment. It may happen that groomers may be the offenders themselves, but in some cases it may not be so. Groomers may use their victims to do many offensive works, including alluring more innocent netizens, circulating contents which may finally prove dangerous for others and so on. Groomer's role in anti-national or terrorist activities is also presently recognised, especially in the cases such as gross propaganda by the Islamic State (IS). Consider their methods of recruiting through internet and response for the same from the youth, who may be groomed to join them through online acquaintance with the IS recruiters.

However, there is a large-scale belief that online grooming is done for the children and youth especially for committing sexual offences on the internet (O'Connel, 2009; Wall, 2007). Researches show how groomers may collect data about the possible victim, contact them and exploit them either for their own sexual gratification or for monetary profit or for both (Zeynep, 2008; Wachs, Wolf & Pan, 2012). Some empirical researches have also shown the sort of communicative languages that are used to win the trust of young children (Wachs et al., 2012); why children fall prey to the groomers and what the consequences of such grooming are. But simultaneously, there are dating scams (Rege, 2009), creation of fake avatars (Halder, 2013a), phishing scams and instances such as recruiting for criminal or terrorist gangs as happened in the case of IS recruitments. These are the instances showing that online grooming happens for committing crimes against women, including transgender women as well. In this chapter we will be discussing about the role of online grooming in cyber crimes against women.

Methods, Platforms and Definition of Online Grooming

Online grooming may necessarily involve two or more individuals who are connected to each other by digital communication technology and who may have never met before. As researchers, such as Wall (2007), O'Connel (2009) and Hof and Koop (2011), pointed out the method of online grooming may be used for exploiting children for sexual offences. Due to the large-scale use of online grooming as a method for sexual exploitation of children and youth over the internet, in recent times, online grooming has often been related to sexual solicitation (Schrock & Boyd, 2008). But some researchers have also shown the association of grooming with bullying (Wachs et al., 2010) or webcam trolling (Kopecky, 2015). Researchers based on their own findings developed various definitions of online grooming; Wachs et al. (2012) developed a definition of online grooming which states,

> Cyber grooming means establishing a trust-based relationship between minors and usually adults using ICTs to systematically solicit and exploit the minors for sexual purposes. The three components repetition, misuse of trust, and the specific relationship between victim and cyber groomer must be considered to distinguish the phenomenon of cyber grooming from a single occurrence of sexual solicitation or exploitation.

Schrock and Boyd (2008) showed that the online grooming process may involve some deception to coerce the victim for sexual conversation, (p. 16), and the online grooming process may also involve use of webcams, directing the victim to send sexted images/video clippings and so on (p. 35). However, we argue that online grooming cannot and should not be restricted to children only. Groomers may target new users irrespective of their gender: women, youth as well as children who may be in a delicate psychological condition (Halder & Jaishankar, 2011; O'Connell, 2009, Schrock & Boyd, 2008; Wachs et al., 2012), susceptible to risky approaches by strangers on the internet. Consider again the cases of phishing; from our practical experiences we have seen that victims (irrespective of their gender) are first contacted with an alluring mail or message through SMS. In some cases the pattern of the mails or the messages may be simple form fill-up types, where the victim may be asked to provide date of birth, residential address and so on. In such cases, if the victim responds to such mails/messages, they may not be contacted by any subsequent mail/message but their information may be used to access their online banking facilities or even email hacking. But in some other cases, victims may be contacted by some personal mail/message whereby they may be asked to send money for the perpetrator who poses as a victim of theft, and stuck in a foreign land, or by fortune mailers, who may target victims by telling them that they wish to donate some fortune since they do not have any heir. Consider also the lottery scam or job scam cases, the mail/message, including SMiShing, vishing and so on, may be designed to allure the victim after two or three communication exchanges, each of which may look extremely promising to the victim. But at the end, the victim may have lost money only to understand how much he/she has been befooled. Men and women can both be victims of phishing, vishing, SMiShing, job and lottery scams.

Similarly, consider dating frauds (Rege, 2009). There are a number of dating sites where one can create profiles, upload pictures and let people build online emotional relationship. Perpetrators may use these opportunities to contact the possible victim and gain her trust only to misuse it. There are examples where victims have been cheated by the perpetrators when they gave in to pleas for monetary assistance by the perpetrators,[1] or by sexting where the perpetrators wanted to save some 'private photos' of the victims only to proceed for sextortion,[2] or where victims were

---

[1] From the personal experience of authors as cyber victim counsellors and researchers.

[2] Ibid.

groomed to perform some graver offence in the physical space such as murder.[3] Basing upon such patterns of the effects of grooming, we in our earlier publication titled 'cyber crime and the victimization of women: laws, rights and regulations' have expanded the scope of online grooming to include crimes against adult women. In the model policy guidelines prepared in this book, we provided a model definition for online grooming which states, 'cyber grooming may mean constant interactions/communications with any individual focusing on sexual conducts or other unethical or illegal conducts in a camouflaged manner with a purpose to misuse the digital presence and/or identity of the respondent herself or personal information provided by her' (Halder & Jaishankar, 2011, p. 131).

Cyber grooming, however, must not be confused with cyber stalking. Though both the concepts involve some common elements such as shadowing and repeated contacts only to create harassment, the underlying difference lies in the condition of psychological stress level of the victim. In cyber stalking, the victim may feel extremely uncomfortable, irritated or appreciate danger from the very beginning or may grow the feeling danger gradually (Bocij, Griffiths & McFarlane, 2002; Brenner, 2004; Ellison & Akdeniz, 1998). Many jurisdictions including United States, United Kingdom, Canada and India have developed their anti-stalking law on these essential grounds (Halder & Jaishankar, 2011). In cases of cyber grooming, the victim may feel extremely relaxed and safe with the groomer and may seek his attention continuously, which the groomer uses for his own benefits. Groomers may randomly select their victims either by random contacts or by extensive data mining in the social networking sites. Halder (2013b, pp. 86–89) has observed that there are two ways for data mining: (a) data revealing by the victim herself and (b) socialising with friends and acquaintances of the victim and secretly spying the victim's online activities. While the latter is mostly applicable for cyber stalking incidences, the groomers may use this method to find more victims or for subsequent stalking of the victim. It needs to be understood that the social networking sites, particularly, provide wide opportunities for data revealing by the data handlers, that is, the users of the profiles. Both, Facebook and Twitter, allow users to update about their professional designation, publish private photos, speak about personal feelings using emoticons and share their opinion in the timelines of other 'friends'. Further, these social media platforms also allow users to tag people in their albums and time line updates, create groups and

---

[3] Ibid.

include people without actually getting consent from them. Even though all social media platforms including Facebook and Twitter periodically revise their privacy statements, the underlying meaning is clear: while creating a profile an account holder is guided to the privacy policies by the concerned websites. The account holder is also made aware that the personal data may be breached by third party if he/she does not wish to use the security options that are provided in each occasion of publishing his/her updates, photos or any other information that he/she prefers to share from other profiles. Such security options include choices for making the update available for 'public', or for 'friends' or for 'close friends'.[4] But there are numbers of loopholes; for example, unless the user is opting for 'hiding mode' (by clicking on options for not allowing the particular website to allow search engines to show the full profile link), the screen name and the profile picture of the user can be visible to third parties even if she opts for personal mode for her time line updates, albums and so on. Again, in cases of unaware or ignorant users who may not use privacy options, the social networking sites may immunise themselves from the tortuous liability by putting the onus on the users themselves to 'save' themselves.

Further, in India, data mining may also happen in matrimonial websites. We note that while there are not much report on adult dating sites and related crimes in India, there are numbers of matrimonial websites, which may partially serve this purpose, where prospective brides and grooms may upload their profiles and socialise. Many of such websites make it mandatory to register with them with personal information to search for partners, and thereby restrict search options for non-members. This may prevent anonymous harassment. But simultaneously, there are not many options for protecting privacy about the information which may have been revealed by the prospective bride/s in their own profiles. Harassers may still use fake names and identity to get connected with women, build their confidence in them and may financially and emotionally cheat them. This is evident from the 'Advisory for functioning Matrimonial Websites', which was uploaded by Ministry of Women and Child Development in their official webpage.[5]

However, this trend of data mining by the groomer and data revealing by the general ICT users may be found in any ICT-based platforms.

---

[4] For more, see privacy basics of Facebook athttps://www.facebook.com/about/basics/and of Twitter at https://support.twitter.com/articles/20170134

[5] The Advisory is available at http://wcd.nic.in/acts/advisory-functioning-matrimonial-websites (Accessed on 7 July 2016).

For example, people (including women and teenagers) may circulate their phone numbers among their friends without apprehending how her number may be circulated to unknown persons due to numerous technological tricks including phone hacking, unauthorised use of phone by others or playing childish tricks with mobile messaging services by children who may be unaware of safety issues (Halder & Jaishankar, 2014). It has been observed that many women may keep their WhatsApp profiles 'public' or the particular number may reach strangers who may have randomly called numbers and stored the numbers in their devices (Halder & Jaishankar, 2015a). Such behavioural pattern regarding privacy may push women and girls to become victims of groomers. As such, digital privacy of women and children may also be susceptible due to Big Data revolution on the internet.

As has been mentioned earlier, women and girls as 'data controllers' of their own data and information (Koops, 2011), may continuously feed the Big Database of the internet companies with their updates, which may be used as 'meta data' (Koops, 2011). Groomers while randomly searching for their victims may take note of the behavioural pattern of the possible targets; for example, sharing selfies taken in different geo locations may indicate that the woman may be adventurous, but may be lonely and may need some virtual companion to share her experiences; sharing lonely, sad or depressed emoticons may indicate that the person concerned may be in a delicate psychological state where she can be trapped by kind, caring words; sharing status updates for workplace stress may indicate that the person concerned could be trapped by communication which shows sympathy to her condition and sharing similar experiences (by way of made up stories) by the groomer. There are also numerous instances where housewives were trapped and groomed by the perpetrators who may have contacted the women after seeing their status updates, posts in group discussions or forums where they would have expressed unhappiness about their family.[6]

Causes and Effects of Grooming

Majority of the researchers are of the opinion that online grooming may be done by a predator who may be a paedophile; his ultimate aim in grooming his target victims may be sexual gratification of self

[6] From the personal experiences of the authors.

(Berson, 2003; O'Connel, 2009; Schrock & Boyd, 2008; Wall, 2007). These researchers have also opined that groomers can be associated with gangs who target children and youth for paedophilic contents and they may gain profit from such contents. As we expanded the scope of the concept of online grooming to adult grooming in our earlier publication (Halder & Jaishankar, 2011), we observed that adult women may also fall victims of online groomers who may groom their victims for sexual satisfaction of self by unethical means, monetary gain by the contents so received or for monetary gain by deceiving or cheating. Similarly, causes of online grooming may be seen from the perspective of the victim precipitation as well. Most of the researchers including Wall (2007), O'Connel (2009) and Schrock and Boyd (2008) have opined that victims of online grooming may be receptive to the groomers because they needed the attention that the groomers deceitfully showered on them. As such, there may be two main causes (see Figure 4.1) that motivate grooming.

It may be understood that perpetrators as groomers may necessarily use all the advantages of digital communication technology including being anonymous. The perpetrators may contact those victims who either directly or indirectly express their loneliness, need for attention or financial assistance. For example, for teenagers or young women, the

Figure 4.1:
Causes motivating grooming

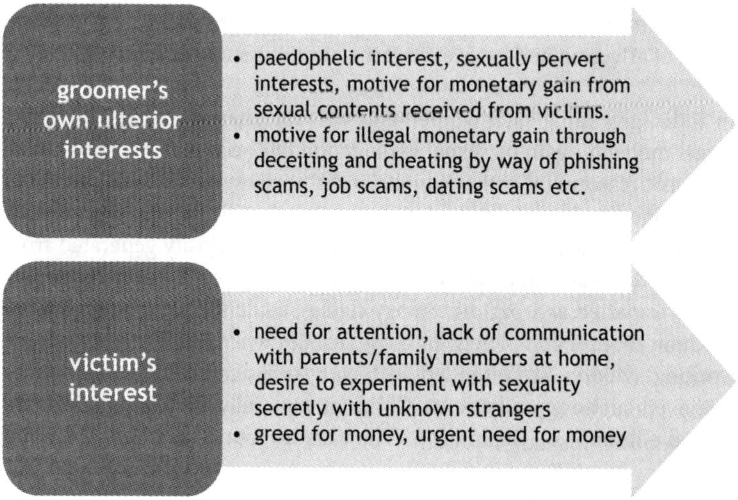

groomer's own ulterior interests	• paedophelic interest, sexually pervert interests, motive for monetary gain from sexual contents received from victims. • motive for illegal monetary gain through deceiting and cheating by way of phishing scams, job scams, dating scams etc.
victim's interest	• need for attention, lack of communication with parents/family members at home, desire to experiment with sexuality secretly with unknown strangers • greed for money, urgent need for money

Source: Authors.

perpetrator groomers may simply start the conversation in a non-sexual way, which may later turn into regular communication asking the victim to send nude photographs or come to the webcam-based chat such as Skype.[7] The perpetrators may share fictitious stories with the girls and women to win their confidence. Women, including single or divorced, may be allured to speak about their sexual expectations, domestic abuse or workplace harassment. There are cases where the victims may be asked to come to video chat either on Facebook or on Skype or in similar webcam-based chat messengers, but the perpetrators may not switch on their camera devices. In some cases, women may be asked to share their personal bank account numbers, in a similar way as phishing or SMiShing or vishing occurs. The question is why do the victims become receptive to the groomers who are strangers to them? To answer this question, victims of grooming may be categorised into three groups:

- Group A: Who are ignorant of internet safety rules and who may be new users or first-generation users of internet and digital communication technology in their families.
- Group B: Mostly teenage girls, who are in a transition period from adolescence to adulthood and feel that they need more virtual friends to share their secrets than real life friends, the latter may reveal their secrets to their parents or to their elders or teachers.
- Group C: Who may be adult women, in need of emotional comforts as well as monetary assistance, and who may be extremely vulnerable to give into any person who communicates with a touch of affection and care, even if the communicator is unknown.

In India, grooming such women and girls for ulterior motives including illegal monetary gain or sexual exploitation has become easier because of two basic reasons: (a) orthodox patriarchal social system and (b) greed for easy money. In India, girls and boys in many families are not encouraged to have sex education at pre-puberty stage. The curiosity generated from childhood remains unanswered. Even though in many schools sex education is imparted as a part of biology classes, students may not be allowed to know about it completely. In most families where both the parents are working, children are often left with gadgets instead of close relatives or caregivers such as grandparents. Children, especially girls, find their unanswered questions on the internet. The vacuum created due to the absence

---

[7] From the experiences of the lead author.

of communication between parents and children pushes them to communicate with strangers. Further, in many cases, we have seen that girls are taught not to speak about their adolescent sexual expectations and fantasies either at home or at school. Busy parents may never be able to understand the slow changes in the psychology of their daughter. Their attempt to speak to their parents may meet with harsh replies including scolding or confining them at home. Consider some standard communication styles that the groomers generally use, these may include sympathetic comments such as 'you don't deserve how they treat you' or 'I have also been treated like you' or 'you are looking beautiful in your pictures'—communications which may easily win the trust of girls who look for care and affection from outside their known hostile environment.

Women especially married but economically dependent or those who are undergoing severe depression in their relationship with spouses may also go through similar state of mind. Consider cases of women who are in the process of separation and make 'friends' on social media such as Facebook, who shower care and affection through chat sessions. Such women are often made to believe that they are abused for no fault of theirs and they deserved better life partners. We have dealt with victims who had groomers supposedly from countries like United Kingdom, Canada, Australia and United States. Women in such cases felt elated to know that men from different countries are praising their beauty, sexual appeal and professional skills. Women in such conditions may not only be showered praises for their physical appearance and sympathy for their psychological conditions, but also fictitious job offerings or business proposals.

Effects of grooming may necessarily be illegal and unethical gain for the groomers. Groomers may not only be able to convince the victim to voluntarily share their private images including nude and sexted images, they may also create a network using children as well as adults to share images of their friends without letting these friends know about it. This way, the groomers may keep the continuous feed of sexually explicit images alive. In some cases, these images may be delivered to adult entertainment sites. Groomers may also necessarily adopt the method of sextortion, a process whereby the victims may be threatened to pay a hefty amount to keep their sexted or regular images safe with the groomers and not to send them as sexually explicit materials either to the adult networking sites or to general social media. In cases where the victims are induced to accept business proposals, they may be encouraged to part with heavy amounts initially only to pay more later in the name of sextortion or blackmailing as the victims may be threatened by the groomers to expose the communication details to the husbands or immediate family members or to their workplaces either through private digital communication or through social media. Grooming may thus not only result in sexual offences over the internet but also take its own path by way of stalking, creation of fake avatars, voyeurism and of course phishing and cheating. Mostly these groomers use fake identities and sometimes real identities as well, which are created to groom their victims, especially women for various ulterior purposes, including flirting, sexual gratification and monetary gains; the grooming method can further be explained by three case studies:

(i)   As a report published in *The Times of India* suggests, a 22 year old man from Bangalore apparently duped a young woman through Facebook and extorted nearly ₹7 lakhs. It was apparently a clean and simple Facebook friendship at the beginning, which grew into an emotional bonding between the victim and the perpetrator as the later not only gained confidence of the woman to believe him as an upcoming cinema hero, he also extracted a huge sum of money from her. He also pestered her to meet in real life and clicked pictures together. The victim was also threatened that her pictures with him would be released on internet if she did not oblige him to give more money. On complaint from the victim, the police arrested him and deleted the pictures of the victim from his devices. The report, however, did not mention about the provisions that have been used to arrest the accused.[8]

(ii) In another report published in NDTV news, the police had busted a racket which used matrimonial sites to befriend prospective brides only to cheat them financially. The fraudsters apparently used to contact women by posing as NRIs. As the report further suggested, the perpetrators used foreign SIM cards along with VoIP. The victim woman was duped by the fraudsters who created a fake profile of a doctor working abroad. The victim's confidence was won by constant communication. The victim was further 'won over' when the fraudster informed her that he was sending gifts including jewellery to her address. The situation

---

[8] See Kalkodi. R (June 19, 2016). Facebook friend blackmails college girl, extorts ₹7 lakh from her. *Times of India*. Available at http://timesofindia.indiatimes.com/city/bengaluru/Facebook-friend-blackmails-college-girl-extorts-Rs-7-lakh-from-her/articleshow/52815508.cms (Accessed on 19 June 2016).

turned to be that like a typical financial cheating case or phishing when the victim received calls from so-called customs officers to clear the customs duty of the package. She was asked to pay huge sums to get the packages. The victim then complained to the police who found out that the fraudsters were cheating women in this fashion.[9]

While these are just a few examples of how groomers use the victims to win their confidence only to gain money illegally, there are hundreds of examples of how groomers may target young girls and women to sexually abuse them in the electronic form.

Challenges and Regulation

The main challenge that the police, prosecution or the counsellors dealing with cyber crimes, especially crimes against women, may face is acknowledging the role of the groomers, the grooming mechanism and the effect of grooming as separate incidences that can individually count as offences. It is often seen that victims of grooming feel extremely reluctant to lodge any police report fearing their own voluntary involvement in the victimisation process. They may take up irrational coping mechanism such as tracking and hacking or trying to hack the groomer's profiles or email id to remove the contents, including the images as well as the chat logs, texts, scanned copies of bank details, personal identification cards and so on that may have been conveyed by the victims themselves. This actually invites more trouble for the victims as the groomers may become enraged by this and may try to do more harm (Halder & Jaishankar, 2015b).

It is sadly noted that there are so far no reported case law to show how prosecution in India has dealt with the act of the grooming of the adult women alone. However, the scenario is different when it comes to children. The IT Act, 2000 (amended in 2008) was the first provision to

---

[9] See PTI. (6 July 2015). Woman duped of ₹48 lakh through matrimonial website, 3 arrested in Gurgaon. Available at http://www.ndtv.com/gurgaon-news/woman-duped-of-rs-48-lakh-through-matrimonial-website-3-arrested-in-gurgaon-778556 (Accessed on 19 June 2016).

touch upon the issue of grooming children for sexual abuse on the internet. S.67B(c) states that

> Whoever cultivates, entices or induces children to online relationship with one or more children for and on sexually explicit act or in a manner that may offend a reasonable adult on the computer resource, shall be punished on first conviction with imprisonment of either description for a term which may extend to five years and with a fine which may extend to ten lakh rupees and in the event of second or subsequent conviction with imprisonment of either description for a term which may extend to seven years and also with fine which may extend to ten lakh rupees.

Subsequently, Protection of Children from Sexual Offences Act, 2012, narrowly touched the issue of grooming especially in S.11 (VI) (sexual harassment and punishment therefore), which says a person is said to commit sexual harassment upon a child when such person with sexual intention entices a child for pornographic purposes. S.12 prescribes punishment for this, which is imprisonment for a term which may extend to three years along with fine. Further, S.13 of the POCSO Act may also be used, especially to bring charges for using the child for pornographic purposes. S.15 (punishment for storage of pornographic materials involving child) can also be included in this regard since grooming may necessarily include storing of sexually explicit contents of the child victim. But reported cases on the process of grooming are extremely rare in India not only for girls but also for women. S.66D of the IT Act, 2000 (amended in 2008) provides some solution to prevent creation of impersonating profile. It states,

> Whoever, by means of any communication device or computer resource cheats by personation, shall be punished with imprisonment of either description for a term which may extend to three years and shall also be liable to fine which may extend to one lakh rupees.

The object of this section is to prevent personation for cheating. But it the drafting of this section does not suggest whether it can be used for cases where there is no illegal monetary gain or loss, but only emotional injuries suffered by the victim due to the deceptive communication of the fraudster. The victim may find solace in S.66D of the IT Act, 2000 (amended in 2008); only this Section may be interpreted in its linguistic meaning of cheating. But along with this, the Section must also be accompanied by provisions like the now defunct Section 66A(b) and

66A(c), which prohibits sending any information through computer resources, communication devices and/or electronic mails/messages which the sender knows to be false, but sends it to cause especially annoyance, inconvenience, danger, insult, injury and criminal intimidation. However, it needs to be further noted that S.66A(b) of the IT Act was declared unconstitutional by the Supreme Court in 2015 in the case of Shreya Singhal v. Union of India & others, 2013, mainly because the provision did not provide any definition of the terms used therein including the concept of 'injury' (including emotional injury). The concept of 'injury' however has been explained under Section 44 of IPC which extends the meaning of the term to cover mental distress by stating that 'the word 'injury' denotes any harm whatever illegally caused to any person, in body, mind, reputation or property.' But as stated above, there are not much reported cases to show how the courts would have interpreted the laws, especially S.66D of IT Act, 2000 (amended in 2008) along with traditional penal laws including Sections 415 of IPC. It says,

> Whoever, by deceiving any person, fraudulently or dishonestly induces the person so deceived to deliver any property to any person, or to consent that any person shall retain any property, or intentionally induces the person so deceived to do or omit to do anything which he would not do or omit if he were not so deceived, and which act or omission causes or is likely to cause damage or harm to that person in body, mind, reputation or property, is said to 'cheat'.

Explanation attached to it further clarifies that 'a dishonest concealment of facts is deception within the meaning of this section' and S. 416 of the IPC (which states that a person is said to cheat by personation if he cheats by pretending to be some other person or by knowingly substituting one person for another or representing him or any other person is a person other than he or such other person really. Explanation to this section further clarifies that the offence is committed whether the individual personated is real or imaginary person) which may very well suit the cases especially when the grooming and subsequent cheating involves monetary loss.

But there is a wide gap in understanding about effectiveness of laws in cases where the grooming and subsequent cheating does not involve monetary cheating, but results only in injury to the feeling and mental distress. Courts in India have on several occasions held that any individual, who has suffered mental distress due to a broken promise for marriage, may have cause of action for suing the other for causing mental distress and injury.[10] But no precedence have been set for the cases involving online grooming and causing mental distress by breaking the promises. Interestingly in such cases, along with S.66D of the IT Act, 2000 (amended in 2008), the victims can also bring charges for voyeurism under S.354B of IPC along with S.66E of the IT Act, or for creating sexually explicit images under S.67 of the IT Act, 2000 (amended in 2008), along with Ss 499 (defamation), 500 (punishment for defamation) and 509 (punishment for harming the modesty of woman) of IPC in cases where the perpetrator would have published private images of the victim which she may not have wishes to be published unless married to the person concerned, or images of the victim along with himself in compromising situations which may have the potentials to damage to reputation. But the question is, whether the victim can really avail the right to sue the perpetrator for being duped by grooming? Unlike child victims, adults are expected to have intellectual maturity to understand the risk factors involved in online communication. On this very understanding, most of the websites claim for immunity under Section 230 of the Communication Decency Act. In such cases, the victim's rights to claim for damages from the websites become extremely limited. Further, it increases the risk of victim blaming which, in turn, may discourage the victims to proceed further with her claim for justice. This situation could be changed if provisions like S.66A of the IT Act, 2000 (amended in 2008; prescribes punishment for sending offensive messages through communication services etc.) is brought back with proper amendments which may explain the scope of the provision and define the terms properly (Halder, 2015) and if such provision is properly tested by the courts and utilised along with provisions including S.66D of the IT Act, 2000 (amended in 2008) and other provisions mentioned above as per the need of the case.

However, while several provisions are available for regulating online grooming, as stated previously, neither victims emphasise upon the course of grooming while reporting the crimes nor the police officers take proper note of this course of victimisation. It is very much suggested that the women and girls should be aware such hidden patterns of offences on the internet and, if victimised, they must report the whole course of victimisation to the police. Simultaneously, the police must also consider applying these provisions for helping the victim to get proper justice.

[10] See N. Sukumaran Nair and Anr. V. P. Narayanan (1996) 2 MLJ 184.

References

Berson, I. R. (2003). Grooming cybervictims: The psychosocial effects of online exploitation for youth. *Journal of School Violence, 2* (1), 5–18.

Bocij, P., Griffiths, M. D., & McFarlane, L. (2002). Cyber stalking: A new challenge for criminal law. *The Criminal Lawyer, 122*, 3–5. Available at https://www.academia.edu/759647/Bocij_P._Griffiths_M.D._and_McFarlane_L._2002_._Cyberstalking_A_new_challenge_for_criminal_law._The_Criminal_Lawyer_122_3-5 (Accessed 10 May 2014).

Brenner, S. (2004). Cyber crime metrics: old wine in new bottles? *Virginia Journal of Law and Technology, 9*, no. 13, 1–53. Available at http://www.vjolt.net/vol9/issue4/v9i4_a13-Brenner.pdf (Accessed on 10 May 2014).

Ellison, L., & Akdeniz, Y. (1998). Cyber-stalking: The Regulation of Harassment on the Internet. *Criminal Law Review*, December Special Edition: Crime, Criminal Justice and the Internet, 29–48. Available at http://www.cyber-rights.org/documents/stalking_article.pdf. (Accessed on 12 May 2014).

Halder, D. (2013a). Examining the scope of Indecent Representation of Women (Prevention) Act, 1986, in the light of cyber victimization of women in India. *National Law School Journal, 11*, 188–218.

———. (2015). A Retrospective analysis of S.66a: Could S.66a of the Information Technology Act be reconsidered for regulating 'bad talk' in the internet? *Indian Student Law Review (ISLR), 3*, 91–118.

Halder, D., & Jaishankar K. (June, 2011). *Cyber crime and the Victimization of Women: Laws, Rights, and Regulations.* Hershey, PA, USA: IGI Global.

———. (2014). Patterns of sexual victimization of children and women in the multipurpose social networking sites. In C. Marcum and G. Higgins (eds), *Social networking as a criminal enterprise* (pp. 129–143). Boca Raton, FL, USA: CRC Press, Taylor and Francis Group.

———. (2015a). Harassment via WhatsApp in urban and rural India: A baseline survey report (2015). Tirunelveli, India: Centre for Cyber Victim Counselling. Available at http://www.cybervictims.org/CCVCresearchreport2015.pdf (Accessed on 12 January 2016).

———. (2015b). Irrational coping theory and positive criminology: A framework to protect victims of cyber crime. In N. Ronel and D. Segev (eds), *Positive criminology* (pp. 276–291). Abingdon, Oxon: Routledge.

Koops, B. (2011). Forgetting footprints, shunning shadows: A critical analysis of the 'right to be forgotten' in big data practice. *SCRIPTed, 8*(3), 229–256.

Kopecky, K. (2015). Misuse of web cameras to manipulate children within the so-called webcam trolling. *Telematics and Informatics, 33*(1), 1–7. Available at https://www.researchgate.net/publication/278031172_Misuse_of_Web_Cameras_to_Manipulate_Children_within_the_so-called_Webcam_Trolling (Accessed on 12 February 2016).

O'Connell, R. (2009). A typology of cybersexploitation and on-line grooming practices. Available at http://image.guardian.co.uk/sys-files/Society/documents/2003/07/24/Netpaedoreport.pdf (Accessed on 2 February 2015).

Rege, A. (2009). What's love got to do with it? Exploring online dating scams and identity fraud. *International Journal of Cyber Criminology, 3*(2), 494–512.

Schrock, A., & Boyd, D. (2008). Online threats to youth: Solicitation, harassment, and problematic content. Final report of the internet safety technological task force. Enhancing Child Safety and Online Technologies. Available at http://www.danah.org/papers/ISTTF-RABLitReview.pdf (Accessed on 3 July 2015).

Van der Hof, S., & Koops, B.-J. (2011). Adolescents and cybercrime: Navigating between freedom and control. *Policy & Internet, 3*(2), Article 4.

Wachs, S., Wolf, K. D., & Pan, C. (2012). Cybergrooming: Risk factors, coping strategies and associations with cyberbullying. *Psicothema, 24*(4), 628–633.

Wall, D. (2007). *Cybercrime: The transformation of crime in the information age, polity.* Cambridge: Polity Press.

Zeynep, T. (2008). Grooming, gossip, Facebook and Myspace. *Information, Communication & Society, 11*(4), 544–564. DOI: 10.1080/13691180801999050. Available at http://www.tandfonline.com/doi/full/10.1080/13691180801999050 (Accessed on 12 January 2016).

5

Privacy Infringement

The concept of right to privacy for women and girls in relation to electronic media has often been narrowly understood as right to protection against sexual predators. Traditionally, right to privacy has been interpreted as right to be left alone from arbitrary interference in regard to one's person, family, home, reputation and honour. Article 17(1) of the International Covenant on Civil and Political Rights says, 'No one shall be subjected to arbitrary or unlawful interference with his privacy, family, home or correspondence, nor to unlawful attacks on his honour and reputation.' Ancillary provision to Article 17(1) further extends the scope of this right to be included within the meaning of right to equality when it says, 'Everyone has the right to the protection of the law against such interference or attacks.' (Article 17(2) of the International Covenant on Civil and Political Rights.) When conceived within the meaning of internet era, the right to privacy was first assumed as a right against unauthorised access to one's digital property, including computer devices, digital data, emails, social media profiles, intellectual property and so on. With the advent of digital communication technology, the concept of digital privacy infringement also expanded to include unwanted phone calls, monitoring and digital surveillance, and leaking of private information in the publicly viewable platforms. This was further broadened to include publishing revenge porn in the electronic media (Franks, 2015). In sum, while traditionally in real life infringement of privacy has been seen as a right to be left alone with dignity, the same has been construed when seen from the perspective of electronic media. Infringement of right to privacy may be treated as the heart of the problem in relation to cyber crimes irrespective of gender. This observation can be explained with the help of the analysis of the term 'data' as has been defined by S.2(o) of the IT Act, 2000, amended in 2008; this definitions is as follows:

> 'Data' means a representation of information, knowledge, facts, concepts or instructions which are being prepared or have been prepared in a formalized manner, and is intended to be processed, is being processed or has been processed in a computer system or computer network, and may be in any form (including computer printouts magnetic or optical storage media, punched cards, punched tapes) or stored internally in the memory of the computer.

As the definition suggests, data can be static or mobile, can be raw or can be processed, modified either with the computing technology or by the aid of digital communication technology. Presently, computer devices or devices enabled with digital computing including smartphones, digital cameras, tablets and so on can all be storage devices and all of them are vulnerable for unauthorised access even if they are not connected with the Wi-Fi or any other mode with other computer devices located at distant geographic locations. It may need to be understood that unauthorised access to the device may itself infringe the privacy of not only the owner of the device by way of accessing his or her data stored in it, but such unauthorised access may also infringe the privacy of others by way of manually operating the device and making use of the data thus created in an unethical manner, or by way of operating on remote control basis. The motive and effect of privacy infringement in the electronic media can thus be either sexual or non-sexual (see Figure 5.1).

As seen from Figure 5.1, while in the first case, the motive for infringement for privacy can be taking revenge over a jittery emotional affair or sexual gratification by way of paedophilia or consuming adult porn or profit-making through commodification of personal information including images, the effects of the same can be reputation damage for the victim, withdrawal effect, development of suicidal tendency or increased risk to physical security of the victim and his/her family members. In the second case, when the motive is not sexual, the perpetrator/s can breach the privacy for illegal monetary gain by various fraudulent ways for gratification of workplace jealousy. There are also instances of privacy breach for establishing solid grounds for court cases for family matters including divorce or separation issues. Apart from this, such sorts of privacy infringement may happen in the name of surveillance as well. The effects of these may or may not be similar to those types of privacy infringement which are motivated by sexual reasons. However, such sorts of privacy breach may necessarily result in monetary loss by the victims, facing court cases or corporate data breach if the victim is a company.

Figure 5.1:
Motives and effects of privacy infringement in the electronic media

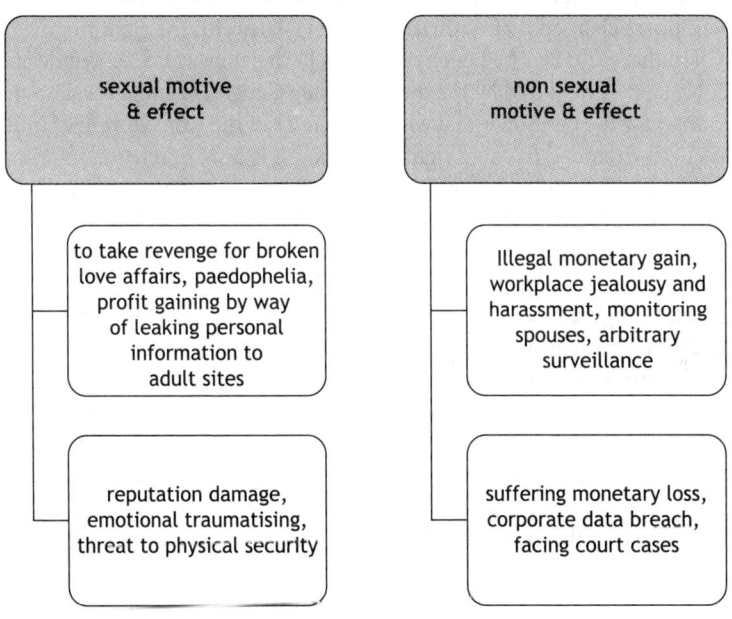

sexual motive
& effect

non sexual
motive & effect

to take revenge for broken
love affairs, paedophelia,
profit gaining by way
of leaking personal
information to
adult sites

Illegal monetary gain,
workplace jealousy and
harassment, monitoring
spouses, arbitrary
surveillance

reputation damage,
emotional traumatising,
threat to physical security

suffering monetary loss,
corporate data breach,
facing court cases

Source: Authors.

From the above, it may be understood that there are certain patterns of privacy infringement, especially for women and girls. It is an unfortunate fact that women in South Asia, especially from Indian subcontinent, are extremely conscious about their image in their own communities, so are their families. Any damage to reputation or even anticipation of the same by way of spreading of any derogatory comment to the character of the woman concerned, may prove extremely dangerous not only for her but for her entire family. Consider the cases of honour killing when women in many parts of India marry according to their own choice, or may have developed an emotional relationship with a man who would not be approved by her family or her community; the feeling or anticipation of shame may make the woman and her family members to take extreme steps. Similarly, any sort of privacy infringement by way of electronic media may also prove extremely dangerous for women. We have come across cases where women have undergone serious mental trauma in anticipation of damage to their reputation, especially for marriage market, due to digital breach of privacy. But, even though the effects could be so severe, there are no focussed laws to establish breach of digital privacy or digital breach of privacy as violation of fundamental right to privacy. This was noticed by the Supreme Court in a recent case regarding the constitutional validity of Aadhaar scheme since petitioners claimed that Aadhaar scheme violates citizen's right to privacy (Choudhary, 2015). The bench of Justices J. Chelameswar, S. A. Bobde and C. Nagappan were told by the then Attorney General of India and also the counsel for the petitioner that while Article 21 of the Constitution of India has been extended to cover right to privacy, it is only in relation to criminal proceeding and search and seizure by the government. This particular point was recognised in the case of Kharak Singh v. State of UP,[1] which has remained a landmark judgment in privacy jurisprudence in India till now. However, even though right to privacy is not a fundamental right in India, in case of digital breach of privacy, India has developed several laws, some of which are exclusively for women. In this chapter, we will discuss about the patterns of privacy violation in the electronic media, some of which are recognised by these laws and some of which still deserve legal recognition in India. As may be seen in Figure 5.2, patterns of privacy infringement in the electronic media can be of three particular types. Such patterns of privacy breach may happen to any individual irrespective of gender. But for the purpose of this book, the discussions are made more gender oriented.

Figure 5.2:
Pattern of Privacy Infringement by Electronic Media

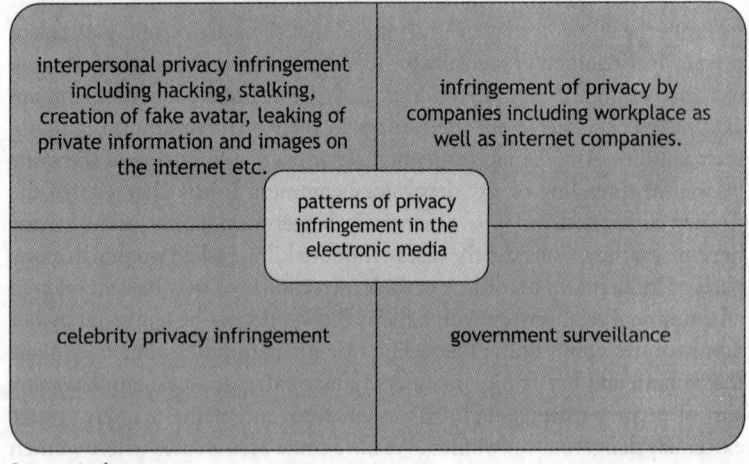

interpersonal privacy infringement including hacking, stalking, creation of fake avatar, leaking of private information and images on the internet etc.

infringement of privacy by companies including workplace as well as internet companies.

patterns of privacy infringement in the electronic media

celebrity privacy infringement

government surveillance

Source: Authors.

[1] Kharak Singh v. the State of UP (1964) 1 SCR 332.

Interpersonal Privacy Infringement

These kinds of privacy infringements are carried out by acquaintances of the victims whom she would have known personally either as a friend, or relative, or colleague or even as competitor. The following are some of the patterns which may fall within this category.

Unauthorised Access to Data, Computer Devices and Disrupting the Access to Network

This sort of digital privacy infringement is generally termed as hacking. The concept of privacy infringement by way of unauthorised access to digital data was further widened by including unauthorised modification of the data that has been accessed without authorisation. In many jurisdictions including the United States, United Kingdom, Canada, Australia and also India, such of infringement of digital privacy have been criminalised. It needs to be understood that Indian laws, especially IT Act, 2000 (amended in 2008) does not mention the term 'hacking' while regulating such sorts of privacy breach. Further, depending upon the remedies available for such misdeeds, the IT Act offers both civil as well as criminal regulating provisions. The regulatory provision in the civil nature is stated under S.43, which is exhaustive and it terms the offence as damage to computer, computer system, data, network and so on. It says,

> If any person without permission of the owner or any other person who is in charge of a computer, computer system or computer network:
>
> (a) accesses or secures access to such computer, computer system or computer network or computer resource;
> (b) downloads, copies or extracts any data, computer database or information from such computer, computer system or computer network including information or data held or stored in any removable storage medium;
> (c) introduces or causes to be introduced any computer contaminant or computer virus into any computer, computer system or computer network;
> (d) damages or causes to be damaged any computer, computer system or computer network, data, computer database or any other programs residing in such computer, computer system or computer network;

    (e) disrupts or causes disruption of any computer, computer system or computer network;

    (f) denies or causes the denial of access to any person authorised to access any computer, computer system or computer network by any means;

    (g) provides any assistance to any person to facilitate access to a computer, computer system or computer network in contravention of the provisions of this Act, rules or regulations made thereunder,

    (h) charges the services availed of by a person to the account of another person by tampering with or manipulating any computer, computer system or computer network,

    (i) destroys, deletes or alters any information residing in a computer resource or diminishes its value or utility or affects it injuriously by any means (inserted vide ITAA-2008);

    (j) Steals, conceals, destroys or alters or causes any person to steal, conceal, destroy or alter any computer source code used for a computer resource with an intention to cause damage, he shall be liable to pay damages by way of compensation not exceeding one crore rupees to the person so affected. (change vide ITAA 2008)

The section further provides some explanations where the following terms are explained and defined:

1. *Computer Contaminant* means any set of computer instructions that are designed (a) to modify, destroy, record, transmit data or program residing within a computer, computer system or computer network; or (b) by any means to usurp the normal operation of the computer, computer system or computer network;

2. *Computer Database* means a representation of information, knowledge, facts, concepts or instructions in text, image, audio, video that are being prepared or have been prepared in a formalised manner or have been produced by a computer, computer system or computer network and are intended for use in a computer, computer system or computer network;

3. *Computer Virus* means any computer instruction, information, data or program that destroys, damages, degrades or adversely affects the performance of a computer resource or attaches itself to another computer resource and operates when a program, data or instruction is executed or some other event takes place in that computer resource;

4. *Damage* means to destroy, alter, delete, add, modify or re-arrange any computer resource by any means;

5. *Computer Source Code* means the listing of programs, computer commands, design and layout and program analysis of computer resource in any form.

Apart from this provision, S.66 of the IT Act prescribes criminal remedies for such offences and states that, 'If any person, dishonestly, or fraudulently, does any act referred to in section 43, he shall be punishable with imprisonment for a term which may extend to two to three years or with fine which may extend to five lakh rupees or with both.'[2] However, in certain cases where unauthorised access to the data is gained through fraudulent measures, including making use of digital signature or unique identification such as passwords and so on, S.66 and also S.43 must be read along with S.66C, which prescribed punishment for identity theft. Such sorts of methods are mostly used especially in financial cheating cases including phishing.[3] However, it would be wrong to say that cyber crime against women does not include phishing. We have come across many instances where women and transgender women have also suffered heavy financial loss due to phishing, which involved fraudulently extracting ATM/debit/credit card details, online banking details and so on. However, in our experience, most of such phishing or financial cheating cases have occurred after the victim was groomed by the perpetrators.[4]

There are many instances of hacking and hacking-related offences victimising women in India. These may include hacking into a woman's email ID or social media profile or even computer device to get private information, including private pictures of the victim and then present them in a modified fashion to victimise her.[5] Unauthorised access to

---

[2] Explanation attached to this provision says (a) the word 'dishonestly' shall have the meaning assigned to it in Section 24 of the Indian Penal Code; (b) the word 'fraudulently' shall have the meaning assigned to it in Section 25 of the Indian Penal Code.

[3] See Chapter 4 for detailed discussion on phishing and various types of financial cheating through electronic media.

[4] For detailed discussion on grooming, see Chapter 4.

[5] See for example, Mehta. A. (March 2, 2011) Spurned youth posts obscene pix of girlfriend. *The Times of India.* Available at http://timesofindia.indiatimes.com/city/jaipur/Spurned-youth-posts-obscene-pix-ofgirlfriend/articleshow/7605208.cms (Accessed on 21 May 2015). In this case, the perpetrator hacked into the email account of the victim and accessed private photographs to misuse them on other websites.

spouse's emails is another such instance. Social media profiles have also become a very common method to get information about the spouse for bringing solid grounds for separation or divorce. In such cases, it is often asked whether accessing the email accounts, social media profiles or any other data within the meaning of S.2(o) of the IT Act of the spouse by another spouses (especially when they are proceeding towards separation) may amount to unauthorised access to the data. It was held in the case of Vinod Kaushik & another v. Nidhi Joshi & others[6] that such acts by spouses may amount to violation of privacy by way of unauthorised access to data, even if the passwords were known. The observation of Shri Rajesh Agarwal (the then adjudicating officer under IT Act, 2000 in Maharashtra) in this case is worth mentioning. The observation is as follows:

> As far as the question of knowledge of password is concerned, it is quite clear from the papers produced by Respondent No. 1 that Complainant No. 2 (husband) had shared passwords with her and also mentioned to her that password of Complainant No. 1 is the same as that of Complainant No. 2. The records produced by Complainants do not prove that they changed the passwords. Hence, a reasonable conclusion is that Respondent knew the passwords, and she took Complainant by surprise by accessing their Gmail accounts, looking at dozens if not hundreds of emails and chat sessions, and forwarding/printing those emails and chat sessions which she thought would help her in the Dowry case. Respondent heavily argues that there is a 'bond of trust' between husband and wife and hence she had right to access the emails. As the emails have been accessed after this bond of trust was broken, and dowry case was lodged, and husband arrested, I find no merit in this argument. Section 43 of IT Act clearly applies, regarding unauthorized access. The respondent has not only accessed the email account of her husband, but also her father-in-law's chat sessions with his relatives and friends. Thus, she has violated the privacy of not only the Complainants, but also of their friends and relatives, who had no stretch of imagination, authorized her to look into these private chat sessions. Even in family or company premises, if someone has forgotten to log out, and another person comes across the open emails when he/she tries to log into their own Gmail (or other email of Facebook or Skype etc.) account, the normal expectation is that the new person will immediately log out and not snoop into other emails or chat sessions. Thus it makes a vast difference whether you glance at an open email, or log into a closed email box

---

[6] See Vinod Kaushik & another v. Nidhi Joshi & others, Complaint no.2 of 2010. Available at https://it.maharashtra.gov.in/Site/Upload/ACT/Madhvika%20Vs%20Kaushik-Rajesh%20Aggarwal.pdf

using a password and look at the emails. This is similar to the difference between looking at an open letter lying around versus opening a sealed envelope which clearly is meant for somebody else. Hence regardless of the fact whether the Respondent No. 1 knew the passwords, or made intelligent guesses, or used some software to crack the passwords, it is clear that she unauthorisedly accessed the emails and chat sessions, and violated the provisions of IT Act. The Respondent had no authority to open these Gmail accounts, especially of her father-in-law and downloading his chat sessions. If she had any suspicion that material evidence of wrongdoing could be found, she should have approached the Police regarding this, and let the investigative agencies take action per law.[7]

In this case, Shri Agarwal however excused her from paying the compensation as has been prayed for by the petitioners. But considering that this amounts to identity theft under S.66C of the IT Act,[8] the respondent was indicted and was ordered to pay a token amount towards State Treasury. It may be mentioned that this observation stands for victims/petitioners in the same manner if the same are women.

Cyber Stalking

Cyber stalking has been traditionally construed as a behavioural misconduct in the cyber space. According to Bocij, Griffiths & McFarlane (2002) cyber stalking is

A group of behaviours in which an individual, group of individuals or organization, uses information and communications technology to harass one or more individuals. Such behaviours may include, but are not limited to, the transmission of threats and false accusations, identity theft, data

---

[7] See page 5 and 6 in the order in Vinod Kaushik & another v. Nidhi Joshi & others, Complaint no. 2 of 2010. Available at https://it.maharashtra.gov.in/Site/Upload/ACT/Madhvika%20Vs%20Kaushik-Rajesh%20Aggarwal.pdf

[8] S.66C of the IT Act, 2000 (amended in 2008) speaks about punishment for identity theft and it says,

Whoever, fraudulently or dishonestly make use of the electronic signature, password or any other unique identification feature of any other person, shall be punished with imprisonment of either description for a term which may extend to three years and shall also be liable to fine which may extend to rupees one lakh.

theft, damage to data or equipment, computer monitoring, the solicitation of minors for sexual purposes and confrontation.

However, Brenner (2004) correctly pointed out that '[i]n a sense, cyber stalking and cyber harassment are lineal descendants of the obscene or annoying telephone call offenses that were created roughly a century ago, to address harms resulting from the misuse of a nineteenth century technology.' Laws regarding cyber stalking first originated in the US, whereby scopes of physical stalking laws were extended to cover cyber stalking. Legally, cyber stalking was recognised as an offence only in early 1990s. In 1993 Michigan Criminal Code criminalised stalking, including cyber stalking, for the first time.[9] Cyber stalking was considered as 'harassment' through the US laws,[10] which defined the term 'harassment' as 'conduct directed towards a victim that includes repeated or unconsented contact that would cause reasonable individual to suffer emotional distress, and that actually causes the victim to suffer emotional distress.'[11] The Michigan Criminal Code further explained that 'unconsented contact' could mean 'sending unsolicited and unwanted mail or electronic communications to the victim.'[12] Presently many provinces of the United States have enacted anti-cyber stalking laws, which explained cyber stalking in the similar connotation as harassment. With the birth of Violence Against Women and Department of Justice Reauthorization Act, 2005, which amended Section 2261A of Title 18, USC through Section 114[13] the concept of *cyber stalking* was further explained clearly. The term

[9] Michigan Criminal Code, Stalking: Section 28.643(8), definitions. 1993 Section 411h. Available at http://www.haltabuse.org/resources/laws/michigan.shtml (Accessed on 12 December 2013).

[10] Ibid.

[11] Para (b) (2) of Section 2701 of Chapter 121, USC 18(Part I).

[12] Michigan Criminal Code, Stalking: Section 28.643(8), definitions. 1993 Section 411h. Available athttp://www.haltabuse.org/resources/laws/michigan.shtml (Accessed on 12 December 12).

[13] This provision explained the procedure of physical and cyber stalking which may be criminalised. It said,

Whoever (1) travels in interstate or foreign commerce or within the special maritime or territorial jurisdiction of the United States, or enters or leaves Indian country, with the intent to kill, injure, harass or place under surveillance with intent to kill, injure, harass or intimate another person and in the course of, or in the result of such travel places that person in reasonable fear of the death of, or serious bodily injury to, or causes

'cyber staking' is still not defined by any particular legal provision in the United Kingdom.[14] Provisions including Ss.2–7 of the Protection from Harassment Act (PHA), 1987[15] are presently used as the regulatory provision for stalking and cyber stalking. Even though PHA does not specifically define the term 'cyber stalking', the Crown Prosecution Service (CPS) provides an exhaustive definition of cyber stalking based upon the frame work of S2A(3). It says,

> Harassment can take place on the internet and through the misuse of email. This is sometimes known as 'cyber stalking'. This can include the use of social networking sites, chat rooms and other forums facilitated by technology. The internet can be used for a range of purposes relating to harassment, for example: to locate personal information about a victim; to communicate with the victim; as a means of surveillance of the victim; identity theft such as subscribing the victim to services, purchasing goods and services in their name; damaging the reputation of the victim; electronic sabotage such as spamming and sending viruses; or tricking other internet users into harassing or threatening a victim.[16]

---

substantial emotional distress to that person, a member of the immediate family (as described in S.115) of that person, or the spouse or intimate person of that person; or (2) with the intent (A) to kill, injure, harass or intimidate another person, or cause substantial emotional distress to a person in another State or tribal jurisdiction or within the special maritime jurisdiction or territorial jurisdiction of the United States; or (B) to place a person in another State or tribal jurisdiction or within the special maritime jurisdiction or territorial jurisdiction of the United States in reasonable fear of death or is serious bodily injury to (i) that person; (ii) a member of the immediate family (as defined in Section 115 of that person; or (iii) spouse or intimate partner of that person; uses the mail, any interactive computer service, or any facility of interstate or foreign commerce to engage in a course of conduct that causes substantial emotional distress to that person or places that person in real reasonable fear of the death of, or serious bodily injury to, any of the persons described in clause (i) through (iii) of subparagraph (B).

[14] See discussions on stalking in the website of Crown Prosecution Service. Available at http://www.cps.gov.uk/legal/s_to_u/stalking_and_harassment/#a02b (Accessed on 14 May 2014).

[15] See the provisions related to harassment in the Protection from Harassment Act, 1987. Available at http://www.legislation.gov.uk/ukpga/1997/40/contents

[16] Ibid.

In India, there were no cyber stalking laws until 2013. There were huge confusions regarding what constitutes cyber stalking. In our earlier publication, we created a functional definition of cyber stalking, which is as follows: 'In one word, when 'following' is added by mens rea to commit harm and it is successfully digitally carried out, we can say cyber stalking has happened' (Halder & Jaishankar, 2010; Halder, 2015). It may further be noted that there can be two stages of cyber stalking: (a) pursuing digitally by shadowing, collecting information about the victim and so on for monitoring to harm the victim and (b) digitally communicating the threat to infringe the privacy to the victim (Halder, 2015). In 2013, vide Criminal Law Amendment Act, 2013, the Indian government introduced anti-stalking law (covering cyber stalking as well), through S.354D, IPC whereby these two stages of cyber stalking were included. The provision states,

> Any man who follows a woman or contacts or attempts to contact such woman to foster personal interaction repeatedly despite a clear indication of disinterest by such woman or whoever monitors the use by a woman of the internet, email or any other form of electronic communication or watches or spies a person in a manner that results in fear of violence or serious alarm or distress, in the mind of such woman or interferes with the mental peace of such woman, commits the offence of stalking.

Further, provisions added to this Section states,

> Provided that such conduct shall not amount to stalking if the man who pursued it proves that—it was pursued for the purpose of preventing or detecting crime and the man accused of stalking had been entrusted with the responsibility of prevention and detection of crime by the State; or it was pursued under any law or to comply with any condition or requirement imposed by any person under any law; or in the particular circumstances such conduct was reasonable and justified.

As such, cyber stalking by way of email, social media monitoring and repeated phone calls, including missed calls, can also be regulated under this provision. However, it is interesting to note how the police officers perceive the cases of missed calls as stalking. In a recent press release, it was seen that Bihar police was considering applying S.354D IPC for cases where women complaint of repeated missed calls. But simultaneously, it was also directed that this provision must be used and cognizance must be taken when it is a case of 'repeated missed calls' and not just one or two missed calls.[17] This is now being followed in almost all parts of India. However, the reporting in such cases is extremely less.

It may be noted that victim also plays a crucial role in aiding stalking by way of data revealing either knowingly or unknowingly due to data swelling technology. In such cases, victim's role as data controller must not be ignored. But for the same, the victim must not be blamed. Even though victims may take precautionary measures like distributing the data and information only to known acquaintances or blocking the unwanted contacts and so on, on the internet and digital communication era, such sorts of precautionary steps to protect privacy may not always be fruitful. It is for this very reason that stalking is considered as one of the most important process of privacy infringement in the digital era. The police and the prosecution must see the aspect of how the data or information was misused by the stalker and why. When dealing with cyber stalking cases, the police must see it from the aspect of the two stages of stalking as mentioned by the lead author. In this process, it becomes necessary to include provisions including S.503 of IPC (criminal intimidation) and 506 of IPC (punishment for criminal intimidation), since stalking may necessarily include intimidation as well. Further, the police also needs to see whether the process of stalking involved unauthorised access to the data of the victim. In such cases, provisions like Ss. 43, 66 and 66C must be applied depending upon the facts of the case. Even if S.354D of IPC is inclusive of the procedure of stalking, it has not amended the IT Act. Hence, it becomes necessary to include several provisions from the IT Act. Further, it must be remembered that S.354D of IPC limits the gender of the stalker only to men. It therefore becomes necessary to include provisions from IT Act in case the stalker is a woman. It must also be noted that in case the victim is a minor, S.11 (iv) of the POCSO Act must also be applied if stalking is done as a course of sexual harassment to the girl concerned.

However, S.354D as a cyber stalking law still needs to be properly analysed, examined, expanded and amended by the courts. This provision is a woman centric law and does not provide complete security to the victim because it is a bailable offence, and the only available retributive punishment is jail-term which can extend to one year to three years and fines. Cyber stalking under this Section becomes non-bailable only in the

---

[17] See, PTI. (September 24, 2014). Giving repeated missed call to women is stalking, attracts jail term. *The Hindu*. Available at http://www.thehindu.com/news/national/other-states/bihar-police-giving-repeated-missed-call-to-women-is-stalking-attracts-jail-term/article6442286.ece (Accessed on 7 June 2016).

case of second conviction. The punitive sentence extends to five years of jail term with fine. But one must understand that there remains opportunities for the stalker to come back and harass (and even take revenge for the police complaint) the victim if and when the stalker manages to get bail or finishes his jail term. This may happen for a number of reasons, including anonymity to identity of the stalker, no action by the service provider to monitor the stalker's profile/s and so on (Halder, 2015). In countries like the United States and United Kingdom, cyber stalking provisions essentially carries 'no contact order' as a civil remedy to restrict the stalker from contacting the victim for a considerable period (Halder, 2015, p. 120). Indian laws on cyber stalking (both in S.354D IPC and S.11 (iv) and 12 of the POCSO Act) do not mention anything about such 'no contact order'. It must be under understood that while victims of cyber stalking may necessarily be benefited by retributive sentencing especially for the effects of the act, that is, cyber stalking, the most important need of the victims is definitely to be protected from any sort of contact by the stalker (Halder, 2015). Further, while applying the provision, the courts must also be cautious about the provisos attached to it, which exempts certain types of 'surveillance' from the scope of the term 'cyber stalking' as have been explained by this provision (Halder, 2015, pp. 118–119). The courts in India have not got much scope to test the effectiveness of this law yet. It is expected that if the courts take up more cautious views to protect the interest of the victims as per the opinion of these authors, the objective of the law may be fulfilled.

Privacy Infringement Through Creation of Fake Avatars

The lead author defines fake avatars as

A false representation of the victim, which is created by the perpetrator through digital technology with or without the visual images of the victim and which carry verbal information about the victim which may or may not be fully true and it is created and floated on the internet to intentionally malign the character of the victim and to mislead the viewers about the victim's original identity. (Halder 2013, p. 197)

As can be seen from the definition, fake avatars are generally created either as a result of unauthorised access to data or of stalking to harass and defame the victims. This is a way of infringement of privacy, especially when the victim's personal information is revealed without proper authorisation by the victim. Fake avatars can be caused due to sexual as well as non-sexual motives. Examples of creation of fake avatars can be posting false information of the victim in the social media, posting her morphed images in the adult networking sites or even floating defamatory and unreal, derogatory information about her either through emails, blogs, chat logs or through mobile communication apps such as WhatsApp. Creation of fake avatars, therefore, cannot be limited to sexual harassment cases alone. When a victim complaints about creation of any sort of defamatory images, fake profiles or leaking of private information on the internet, it may be construed as creation of fake avatar, and appropriate provisions must be applied depending upon the factors of the case.[18]

As such, when the fake avatar is created by unauthorised access to data, fraudulent use of unique identification features and so on, the police officer must consider applying S.43, 66 and 66C of the IT Act. Depending upon the effect of the creation of fake avatar, the officer concerned, must also consider applying laws related to defamation including S.499 and 500 of IPC and necessarily S.509 of IPC since it may harm the modesty of woman concerned. If the fake avatar created is of the nature of sexual offences, the officer concerned must consider applying related laws including S.67 (punishment for publishing or transmitting obscene material in electronic form), 67A (punishment for publishing or transmitting of material containing sexually explicit act etc. in electronic form), 67B (punishment for publishing or transmitting of material depicting children in sexually explicit act, etc. in electronic form; in case the victim is a minor), 66E (punishment for violation of privacy) of the IT Act as well as relevant provisions from the IPC including S. 354C of IPC (voyeurism and punishment for the same). In case the victim is a minor girl and such fake avatars are used for the creation of pornographic materials, the police must consider applying S.13 (use of child for pornographic purposes) and S.14 (punishment for using child for pornographic purposes) of the POCSO act along with S.11 (sexual harassment) and S.12 (punishment for sexual harassment) of the POCSO Act. However, as fake avatars can be results of stalking or unauthorised access to data, in all the earlier mentioned situations, the officer concerned must examine the evidences, motives and so on thoroughly for applying provisions meant for stalking or unauthorised access to data.

---

[18] A detailed discussion on how to deal with fake avatars has been done in the later chapters.

Revenge Pornography

In our earlier publication (Halder & Jaishankar, 2013), we have defined revenge porn as

> [A]n act whereby the perpetrator satisfies his anger and frustration for a broken relationship through publicizing false, sexually provocative portrayal of his/her victim, by misusing the information that he may have known naturally and that he may have stored in his personal computer, or may have been conveyed to his electronic device by the victim herself, or may have been stored in the device with the consent of the victim herself; and which may essentially have been done to publicly defame the victim.

Victimising by way of revenge porn has become a common phenomenon in India now. It needs to be understood that while revenge porn essentially creates sexual violence to women on the internet, it necessarily involves voyeurism, hacking and stalking. In India, there is no specific law for regulating revenge porn. But it may be regulated by way of S.354C of IPC (voyeurism), 66E of the IT Act (violation of privacy) and also S.509 of IPC (punishment for harming the modesty of women) since it necessarily harms the modesty of women. Revenge porn must also be seen in the perspective of indecent representation of women.

However, while regulating revenge porn, consideration must be given to the various forms of harassment caused to the victim as well as the infringement of privacy of the victim. Professor Franks, one of the noted forefounders of cyber civil rights movements in the United States thus noted:

> Before 2013, only three states in the US criminalized the unauthorized distribution of private sexual images. As of June 21, 2015, that number has increased to twenty-three, with at least seventeen more states in the process of drafting or passing legislation. That so many states are taking this issue seriously is tremendous progress. It is crucial, however, to ensure that the laws being passed truly protect victims and that they are clear, principled, and constitutionally sound.
>
> Unfortunately, many of these state laws do not fulfill these criteria. A disappointing number of these laws treat nonconsensual pornography primarily as a form of harassment rather than as a privacy violation. These laws require that a perpetrator act with the 'intent to harm or harass' the victim, with some even requiring that the perpetrator be a current or former intimate partner of the victim. To be sure, nonconsensual pornography often plays a role in domestic violence, but making intent to harm or harass an element of the crime does not serve the best interests of domestic

violence victims. Having to prove intent to harm or harass beyond a reasonable doubt will not only be practically impossible for those victimized by strangers; it will often be very difficult in domestic violence cases as well, as perpetrators can claim a number of plausible alternative motives. Nonconsensual pornography is not always about revenge, but it is always about privacy. It is for good reason that privacy laws, from trespass laws to confidentiality requirements to prohibitions against voyeurism, do not require that perpetrators be motivated by intent to harm or harass the victim. The knowing violation of privacy is the substance of the harm. The folly of requiring intent to harm or harass in nonconsensual pornography laws is made clear by considering how none of these (actual) cases would constitute a crime under such a definition:

- Anonymous posters distributing private, intimate photos stolen from more than a hundred celebrities, in the hopes of obtaining Bitcoin or elevating social status;
- A California Highway Patrol officer passing around intimate pictures obtained from a female arrestee's cellphone as part of a 'game' among officers;
- Penn State fraternity brothers uploading photos of unconscious, naked women to a members-only Facebook page for entertainment purposes;
- Revenge-porn site owners like Hunter Moore and Craig Brittain publishing thousands of private, sexually explicit private images for profit and entertainment.

Intent to harm requirements aren't just bad policy; they are also bad law. Though some claim that such requirements are necessary to ensure compliance with the Constitution, the exact opposite is true: arbitrary distinctions about motive create constitutional issues instead of resolving them. Prohibiting disclosures of sexually explicit images only when they are made in the hopes of causing distress while allowing disclosures made in the hopes of obtaining profit or providing entertainment renders a law vulnerable to objections of both under-inclusiveness and viewpoint discrimination under the First Amendment.

These and other problems with many of the state laws regulating nonconsensual pornography, combined with jurisdictional limitations poorly suited for this borderless crime, make the need for a federal criminal law clear. A federal criminal law is necessary not only to provide a single, clear articulation of the relevant elements of the crime, but also to signal society's acknowledgement and condemnation of this serious wrongdoing.

In April 2015, Senator Al Franken, who serves on the Senate Judiciary Committee's subcommittee on Privacy, Technology and the Law, called on the FBI to 'provide information on any limitations in current law...that may have prevented the FBI from conducting investigations and making arrests in cases of nonconsensual disclosure of sexually explicit images.'

Representatives Jackie Speier (D-CA) and Gregory Meeks (D-NY) are addressing those limitations by leading Congressional efforts on a federal criminal provision protecting intimate privacy. For over a year, I have worked closely with their offices to draft the Intimate Privacy Protection Act, with input from the tech industry, civil liberties groups, constitutional scholars, victims, and advocacy groups. The bill is scheduled to be introduced in the near future.

Laws protecting privacy have a long and important history in this country. Privacy is essential to freedom of expression and speech, as well as being fundamental to a democratic society committed to equality and personal autonomy. This is as true for sexual privacy as it is for financial or medical privacy, and a federal bill recognizing this is long overdue (Franks, 2015).

In India, this approach should be followed. Even though S.354C of IPC and also S.66E IT Act are framed to criminalise voyeurism against intrusion of privacy, it needs to be understood that this may not be fully helpful for regulating revenge porn. The parliament must consider making laws for criminalising revenge porn considering all the factors that constitute revenge porn.[19] However, when the police are contacted with any complaint of revenge porn, they must consider applying existing provisions that cover infringement of privacy by way of voyeurism, effects of the same by way of harm on the modesty of woman concerned and the large-scale defamation that may be the ultimate result of revenge porn.

Patterns of Privacy Infringement by Companies

Often, we get to hear how web companies such as Facebook have been involved in data breach of the users. Almost always such data breach is related to the web company's own marketing research policies. The companies may extract data from the user's profiles, updates, browsing habits, purchasing accounts and so on in a camouflaged legal way, especially when such web companies reveal the said policies in their policy guidelines, which are to be signed by the subscribers. In many occasions, internet companies have defended this by showing that some clauses which mentions that these data would not be revealed to third parties. As researchers have observed, there is a constant commodification of personal information' (Tavani & Grodzinsky, 2002) by intermediaries, which

---

[19] See for detailed discussion on nature, effect and functional definition of revenge porn provided later.

may provide wide opportunities for cyber stalking (Halder, 2015, p. 111). Also, private information of the users does get circulated every day by the way of big data policies followed by web companies.

After a perusal of the policy guidelines of the service providers such as Google, Facebook, Twitter, LinkedIn and so on, it can be seen that they provide the users 'options' to secure their information as well as speeches that are expressed through these websites as 'private'; and none of them protect the privacy of the users in regard to the data that are already publicly exhibited with the consent of the owner of the data.[20] It is interesting to note that the privacy policy, which is a part of the contract form between the user and the web-service providers, does not guarantee any prevention for cyber stalking especially in cases when it is expected that the users will read the privacy policies. In other words, the US civil liability laws, which guide the internet giants, impose liability for privacy protection on the internet service providers for the protection of the consumer interest only when the copyright of the customer is infringed. But seeing from the other end, it can be seen that such privacy protection guidelines confer more rights on the users to decide whether to be accessed or not (Glancy, 2000). As such, the option of being available 'publicly private' (i.e., being in the social media and sharing limited information such as one's details including present geo-information, marital status and so on with the worldwide audience and sharing some chosen information such as personal photographs, personal favourites or opinions and so on with only 'friends') depends upon the choice of the privacy setting by the user and on the way he/she likes to project him/herself. However, at the same time, the choice of being 'privately private' (i.e., being connected with close friends in the social media but not sharing anything about him/herself) is always challenged by the privacy set ups and the concept of 'private environments'. In this regard it is necessary to understand about

---

[20] All of these websites rely upon the US copyrights laws, especially Section 512 of the Digital Millennium Copyright Laws, which creates Safe Harbor Policy. This provision is especially used for preventing intellectual property infringement against the users and also for developing and implementing the privacy policy for the users. Apart from these, all of these sites exercise due diligence by providing 'safety tips' to the users, which may protect their accounts against privacy infringements. Some of such safety tips are as follows: Advise for changing passwords and easy options for such action; options for reporting if and when the user feels that the password has been 'stolen' or misused; advise to not click on 'unknown' links and 'scraps' as preventive measure to protect the user's computer from malware attack; advise for not to release personal sensitive data and so on.

privacy, immunity cloak and due diligence used by the websites concerned and their origin, which is discussed in detail in Chapter 7.

It must also be noted that along with intermediary liability towards due diligence, consideration must be given to the wider database concept followed by the web companies. It may also be noted that the social medias, email/message/digital communication service providers and search engines may be part of a wider database which can share the information of the user if the user wishes to (Armbarst et al., 2009); for example, a Facebook user can log in to Academia.edu—a site meant for sharing academic interests, scholarly articles published by the users themselves—with the username and password used for his/her Facebook profile. All that the user needs to do is to confirm participation in the site through his/her email ID.

Apart from web companies, privacy of infringement may also happen by leaking of personal data by concerned organisations such as workplace, hospitals, educational institutions and commissioned private organisations who work on behalf of the government to collect data from the public. This last instance was particularly apprehended by the petitioners in the recent case relating to constitutional validity of the Aadhaar scheme (Choudhary, 2015). In countries such as United States, United Kingdom and so on, instances of privacy breach by way of data leaking have often been noted. In India, there are instances where email IDs and relevant information of supporters of net neutrality were leaked and these emails IDs were exposed by none other than the Telecom Regulatory Authority of India (TRAI) website, which was alleged to have been hacked.[21] In such kinds of privacy breach, women are more prone to be victimised due to the social structure of the nation. As has been stated earlier in this chapter, leakage of any sensitive information about women and girls in any form in electronic media may prove dangerous not only for the victim concerned but also for her family. In such cases, the victims must also consider including the companies for failure to protect the private data in their reports to the police. S.43A of the IT Act prescribes payment of compensation for such failure by the body corporates.[22] While this provision prescribes civil penalties, Ss. 72 and 72 A of the IT Act prescribes

---

[21] See Khandelwal, S. (April 27, 2015). TRAI leaked over million email addresses; anonymous India takes revenge. Available at http://thehackernews.com/2015/04/net-neutrality-trai-emails.html (Accessed on 7 June 2016).

[22] For detailed discussion on this provision, see Chapter 7.

criminal penalties for breach of such data by any individual (in case of earlier) and body corporate (in the latter case).

The other group of potential victims for such sorts of infringement of privacy by companies is celebrities and public figures including actors, politicians, celerity journalists and so on. There is a huge internet market for gaining profit by selling or distributing private images of such celebrities, especially women. The recent case of leaking of hundreds of nude photos (some of which are sexted images, some are nude selfies) of female celebrities, mostly from the Hollywood, is noteworthy in this regard. Such sorts of privacy breach not only cause different forms of victimisation to the women concerned, but also may hamper healthy growth in their professional field. Even though many would be of the opinion that such situations are immediately used for increasing the publicity of the film done by such actors, in reality, it may not be so, especially if the image or distribution of the same violates any existing law/s. In this particular case many such celebrity victims of nude photo scandal preferred to bring a formal legal suit against Google as a web company as it had allegedly failed to note and monitor such huge privacy breach (Hern & Rushe, 2014). Google however, after receiving legal notice from the victims, removed many of the images and took action to prohibit further circulation of such private images. In India, there are some sparing incidences of similar privacy breach where celebrities are targeted, in most cases, it could be seen that they the concerned actresses have filed police cases. If the news reports are analysed it will be seen that the police reports are generally directed to track the offenders and remove the contents from the websites. Even though in India we have S.79 (exemption from liability), especially clause 2(c) of the same which prescribes intermediary's liabilities regarding due diligence, and several intermediary guideline regulations regarding privacy protection of the individuals,[23] very rarely victims of privacy infringement include the intermediaries in their police reports, especially when their 'take down' reports are ignored or not complied with by the intermediaries.

But what is important to note here is the victim of such privacy breach may not avail any legal remedy when their certain information (which have been breached or which may have been used to harass the victims) are already revealed in the public websites or public gazettes. Such information does not fall under the category of 'private information'. However, even in such cases, there is still a remedy available when such

---

[23] Ibid.

information is misused to victimise the person concerned in other forms of cyber crimes or any other offline crimes, including causing security risk, monetary loss or defamation. Further, Right to Information Act, 2005 also provides certain exceptions whereby people can restraint from giving away personal information as a right to information to the information seeker.[24]

[24] S.8 of the Right to Information Act, 2005 discusses the exemptions. It states as follows:

(1) Notwithstanding anything contained in this Act, there shall be no obligation to give any citizen—

(a) information, disclosure of which would prejudicially affect the sovereignty and integrity of India, the security, strategic, scientific or economic interests of the State, relation with foreign State or lead to incitement of an offence;

(b) information which has been expressly forbidden to be published by any court of law or tribunal or the disclosure of which may constitute contempt of court;

(c) information, the disclosure of which would cause a breach of privilege of Parliament or the State Legislature;

(d) information including commercial confidence, trade secrets or intellectual property, the disclosure of which would harm the competitive position of a third party, unless the competent authority is satisfied that larger public interest warrants the disclosure of such information;

(e) information available to a person in his fiduciary relationship, unless the competent authority is satisfied that the larger public interest warrants the disclosure of such information;

(f) information received in confidence from foreign Government;

(g) information, the disclosure of which would endanger the life or physical safety of any person or identify the source of information or assistance given in confidence for law enforcement or security purposes;

(h) information which would impede the process of investigation or apprehension or prosecution of offenders;

(i) cabinet papers including records of deliberations of the Council of Ministers, Secretaries and other officers: Provided that the decisions of Council of Ministers, the reasons thereof, and the material on the basis of which the decisions were taken shall be made public after the decision has been taken, and the matter is complete, or over: Provided further that those matters which come under the exemptions specified in this section shall not be disclosed;

Government Surveillance

This pattern of privacy infringement has become most notable since whistle blowers like Snowdon and Assange exposed many sensitive issues of the US Government. Many defenders of privacy rights consider government surveillance as one of the most dangerous pattern of privacy breach. This is because almost all laws dealing with privacy protection in the digital media have exception clause which exempts surveillance by the government from criminal or civil liabilities. India is no exception. While S.43 and 43A, 66, 66c, 66E, specifically, and 67, 67A, 67B, indirectly, speak for protection of privacy, there is laws such as S.69,

---

(j) information which relates to personal information the disclosure of which has no relationship to any public activity or interest, or which would cause unwarranted invasion of the privacy of the individual unless the Central Public Information Officer or the State Public Information Officer or the appellate authority, as the case may be, is satisfied that the larger public interest justifies the disclosure of such information: Provided that the information which cannot be denied to the Parliament or a State Legislature shall not be denied to any person.

(2) Notwithstanding anything in the Official Secrets Act, 1923, nor any of the exemptions permissible in accordance with Sub-section (1), a public authority may allow access to information, if public interest in disclosure outweighs the harm to the protected interests.

(3) Subject to the provisions of clauses (a), (c) and (i) of Sub-section (1), any information relating to any occurrence, event or matter which has taken place, occurred or happened twenty years before the date on which any request is made under Section 6 shall be provided to any person making a request under that section: Provided that where any question arises as to the date from which the said period of twenty years has to be computed, the decision of the Central Government shall be final, subject to the usual appeals provided for in this Act.

S.9 further states that

Without prejudice to the provisions of Section 8, a Central Public Information Officer or a State Public Information Officer, as the case may be, may reject a request for information where such a request for providing access would involve an infringement of copyright subsisting in a person other than the State.

and its series, including Ss. 69A and 69B which provides power to issue direction for monitoring or decryption of any information through any computer resource on the grounds as mentioned in Article 19(2) of the Constitution (S.69), power to issue direction for blocking public access of any content on the grounds aforementioned (S.69A) and power to issue direction for monitoring and so on of any computer resource for cyber security especially (S.69B). It may be necessary to point out here that these provisions are generally used for the reasons mentioned therein, and they have been used in recent past especially for preventing further occurrence of big-scale national unrest such as spreading rumours that may instigate riots. Presently, these provisions are used mainly during sensitive period including general elections or for period when sensitive cases are being heard by the courts and so on to prevent widespread violence. In Shreya Singhal's case, petition was also made to declare S.69A unconstitutional. But the courts held that unlike S.66A, S.69A is well guarded by reasons as well as by Information Technology (procedure and safeguards for blocking for access of information by public) Rules, 2009. Hence it is valid. Similarly, as S.69 and 69B as well as S.79 are supported by various intermediary guidelines rules of 2011, they cannot be and should not be misunderstood and misused as S.66A had been. But we argue that this does not mean that government surveillance is absolutely safe when it comes to protection of privacy. The incidences of Delhi metro CCTV footage leak are glaring examples of such negative effects of government surveillance. In both these incidences, CCTV footage of intimate moments of the man and woman that were captured and stored as parts of general CCTV surveillance in public places, were leaked on the internet and especially on porn websites.[25] Till August 2015, the images under the tag 'Delhi metro CCTV footage' were still available on the internet.

It must also be mentioned that S.354D of IPC, which is a very much relieving privacy protection law for women, is not free of this flaw either. The provisos attached to it lay down certain exceptions including government surveillance as has been mentioned above. Hence, it is expected that these laws must be used cautiously. Otherwise, it may turn extremely fatal not only for the victims, but also for the society as a whole.

---

[25] See, IANS. (July 23, 2013). Delhi Metro video of intimate couple leaked, again. *The Hindustan Times*. Available at http://www.hindustantimes.com/newdelhi/delhi-metro-video-of-intimate-couple-leaked-again/article1-1097064.aspx (Accessed on 7 June 2015).

References

Armbarst, M., Fox, M., Griffith, R., Joseph, A. D., Katz, R. H., Konwinski, A., Lee G., Patterson, D. A., Rabkin, A., Stoica, I., & Zaharia, M. (2009). Above the clouds: A Berkeley view of cloud computing. Technical Report No. UCB/EECS-2009-28. Available at http://www.eecs.berkeley.edu/Pubs/TechRpts/2009/EECS-2009-28.html (Accessed on 11 May 2014).

Bocij, P., Griffiths, M. D., & McFarlane. L. (2002). Cyber stalking: A new challenge for criminal law. *The Criminal Lawyer, 122*, 3–5. Available at https://www.academia.edu/759647/Bocij_P._Griffiths_M.D._and_McFarlane_L._2002_._Cyberstalking_A_new_challenge_for_criminal_law._The_Criminal_Lawyer_122_3-5 (Accessed 10 May 2014).

Brenner, S. (2004). Cyber crime metrics: Old wine in new bottles? *Virginia Journal of Law and Technology, 9*(13), 1–53. Available at http://www.vjolt.net/vol9/issue4/v9i4_a13-Brenner.pdf (Accessed on 10 May 2014).

Choudhary, A. (22 July 2015). No fundamental right to privacy to citizens: Centre tells SC. *The Times of India.* Available at http://timesofindia.indiatimes.com/india/No-fundamental-right-to-privacy-to-citizens-Centre-tells-SC/articleshow/48171323.cms (Accessed on 22 July 2015).

Franks, A. (22 June 2015). How to defeat 'revenge porn': First, recognize it's about privacy, not revenge. *The Huffington Post.* Available at http://www.huffingtonpost.com/mary-anne-franks/how-to-defeat-revenge-porn_b_7624900.html?ir=India&adsSiteOverride=in (Accessed on 2 July 2015).

Glancy, D. (2000). At the intersection of visible and invisible worlds: United States privacy law and the internet. *Santa Clara High Tech. L.J., 16*, 357. Available at http://digitalcommons.law.scu.edu/chtlj/vol16/iss2/8 (Accessed on 10 May 2014).

Halder, D. (2013). Examining the scope of indecent representation of women (Prevention) Act, 1986, in the light of cyber victimization of women in India. *National Law School Journal, 11*, 188–218.

———. (2015). Cyber stalking victimisation of women: Evaluating the effectiveness of current laws in India from restorative justice and therapeutic jurisprudential perspectives. *TEMIDA, 18*(3–4), 103–130: doi: 10.2298/TEM1504103H

Halder, D., & Jaishankar, K. (2010). Cyber victimization in India: A baseline survey report. Tirunelveli, India. Centre for Cyber Victim Counselling. Available at http://www.cybervictims.org/CCVCresearchreport2010.pdf (Accessed on 11 January 2016).

———. (2013). Revenge porn by teens in the United States and India: A socio-legal analysis. *International Annals of Criminology, 51*(1–2), 85–111.

Hern, A., & Rushe, D. (October 2, 2014). Google threatened with $100m lawsuit over nude celebrity photos. *The Guardian.* Available at http://www.

theguardian.com/technology/2014/oct/02/google-lawsuit-nude-celeb-rity-photos (Accessed on 2 May 2015).

Tavani, H. T., & Grodzinsky, S. (2002) Cyberstalking, personal privacy, and moral responsibility. *Ethics and Information Technology, 4*(2), 123–132. Available at http://www.redwoods.edu/instruct/jjohnston/Philosophy20/Readings/Issues/CyberstalkingMoralResponsibility.pdf (Accessed on 9 May 2015).

6

Online Sexual Offences

When we speak about sexual offences on the internet, especially with regard to India, we have seen that this concept is understood within the meaning of pornography and obscenity and these two concepts are often understood as synonymous. Furthermore, when we speak about cyber crimes against women and girls, it is often understood that all sorts of offences may be sexual offences. In fact, it may not be so. There are various sorts of crimes that may happen to women and girls on the internet including bullying, stalking, grooming and so on, which may or may not be sexual in nature. However, because offences that are sexual in nature are mostly reported in India, some of which are recognised by laws and because such offences may cause graver harm to women and girls, and also that the other sorts of offences including bullying, stalking or grooming may result in sexual offences against women and girls, many researchers and legal experts including the judges often tend to overshadow cyber crimes against women with sexual offences.[1]

As may be seen, sexual offences on the internet may have graver impact on the victim, especially for reputation damage. Once the sexually explicit image or obscene content targeted at the woman concerned gets

[1] Consider former Chief justice of India Shri Balakrishnan's speech on cyber crime against women in the 'Seminar on Cyber Crime against Women' public awareness meeting, held at Maharaja College, Ernakulam, on 1 August 2009. Available at http://www.supremecourtofindia.nic.in/speeches/speeches_2009/seminar_-_cyber_crimes_against_women_1-08-09.pdf (Accessed on 9 March 2015). It contained more thoughts about sexual offences.

viral on the internet (which is unfortunately a hard reality), it may travel from one website to another, one device to another, irrespective of physical jurisdiction. It may become extremely difficult for the police to help the victim especially when it travels across jurisdiction and keeps floating on different websites (Citron, 2014). It may also become extremely traumatising for the victim to face the situation again and again when the content resurfaces after a certain gap. It may be noted that all such contents may not be fake avatars created by the perpetrator; it may be a sexted image that has been conveyed by the victim herself to her friends or her boyfriend (Halder & Jaishankar, 2014b) and which may have been leaked due to hacking of any of the recipient's profile or email id or devices, or may have been circulated by the recipient in the form of revenge porn if the latter becomes unhappy with the former (Halder & Jaishankar, 2013). The question is: Who creates sexually objectionable contents on the internet and why does it attract penal offences?

As per Ss.67 (punishment for publication or transmitting obscene materials in the electronic form), 67A (punishment for publication or transmitting sexually explicit materials in the electronic form), 67B (punishment for publishing, transmitting materials depicting children in sexually explicit form) or 66E (punishment for violation of privacy) of the Information Technology Act (2000) (amended in 2008), except S.354C of the Indian Penal Code (IPC) (punishment for voyeurism) or S.13 of the Protection of Children from Sexual Offences Act (POCSO Act) (creation of child pornography), 'whoever' or 'any person' who does these acts, may be liable for punishment. Such a broad term may include not only the perpetrators, but also the women who wish to capture their private moments with their partners, teenagers and young adults who wish to do sexting, and even genuine activists who may ask general people to share objectionable sexual contents for creating general awareness. While the latter may create a debatable issue when transmitting of objectionable sexual offences is done apparently to create general awareness, but may have enough potential to be misused, the former may fall on the other side of law because sexting or sharing objectionable contents in the electronic form in the name of nasty jokes remained in the grey area in the Indian laws.

Publishing or transmitting becomes penal offences in two typical conditions: (a) when it infringes other's right to live with dignity and (b) when it violates the freedom of speech and expression. The former denotes the infringement of victim's rights that are guaranteed by the Constitution and the penal as well as civil laws of the country; the latter denotes the violation of one's own duties and responsibilities to exercise one's rights properly. These are interconnected. But we often find these two concepts overlapping as well. The judicial understanding regarding freedom of speech is expanding in many jurisdictions including India, the United States, the United Kingdom and so on. Creation of sexual contents in the electronic form is often considered as a part of freedom of speech and this has escaped the chilling speech category in many occasions in the United States as well as in India. One of the prime examples of this may be the continuous rejection of the courts in India to throw a blanket ban on the porn websites.[2] It may need to be understood that law cannot suppress healthy sexual desires but can definitely restrict sexual desires or expressions when it harms the rights of others. The crucial question that can be raised here is: Can watching sexual contents at home on the internet by adults be treated as an offence? Presently, the Supreme Court of India is also considering the same question. The answer may be 'yes' when the websites catering to such needs show contents which are legal, the contents are made of actors who are legally eligible to enter contracts for making sexual contents for these websites and there is no violation of human rights, women rights or child right while making, transmitting or selling such contents.[3]

But in reality, the sex sites including YouTube or WhatsApp and so on are often flooded with sexted contents, revenge porn materials, child porn materials and real-life rape videos. In such cases, the courts cannot give a blanket green signal to porn websites as well. Furthermore, in such cases, the courts may need to decide whether to treat such contents as harmful pornography, sexually explicit materials or obscene materials. In numerous news reports as well as court decisions, we have got to see that the police may have booked the offences under provisions meant

[2] It may be necessary to point out that earlier Bombay High Court had refused to put a blanket ban on porn sites. Again, in August 2015, the Supreme Court reiterated the same by stating that neither the government, nor the courts can play as moral policies to restrict an adult from watching porn content within the four walls of his house. (See for more details NDTV. (2015). Can't be present in everyone's bedroom: Centre to Supreme Court on banning porn sites. Published in NDTV on 10 August 2015. Available at http://www.ndtv.com/india-news/cant-be-present-in-everyones-bedroom-centre-to-supreme-court-on-banning-porn-sites-1205677 (Accessed on 10 August 2015).

[3] Such sorts of adult networking sites or porn websites may exempt liability of violating any laws in relation to child abuse or child pornography or even immoral trafficking by using special license forms which permit them to use RFA (restricted for adult) symbols.

for sexually explicit contents (S.67 A of the IT Act) as well as obscenity (S.67 of the IT Act). It needs to be understood that such confusions may ultimately produce bad justice for the victims who brave all social odds to fight the cases till the last. Like, how the concept of cyber stalking cannot and should not be interpreted to mean cyber bullying only, we argue that the concepts of cyber pornography and obscenity should not be interpreted as the same. This chapter is framed to give a clear view for setting such confusions at rest.

Regulable Cyber Pornography

India is known as the first country in the world to present a formal guide to erotica[4] in the form of Kamasutra. Interestingly, we have often come across many interesting queries from domestic as well as international researchers regarding legal scopes to criminalise watching porn when we have temple architectures like Khajuraho which are erotic, sometimes similar to pornographic poses as one gets to see in XXX videos and which attracts a huge amount of tourists irrespective of gender, age and country. However, pornography as a term has remained undefined by laws unlike obscenity for a long time. This has practically led to non-ending questions for law researchers as to whether pornography as a term denotes any offence, and whether it is synonymous with obscenity. But in reality, the terms pornography and obscenity denote two different concepts. According to Russel (1993), pornography denotes 'materials that combine sex and/or exposure of genitals with abuse or degradation in a manner that appears to endorse, condone or encourage such behaviour.' According to Dworkin and MacKinnon (1998), pornography is the 'graphic sexually explicit subordination of women'. According to Malamuth (1999), 'pornography literally means the "writing of harlots" or depiction of acts of prostitutes. It has come to mean materials intended to arouse sexual feelings that may include sexist or violent elements.'

---

[4] According to Neil. M. Malamuth (1999), the word 'erotica' derives its origin from Greek word Eros (Greek god of love) and it refers to 'sexual love'. He says 'it is typically defined as materials intended to arouse sexual feelings that portray mutually consenting pleasurable acts. Some writers emphasise that such materials contain no sexist or violent connotations'.

The term 'pornography' as such has not found any legal definition in jurisdictions including India, the United States, the United Kingdom and so on, unless it is coupled with the term 'child'. Child pornography has remained a concern for a long time and this was reflected in the European Union Convention of Cybercrime, 2001,[5] which pushed the birth of many cyber crime regulations, including that of India. Pornography, however, has been expressed in different terms by legal scholars like Sunstein (1986, p. 592), who defines 'regulable pornography' as one which 'must be (a) sexually explicit, (b) depict women as enjoying or deserving some form of physical abuse and (c) have the purpose and effect of producing sexual arousal'. In India, pornography law, especially cyber pornography law (and not cyber obscenity law) has been framed mainly on the very understanding of the term 'sexually explicit' materials. The linguistic meaning of 'explicit' may be clear, unambiguous, specific, candid or graphic. If we minutely analyse Sunstein's definition of regulable pornography, it may be seen that the reflections of the same may be found in the present Indian laws that regulate cyber pornography; these may include Ss. 67A (punishment for publishing, transmitting materials containing sexually explicit acts in the electronic form), 67B (punishment for publishing or depicting children in sexually explicit acts in the electronic form) of the IT Act, 2000 (amended in 2008), S.13 (using child for pornographic purposes) of POCSO Act, 2012 and so on.

It is a welcome move by the Indian lawmakers to segregate the pornography law by way of creating these provisions from obscenity laws which had existed in the IPC through Ss. 292 (sale of obscene books and so on), 294 (obscene acts and songs in public to annoy other and punishment for the same) of the IPC and again through S.67 of the IT Act, 2000 (amended in 2008) (punishment for transmitting, publishing obscene materials in the electronic form). As may be seen from some earlier cases like that of State of Tamil Nadu v. Suhas Katty, decided in 2004 by the Chief Metropolitan magistrate, Chennai,[6] or the case of

---

[5] Article 9(2) of the EU Convention of cyber crimes, 2001 stated that 'the term "child pornography" shall include pornographic material that visually depicts: (a) a minor engaged in sexually explicit conduct; (b) a person appearing to be a minor engaged in sexually explicit conduct; (c) realistic images representing a minor engaged in sexually explicit conduct.'

[6] For full details of the case, see State of Tamil Nadu v. Suhas Katty. Published on 30 July 2013. Available at http://www.legalserviceindia.com/lawforum/index. php/topic,2238.msg2547.html#msg2547 (Accessed on 5 March 2015).

'sex doctor' L. Prakash, who was booked and arrested in 2001 under various provisions of Indecent Representation of Women (Prevention) Act, the Immoral Traffick (Prevention) Act and mainly S.67 of the IT Act for taking obscene pictures of girls detained in his farm house and posting them on the internet, and was charged with life imprisonment by a 2008 decision by the lower court in Madras, but later acquitted after the Madras High Court modified the award of life sentence since he had already served 13 years of imprisonment,[7] the legal concept of cyber pornography and obscenity was not well developed or properly executed by the courts. However, there are positive developments in this issue now.

When we speak of 'regulable pornography' (Sunstein, 1986), we need to remember that there are other forms of pornographies available on the internet which may be legal. Consider the provisos attached to each of the sections mentioned before; as such, as we have mentioned in our earlier researches, '... it is to be noted that pornography may not be treated as a crime when a woman who is depicted as a model therein, consents for her involvement' (Halder & Jaishankar, 2011, p. 30). These may involve online porn videos acted by adult porn actors who are legally eligible to enter into contracts for the creation/production of such porn contents for porn websites. In fact, when one opens any adult entertainment site/s, he or she may see an exemption from the liability clause, either in the 'frequently asked questions' (FAQ) menu or in the 'terms of services' menu or in the Digital Millennium Copyright Act (DMCA) notice menu or in the 'privacy' menu where the website declares its immunity clauses along with the notifications, such as, it is not liable for the videos uploaded by the subscribers, the actors are not minors, the site follows DMCA take down policies and so on. Several US-based sites may also show the 'Restricted for adult' (RFA) symbol.

In this context, mention must be made of the case of Kamalesh Vaswani v. Union of India & others (2013),[8] which is still pending for further hearings in the courts. In this Public Interest Litigation (PIL) filed by the petitioner, it was mentioned that there was a lacuna in the anti-pornography law which has allowed extreme penetration of porn videos into the Indian society and it has caused grave harm to the youth, especially minor

---

[7] For more, See Jesudasan, D. (2015). Convict in cyber porn case released. Published in *The Hindu* on 26 April 2015. Available at http://www.thehindu.com/news/cities/chennai/convict-in-cyber-porn-case-released/article7142399.ece (Accessed on 9 June 2015).

[8] Writ Petition (Civil) No. 177/2013 in the Supreme Court of India.

children. There are social opinions that viewing pornography in a way motivates more sexual offences in the society, especially rape, sexual molestation of women and girls and also bestiality. The same opinion was also expressed in the above-mentioned case. It is an unfortunate fact that while the laws in India has categorically criminalised publishing, transmitting pornography by way of sexually explicit contents in the electronic forms or using children for making pornographic contents, there is no law to ban viewing of pornography in private by the adults. The Bombay High Court judgement in Vinay Kumar & Others v. State of Maharastra (2010)[9] is noteworthy in this regard. In this case, the Bombay High Court held that watching pornographic contents inside the four walls of one's private residence is no offence especially when the contents, the digital form, CD etc. are not meant for sale, hire, distribution etc.

The Concept of Non-consensus Pornography or 'Forced Pornography' and 'Fake Avatar'

A porn content can be an offensive content when it is non-consensus pornography or 'forced pornography' and 'Fake avatar'. The decision of the Bombay High Court as discussed previously cannot and should not govern the general mindset about regulations regarding pornography, especially when it is non-consensus pornography or 'forced pornography' (Halder & Jaishankar, 2011).

In our earlier publication, we spoke about 'forced pornography' by explaining it as follows:

> Forced pornography ... constitutes a crime in itself when the woman is either made a target without her knowledge or made to give her consent under threat. Forced pornography involves the following elements: Voyeurism including stealing the victim's personal pictures, or capturing her images which may or may not show the victim in compromising positions through secret camera and using the same for; using the visual images of the victim (either the original picture or the morphed image) without her permission

---

[9] Vinay Kumar & Others v. State of Maharastra, Criminal Application No. 2809 of 2010 in the High Court judicature of Bombay. Available at https://docs.google.com/document/d/1ZyBevXbdC-FXzkSNA9itU5oFjhwO7CNSmZ7_H0Ji_B0/edit?pli=1 (Accessed 2 February 2015).

to create pornographic clippings, gallery etc. for fulfilling sexual gratifications of others in lieu of monetary gains; threatening the victim with dire
consequences and forcefully pressurizing her to consent for either sending
her photographs for pornographic uses or acting as a porno star. (Halder &
Jaishankar, 2011, p. 30)

We further observed:

A woman can be victim of forced pornography when: a) her picture, either
already available in the net or digitally scanned without her consent, is
morphed without her knowledge and distributed to the wider audience
for evil motive; b) her picture is used to digitally design the graphics to
depict her involved in sexual activities with man/groups of men; c) her
picture is used without her consent in adult websites to invite others to
virtually striptease, rape or molest her (Sanders, 2010); d) her profile
has been hacked and her pictures in the profile have been morphed.
Victimization begins when the hacked profile is used to cater the needs
of sexually perverted internet users; e) the harasser captures her private
moments through voyeurism and uses these voyeur images for monetary
gain. (Halder & Jaishankar, 2011, p. 30)

On the basis of these understandings, the lead author further developed
the concept of 'fake avatar' (Halder, 2013). According to the lead author:

One of the most common forms of online harassment of women is depicting the victim through false and derogatory identities mostly through
social websites like Facebook and also through adult websites. While in
the West, Craigslist is also used to expose the personal information including residential address of the victim for tagging her as one who solicits
sex, in India the medium of victimisation is largely restricted to Facebook
and adult websites including porn sites. The typical nature of victimisation includes the creation of a profile of the victim which may contain
picture(s) and personal information including residential addresses,
schooling and graduation information and professional designations. In
most cases such profiles may be left open for public viewing and they are
constantly updated in search engines. Of late, the trend has broadened to
include verbal descriptions of the victim in extremely derogatory words
describing the victim as a 'whore' or 'prostitute' through adult bullying and
trolling in Facebook and Twitter. (Halder, 2013, p. 188)

Consider hundreds of profiles of women TV/cine stars that one gets
to see on Facebook, Twitter or in adult entertainment sites. Even if the

concerned woman may not be a 'porn star' in typical sense, the profile so created may project her as one. Same story runs for hundreds of ordinary women who may have been targeted by predators to paint them in black before the World Wide Web and the society as a whole. The story may be no different for transgender women. There are many such profiles which are created to harass transgender women who may refuse to share their phone numbers or friend requests from men who want them as sex partners through social media. All these profiles or images actually create a different avatar for the victim which is different from her real self. These avatars may stay in the social media for a long time or get spread through mobile message services or through websites to continue to harass women and girls. The lead author termed these avatars as 'fake avatars' and defined the term as:

> a false representation of the victim which is created by the perpetrator through digital technology with or without the visual images of the victim and which carry verbal information about the victim which may or may not be fully true and it is created and floated in the Internet to intentionally malign the character of the victim and to mislead the viewers about the victim's original identity. (Halder, 2013, p. 197)

Creating such images or profiles to harass women in the electronic form has attracted the attention of the lawmakers in several ways. But going through the different laws that would be discussed further in this chapter as well as in other chapters, it may be understood that there is no uniform term for this menace. Different laws address it as 'obscene', sexually explicit, indecent representation or defamatory; these are done to segregate the nature of the contents depending upon the moral understanding of the society, the criminal justice machinery and the judgmental power of the victim to take it as a particular type(s) of right violation(s) or not. The term 'fake avatar' may be used as an umbrella term to address such profiles/images and so on, created to harass women and girls and also men. It may be necessary to understand that fake avatars may be created not only to harass women by floating false images of women and girls in the electronic media and destroying the reputation of the victim, but it may also be created for making profit. If the fake avatar is created in the form of 'forced pornography' whereby the victim is shown in sexually explicit manner, the same can be sold to porn websites as a porn image. One of the finest Indian examples of this could be the case of Baazee.com, where an IIT student, who received the images of teenagers in sexually explicit manner from another teenager (who was apparently angry and frustrated with the victims concerned), sold it to websites to gain profit. Seen from the perspective of the definition of fake avatar, it may be seen that those images apparently presented a false image of the victims as 'porn actors' or girls with lower moral when the victims were not the same in real life.

As such, forced pornography, which may necessarily involve fake avatars and, which falls in the category of regulable pornography can be dealt with under the heads of 'voyeurism', 'creation of sexually explicit content in the electronic form', 'creation of sexually explicit content with children' and 'revenge pornography'.

Voyeurism

Earlier, voyeurism was regulated as per S.66E of the IT Act, 2000 (amended in 2008). This provision is gender neutral and prescribes punishment for imprisonment for a term which may extend to three years or may be slapped with a fine of ₹1 lakh, or may be slapped with both imprisonment and fine. In sum, this provision makes it a punishable act when anyone videotapes, photographs, makes a film or records by any other means, naked or undergarment clad genitals, pubic area, buttocks or breasts of any man or a woman, where the person so captured or videotaped and so on can have a reasonable expectation that (a) he or she could disrobe in privacy, without being concerned that an image of his or her private area was being captured or (b) any part of his or her private area would not be visible to the public, regardless of whether that person is in a public or private place, and/or the person who captures such images, electronically sends the visual image(s) with the intent that it be viewed by person(s) and/or publishes, i.e., reproduces it or intends to reproduce it in the printed or electronic form and makes it publicly available.

Later, with the Criminal Law Amendment Act, 2013, S. 354C was introduced and inserted in the IPC with almost the same wordings, but specifically safeguarding the interest of women. S.354C of the IPC makes it a penal offence for any man who watches, or captures the image of a woman engaging in a private act in circumstances where she would usually have the expectation of not being observed either by the perpetrator or by any other person at the behest of the perpetrator or disseminates such image. The explanation attached to this section further clarifies that 'private act' includes an act of watching or capturing images of a woman engaged in sexual activities which is carried out in a place which, in the circumstances, would reasonably be expected to provide privacy and where the victim's genitals, posterior or breasts are exposed or covered only in underwear; or the victim is using a lavatory or the victim is doing a sexual act that is not of a kind ordinarily done in public. A very important point in this is the mention of 'sexual act' by the woman concerned. The second explanation further clarifies that where the victim consents to the capture of the images or any act, but not to their dissemination to third persons and where such image or act is disseminated, such dissemination shall be considered an offence under this section. There are several news reports regarding voyeurism in the trial rooms in the textile shops, toilets in restaurants, bathrooms in the hotels or even in the women's hostels.[10] All such acts may fall under this provision. S.354C of the IPC prescribes punishment for this which is imprisonment which shall not be less than one year, but may extend up to three years and also fine, in the first instance of conviction. In such case, the offence is non-cognizable and bailable. In the second instance of conviction, the punishment may enhance which shall not be less than three years and may extend to seven years, and the convict is also liable for fine. In such case, the offence becomes cognizable and non-bailable.

Sexting

When we speak of voyeurism, invariably the issue of sexting may arise. Of late, we have been noticing an increase in the tendency among teenage girls, young adult women as well as married couples and live-in couples to get engaged in sexting and also recording sexual acts including penetrating and non-penetrating acts. In our article (Halder & Jaishankar, 2014b), we have explained sexting in the following words:

> Sexting simply means sending and consequently receiving text messages carrying sexual expressions and sexual images through mobile phones. Even though technically sexting may mean any such electronically communicated text message which can include email message as well as mobile phone message, the term sexting is popularly used for indicating mobile phone text messages only. Such sexually explicit communications existed

[10] See the lead author's interview to the media in this regard at Madhukalya, A. 2015. Smriti Irani brings back focus on voyeurism prevailing in our country. Published in DNA on 6 April 2015. Available at http://www.dnaindia.com/india/report-smriti-irani-brings-back-focus-on-voyeurism-prevailing-in-our-country-2075010 (Accessed on 3 July 2015).

since the beginning of web era, where communicating partners can be (i) only adults, or (ii) adult/s-children or (iii) only adolescent teens or (iv) adult-teens. However, the term 'sexting' for the purpose of sexual text messages through the mobile phones became widely famous after a section of media started using the term to highlight the perils of sexual interaction through technology among teens (Roberts, 2005). Presently sexting is used to mean text messages which include individuals' (teens especially) nude pictures or naked private parts like breasts, genitals etc. or even sexually compromising positions of two partners, captured by himself or herself with the help of mobile camera and sending the same to others, who are mostly the creator's friends belonging to the same age group, via mobile phone or email messages or uploading these messages from camera phones to social networking sites. Sexting, for the purpose of mobile phone texting has been defined by many in different ways. As per MySecureCyberspace (2012), 'sexting' means, 'the trend of sending each other sexually explicit or suggestive content, usually photographs.' Jaishankar (2009) defines sexting as 'self photographing nude body or body parts and sending to others, as well texting obscene words to known persons (in most cases) using mobile phone' ... While sexting can take place consensually between people who are in a relationship, it also occurs unknowingly or against the wishes of a person who is the subject of the content (MySecureCyberspace, 2012). Hence, sexting can be defined as an electronic communication which 'includes a variety of risqué stunts'. Nude pictures of the girl sent to her boyfriend by herself, as well as capturing indecent images in a locker room by a stranger and then distributing it to a vast audience can also be included as sexting. This is a popular trend among teens to flirt electronically (MySecureCyberspace, 2012). According to Jayne Hitchcock, President of WHOA (Working to Halt Online Abuse, url: www.haltbause. org), sexting happens 'when someone sends a nude or semi nude picture via cell phone'. (Personal Communication, 19th June, 2012) (Halder & Jaishankar, 2014b, pp. 28–29)

As such, this is the digital way of traditional 'sexy prank talks' between two teens who want to impress each other. Sexting by teens has certain unique characteristics which we documented in this particular article; these are as follows:

- Sexting is done by teenagers of adolescent age (13–18). In cases of 'Sexting among teens', both the original creators as well as the original recipients are teens. In other words, in such cases, adults are not participants.
- Mobile phone with camera is the main device for creating sexting.

- Adolescent teens take pictures of their nude bodies or bare private parts or genitals only and send it to their friends either with some written text messages or without any message as such.
- This may even include taking pictures in compromising situations and sending it to others.
- Majority of sexting cases first start among boyfriends or girlfriends, either on demand or to impress the other person.
- It can also be done by a teen taking picture of other friends including himself or herself and sending it to bulk of friends.
- In some cases, the self-captured or even received pictures are distributed to known or even unknown individuals, either by cell phone or even by email and social networking sites. It is only in this stage that any adult receiver, who receives the message in bulk, accidentally becomes a participator. But the adult is never the first recipient.
- Such distribution can happen even to take revenge due to breaking of emotional relationship.
- Sexting is mainly done by and among children of the same school; however, sometimes there can be involvement of children of different schools also when they know the sender personally or through social networking sites or even when the angry teen wants to spread the picture to a wider audience randomly.
- Sexting is done by teenagers who don't know that it can create legal trouble.
- Sexting can create terrible mental trauma on the creator as well as the recipient. It can even lead the creator to commit suicide. It can also lead some recipients to turn in to instant bullies towards the creator. (Halder & Jaishankar, 2014b, pp. 29–30)

It may be noted that the scope of these characteristics of sexting can be expanded to cover adult sexters as well. In this article, we have also discussed about when sexting can be illegal. We observed:

> Although in this context sexting is generally done between school friends, it's important to note that no matter the circumstance, it is illegal to possess, distribute or manufacture pornography involving anyone less than 18 years of age. Therefore, students who are minors themselves and are found distributing or possessing such images can be found guilty of child pornography … and can face up to 10 years in prison. (Wilson, 2008)

Sexting, having characteristics of child pornography, is being legally considered as a new form of child pornography. From the various reported cases, it can be seen that sexted messages are being misused by distributing them either through similar web based messaging services like WhatsApp or through emails or social networking websites to a wider audience to harass the original sender. Almost every state in the United States has penalised the production, distribution as well as private possession of child pornography, besides the existing federal laws penalising such actions. The two important cases which paved the way for framing sexting as 'child pornography' are Osborne v. Ohio (495 US 103), 1990 and Ashcroft v Free speech coalition 535 US 234 (2002)' (pp. 31–32). We further observe that in India, even though the term 'sexting' has not been recognised by any law as a penal offence or even an issue to be legally concerned about, there are two specific provisions which broadly touch the issue; S. 67B of the IT Act, 2000 (amended in 2008) prohibits and punishes creating, publishing or transmitting material depicting children in sexually explicit activities. This provision also includes grooming of the children for the purpose of creation of child pornographic materials as well as recording of own sexual abuse or that of others.[11] However, while this provision was exclusively meant for regulating child pornography

---

[11] S.67B of the Information Technology Act, 2000 (amended in 2008) states as follows:

> Whoever (a) publishes or transmits or causes to be published or transmitted material in any electronic form which depicts children engaged in sexually explicit act or conduct or (b) creates text or digital images, collects, seeks, browses, downloads, advertises, promotes, exchanges or distributes material in any electronic form depicting children in obscene or indecent or sexually explicit manner or (c) cultivates, entices or induces children to online relationship with one or more children for and on sexually explicit act or in a manner that may offend a reasonable adult on the computer resource or (d) facilitates abusing children online or (e) records in any electronic form own abuse or that of others pertaining to sexually explicit act with children, shall be punished on first conviction with imprisonment of either description for a term which may extend to five years and with a fine which may extend to ten lakh rupees and in the event of second or subsequent conviction with imprisonment of either description for a term which may extend to seven years and also with fine which may extend to ten lakh rupees: Provided that the provisions of Section 67, section 67A and this section does not extend to any book, pamphlet, paper, writing, drawing, painting, representation or

as inclusive in the ITAct, in 2012, a new law, POCSO Act was created to address sexual offences against children exclusively by the Government of India. In this law, S.11 addresses using of children for sexual harassment purposes and this also includes compelling/grooming/making children show their private parts for sexual gratification through digital media. S.13 of this law further makes it punishable to use children for pornographic purposes and S.15 makes it an offence to store any digital child pornographic material for any commercial purposes by any person.[12] But all of these laws predominantly cover child pornography and the issue of sexting particularly (Halder & Jaishankar, 2014b, pp. 36–37).

While in the former paragraphs we have spoken about sexting in regard to children and child pornography, let us go back again to Ss. 67, 67A of the IT Act, 2000 (amended in 2008) and 354C of the IPC to see whether sexting can be considered a crime by adults. If sexting is seen in the light of creating sexually explicit material or obscene material by oneself, it may narrowly attract Ss.67 (punishment for publishing, transmitting obscene materials in the electronic form), in case the images or acts captured and transmitted are prurient to the interest of the society and S.67A (punishment for publishing or transmitting sexually explicit materials in the electronic form), if the images captured and transmitted contain sexually explicit acts or conducts. This is because both these provisions expand their scopes to 'whoever' publishes or transmits the objectionable contents. As we may see from the earlier discussions on sexting, in general, the sexters tend to publish or transmit the sexy-selfies for the viewing of others, especially their partners including boyfriends, husbands, and even to their girlfriends (in case sexting is done by women). But till now, there is no reported case of conviction in sexting cases even for adults in India under the above-mentioned provisions. It may be because sexting is still being considered as a behavioural issue where the sexter may not have the motive to commit any harm knowingly.

---

figure in electronic form—(i) The publication of which is proved to be justified as being for the public good on the ground that such book, pamphlet, paper writing, drawing, painting, representation or figure is in the interest of science, literature, art or learning or other objects of general concern; or (ii) which is kept or used for bonafide heritage or religious purposes Explanation: For the purposes of this section, 'children' means a person who has not completed the age of 18 years.

[12] See Ss.11, 13 and 14 of the POCSO Act, 2012. Retrieved on 11 July 2014. Available at from http://wcd.nic.in/childact/childprotection31072012.pdf

Consider numerous news reports of selfies that are published by Poonam Pandey or Sherlyn Chopra on their social media accounts including Twitter; most of these selfies posted are in the nature of sexting. The sexters not only get huge amount of fan following, but they may also make good money by such sorts of sexting to the World Wide Web through their social media accounts. However, here comes the controversial question of right to express one's own sexual appeal versus duty not to harm anyone, especially minor viewers. In this context, a brief analysis of S.354C of the IPC is necessary. Consider again this particular sentence in the explanation of S.354C of the IPC which says '... or the victim is doing a sexual act that is not of a kind ordinarily done in public'; and again the sentences in the second explanation which says 'where the victim consents to the capture of the images or any act, but not to their dissemination to third persons.' This provision of the section may come as a defence to the sexter from legal liabilities as has been stated in Ss.67 and 67A of the IT Act amended in 2008. It is actually a matter of trust between the sexter and her recipient and of course the ultimate purpose of establishing an admiring or a sexual arousing feeling only with the recipient, that may secure the sexter's rights under S.354C, especially when the second explanation to the provision further says 'and where such image or act is disseminated, such dissemination shall be considered an offence under this section.' Almost in the same line, the celebrity nude-selfie posters or sexters like Poonam Pandey or Sherlyn Chopra may also escape the legal liabilities as has been enshrined in Ss.67 and 67A of the IT Act, 2000 (amended in 2008), especially if they can establish the fact that they do not hold liability for viral spreading of their sexted images on the internet and neither about social media's liability to filter such images for minor users. But in practice, if any person establishes his claim in the line of Ss.67 and 67A of the IT Act, 2000 (amended in 2008) to prohibit and prosecute such celebrity nude-selfie posters, the court needs to take an extremely conscious social decision to safeguard the right of the accused, as well as that of the minor viewers.

The second explanation to S.354C of the IPC further safeguards a woman's interests when she has consented in capturing sexual acts with her partner. As practitioners, counsellors and researchers, we have come across numerous cases where such confidential images have been disseminated without the knowledge or consent of the woman concerned. Such dissemination may happen due to two main reasons: (a) unauthorised access to the device of the woman or her partner which was used to capture/store the images and illegal dissemination of the same for making profit out of it either by way of sextortion,[13] or blackmailing and criminal intimidation and (b) dissemination of the images by the male partner himself due to anger or frustration over the woman and the same dissemination is done in the form of revenge porn.

In case of the former, it becomes the case of voyeurism turned into 'forced pornography', which must be seen as a case of unauthorised access to the electronic devices and also transmission of the same. In such cases, the victim has to lodge a detailed complaint regarding unauthorised access to the electronic device, unauthorised use of the images stored in it and infringement of privacy by way of publishing the compromising pictures. The police officer in such cases must keep it in mind that the victim woman should not be blamed as the creator/publisher of the images. The officer needs to remember that these images were not captured to disseminate for public viewing, but due to unauthorised access to the device or to the computer network, the images have been disseminated. It may be treated as hacking from one angle. We have earlier observed,

> Wall (2007, p. 53) describes hacking as 'deliberate unauthorized access to cyber spaces over which rights of ownership or access have already been established, committed with the primary aim of breaching the integrated security of the computer system'. Earlier, hacking had been used to describe as cyber crimes targeting electronic commerce, and government websites. Slowly the patterns of hacking related to victimization have changed and presently hacking emails, personal non commercial websites or web links, and personal profiles in the networking sites have become a common phenomenon.... It is noted that when hacking forms one of the constituting elements of cyber harassment or cyber crime targeting women, it is done either as a mode to take revenge for broken emotional affairs or for professional jealousy. It could also be the result of digital 'experiments' by pranksters and new users of internet who fail to understand the serious consequences. In cases of nonsexual hacking, it is observed that:

> The hacker can hack the email id of the victim to harass her, reach out to her friends with malicious mails and contents, defame her and debar her

---

[13] Sextortion (Sex + extortion) is a term that is used to denote sexual exploitation of children as well as adults whereby the victim is blackmailed and coerced to continue show/convey sexted selfies, come for webcam chat in nude or semi-nude position and so on.

from further communicating with her acquaintances through her hacked email id.

The hacker may also hack and block the victim's profile pages in various socializing sites. (Halder & Jaishankar, 2011, pp. 27–28)

In such situation, the concerned officer must apply his or her mind to apply provisions such as S.43 (penalty and compensation for damage to computer, computer system and so on), especially subsections (a) (which says, If any person without permission of the owner or any other person who is in charge of a computer, computer system or computer network accesses or secures access to such computer, computer system or computer network or computer resource, then he shall be liable to pay damages by way of compensation not exceeding ₹1 crore to the person so affected), (b) (which says, If any person without permission of the owner or any other person who is in charge of a computer, computer system or computer network downloads, copies or extracts any data, computer data base or information from such computer, computer system or computer network including information or data held or stored in any removable storage medium, then he shall be liable to pay damages by way of compensation not exceeding ₹1 crore to the person so affected) and (c) (which says, If any person without permission of the owner or any other person who is in charge of a computer, computer system or computer network destroys, deletes or alters any information residing in a computer resource or diminishes its value or utility or affects it injuriously by any means, then he shall be liable to pay damages by way of compensation not exceeding ₹1 crore to the person so affected), depending upon the information provided by the complainant/victim along with S.66 of the IT Act (punishment for computer related offences)[14] and S.354C of the IPC, highlighting the second explanation stated in it. But the victim needs to know that while S.43 sees the offence and restitution of justice more from civil perspectives, the IPC may provide criminal punishment not

---

[14] S.66 of the IT Act, 2000 (amended in 2008) says:

If any person, dishonestly, or fraudulently, does any act referred to in section 43, he shall be punishable with imprisonment for a term which may extend to two three years or with fine which may extend to five lakh or with both. Explanation: For the purpose of this section—a) the word 'dishonestly' shall have the meaning assigned to it in section 24 of the Indian Penal Code; b) the word 'fraudulently' shall have the meaning assigned to it in section 25 of the Indian Penal Code.

only for dissemination of the private images without the consent of the victim, but also for infringement of the privacy of the victim. However, we would not very much support the idea of slapping S.67A (punishment for publication, transmission of sexually explicit materials in the electronic form) or 67 (punishment for publication, transmission of obscene contents in the electronic form) in such cases, until and unless these provisions are used to exclusively book the person who has unauthorisedly disseminated the images and not the victim herself (since as mentioned earlier, the scope of these provisions may be extended to book the creators of such images as well).

Revenge Porn

In case such dissemination of porn is the result of revenge, then the case must be seen as a fit case for revenge porn. In India, we do not have any separate anti-revenge porn law till now. In our article, (Halder & Jaishankar, 2013), we have carried out a brief research on revenge porn, which is as follows:[15]

> The terms 'revenge' and 'revenge porn' have been used with reference to cyber victimization mostly to indicate victimization of adult women in the hands of their dating partners or cyber acquaintances in the forms of creation of untrue, ugly and sexually provocative profiles in the internet. The most common mode of creating revenge porn is to use the personal information and the photo of the victim, which may or may not be doctored, and uploading them in various cyber portals to spread the message that the victim is available for the sexual gratification of men. Even though the original porn sites and various social networking portals including the popular ones like the Facebook etc., strictly transfers the onus on the users to contribute only genuine data which does not harm the rights of the others,[16] various examples of violating this very guideline are available in the internet.[17] However, it would be wrong to say that only adult women fall as victim to revenge porn. Children, especially teenage girls in the age group of 14 to 19 are equally vulnerable in this case. (pp. 88–89)

[15] These excerpts are republished here with the permission of the editor of the journal.

[16] See Facebook rules regarding safety. Available at https://www.facebook.com/terms.php

[17] See Barnes v. Yahoo!. Available at http://www.ca9.uscourts.gov/datastore/opinions/2009/05/07/05-36189.pdf

Regarding the characteristics of revenge porn, we have stated as follows:

> Online revenge porn differs from the traditional concept of cyber porn in the sense that the perpetrator intentionally misuses the information about the victim to bring in emotional distress to her. Revenge porn aided by sexting and other non sexted victim aided stuff, is also a perfect way to create huge defamation for the victim. In cases of defamation resulting from sexting the whole cycle can be expressed as given in Figure 6.1.

As Figure 6.1 suggests, the whole cycle involves four major steps, viz.

1. The victim captures her nude/semi-nude picture in her mobile phone or consents for capturing her compromising position with the partner through mobile phone camera or webcam and sends it

Figure 6.1:
Sexting turning into defamation for victims

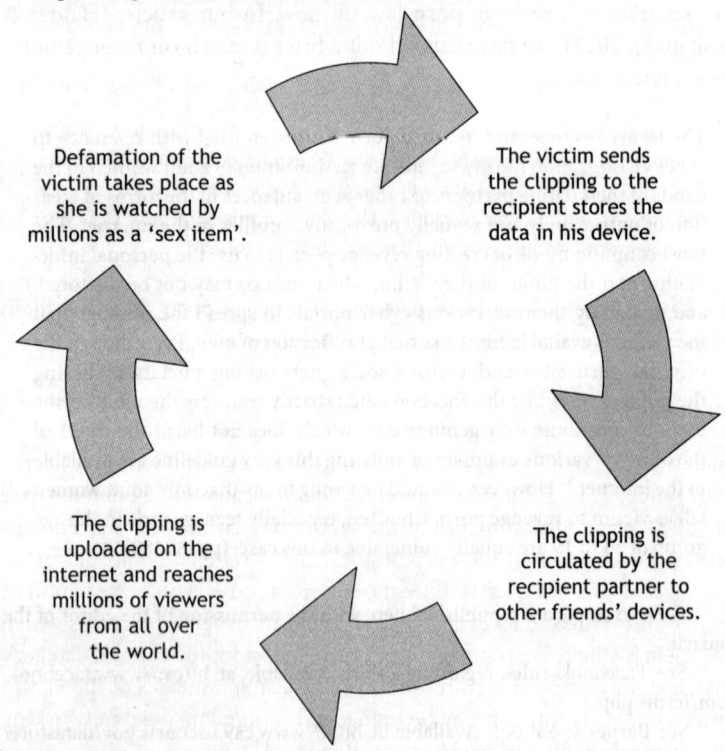

Defamation of the victim takes place as she is watched by millions as a 'sex item'.

The victim sends the clipping to the recipient stores the data in his device.

The clipping is uploaded on the internet and reaches millions of viewers from all over the world.

The clipping is circulated by the recipient partner to other friends' devices.

Source: Authors.

to her chosen partner and the partner stores the image/clipping in his device.

2. The partner may transfer the clipping to his friend(s) because he wants to humiliate the girlfriend as a revenge taking measure.

3. The partner himself or the friends, who are the secondary recipients, may then upload the clippings on the internet.

4. The clipping rapidly captures millions of viewer's attention, who may have watched the clipping, and the original creator may become a 'sex item' and her reputation is severely damaged.

Depending on these basic characteristics, we define online revenge porn as follows:

> It is an act whereby the perpetrator satisfies his anger and frustration for a broken relationship through publicizing false, sexually provocative portrayal of his/her victim, by misusing the information that he may have known naturally and that he may have stored in his personal computer, or may have been conveyed to his electronic device by the victim herself, or may have been stored in the device with the consent of the victim herself; and which may essentially have been done to publicly defame the victim.

> On the contrary, traditional cyber porn is created with the help of professional models who perform for the visual sexual gratification of viewers. The chief aim of traditional cyber porn lies in monetary gain for the creator and distributor (Bartow, 2008). The scope of this definition can cover revenge porn by adults as well. (Bartow, 2008, pp. 89–90)

We have further divided the patterns of revenge porn into two main types, viz., (a) camouflaged porn and (b) teen porn.

(a) Camouflaged Porn

Such sorts of porn images may contain user-generated (George & Scerri, 2007) and also user- adopted contents. The first category of contents may include storing visual images of the victim, which may have been supplied by the victim to the perpetrator. These contents could be sexted messages, email photo attachments, stored pictures which are captured from online video chat sessions or even victim consented pictures which are taken by the perpetrator of the victim. User-adopted content category may include doctored pictures of the victim, stolen images of the victim and so on. Such content may be uploaded on popular social networking sites like Facebook, Orkut, Myspace, Bebo and so on.

These typical camouflaged porns could be created by teenage boys in the above-mentioned social networking sites (SNSs) in the regular fashion as other profiles are created. However, the difference remains in the originality of the information provided therein and the motive behind the creation of the same profile. The profile may thus contain a profile picture which belongs to the victim; the profile name which may depict the victim it may contain the album which may contain the sexted, as well as non-sexted captured pictures which may depict the victim in semi-nude or scantily clad dress. The profile may hugely impersonate the victim as a girl ready for soliciting men of different age groups.

We term it as 'camouflaged porn' because such profiles apparently do not violate the rules and policies of these social networking sites prima facie, as happens in the cases regarding child pornography and they are camouflaged under the disguise of first amendment protection. It must be noted that all the SNSs emphasise on the issue of child pornography from the perspective of child abuse and grooming the child for either offline abuse or online sexual gratification.[18] Of late, Facebook has turned the highlight towards sexted messages from the perspective of bullying.[19] But few have highlighted the issue of using sexted messages or stored messages for creating impersonated profiles which present the characteristics of camouflaged porn.

Camouflaged porn can be created further by circulating the stored data to others through emails or SMSs. This is the most common form of creating revenge porn by teens. Even though this deviant behaviour has been highlighted by many scholars from the perspective of infringement of privacy, it is not dealt from the perspective of creation of teen porn.

(b) Teen Porn

Such sorts of porn are generally found as one of the various categories of porn that are exhibited in adult websites. Nonetheless, these websites showcase safety shields to be protected by the immunity clause of Section 230 of the Communication Decency Act, codified at 47 United States Code (USC), which provides immunity for all types of materials that

---

[18] See Facebook terms on Safety. Available at https://www.facebook.com/terms.php?ref=pf. Also see, Justin. (February 22, 2011). You *received a 'Sext', now what? advice for teens*. Available at http://cyberbullying.us/blog/you-received-a-sext-now-what-advice-for-teens.html

[19] See Facebook tools on safety. Available at https://www.facebook.com/safety/tools

may attract liability of the website[20] through the routine announcement that the porn models are professional models who have consented for such performances; the viewers must certify that they are above 18 and therefore legally eligible for viewing the sites and by the immunity clause provided by Title 512 of the DMCA[21] which states that the contributors must not violate other's rights by infringing the copyrights and privacy of others and so on. But the minute analysis of the policies as well as the mode of execution of these sites may present a different picture. Such sites present a possible platform for the teens to execute revenge over split affairs with the help of stored data like the sexted messages and pictures. Such porn differs from camouflaged porn especially because the contributor openly declares his intention to tag the clipping as a porn clipping and showcase the victim as a true porn model (pp. 91–92).

The scope of these discussions regarding revenge porn can be extended to cover adults as well. Coming to regulating revenge porn, our discussion involved two US-based cases, namely New York v. Ferber (458 US 747 (1982) and a 2011 case involving sexting in Kentucky.[22] We have observed as follows:

Bartow[23] has addressed the issue of revenge porn from the perspective of copyright violations; even though Bartow has made a crucial observation in this reference in regard to revenge porn involving women, her observation stands right for teen victims as well. However, we argue that revenge porn by teens must also be seen from the perspective of individual liability of the perpetrator as well as the victim. As we have mentioned above, revenge porn can involve sexted messages, captured pictures of the victim, as well as self attached non-sexted pictures of the victim. A couple of years back, when the US federal and the provincial governments started

[20] See in general Digital Media Law Project, Immunity for online publishers under the Communication Decency Act. Available at http://www.dmlp.org/legal-guide/immunity-online-publishers-under-communications-decency-act

[21] S.512 of the Copyright Act was added by Title II of The DMCA, 1998 to create four limitations on liability for copyright infringement by online service providers on four categories of conduct by a service provider. For more, see http://www.copyright.gov/legislation/dmca.pdf

[22] See Daily Mail Reporter, Boy of 14 accused of child pornography after convincing girl his age to send him sex text. Published in *Mail Online* on 6 March 2011. Available at http://www.dailymail.co.uk/news/article-1363445/Sexting-case-asks-14-year-old-child-pornogragher.html

[23] See Ann Bartow (2008). Available at http://works.bepress.com/cgi/viewcontent.cgi?article=1030&context=ann_bartow (Accessed on 12 December 2015).

addressing sexting as a new form of self created child pornography[24] scholars including us researched on the possible alternative resolution to the
issue other than criminally prosecuting the creator–sender and the recipient as well (Halder & Jaishankar, 2014). But it must be remembered that
the courts only executed the inherent philosophy of child pornography
prevention laws in cases where both the deviant teens were prosecuted.
The courts basically wanted to show that the creation and distribution of
any material which depicts children in any fashion that creates erotica,
must be prohibited to safeguard the interest of the children and this has to
be carried out even when the act is done as a part of self sexual gratification by adolescent teens. Arguably, this approach of the US courts could be
criticized as many have rightly pointed out that laws meant for protection
of children are being used to punish the children for modern age adolescent behaviour.

Notably, the courts' understanding of the subject stands right when the
image or clipping meant for private viewing, are distributed to third party
for public viewing. But the details of almost all these cases would show that
the secondary 'distributor', who is the primary recipient, did not distribute the data for taking revenge. Therefore the motive was not criminal, but
purely adolescent fun. However, in revenge porn the motive is essentially to
defame the victim and therefore it is criminal. Now the question is; could
a 'child' be prosecuted for harbouring a criminal intention and executing
the same by a law which is meant for matured people? The question could
be analyzed in the light of two famous cases, namely, Ferber's case and the
ongoing Kentucky sexting case. (Halder & Jaishankar, 2014, pp. 93–94)

Both Ferber and the Kentucky case therefore established the fact that
when the substance presents a situation which cannot have any social
value, it may not claim the protection of the first amendment guarantee.
Understandably, publishing with an ill motive, of a still image, or audio–
visual clipping of the sexual performance of a teen, which was meant
strictly for private viewing of the recipient, therefore does not protect
the wrongdoer from the category of unprotected speech. It must be
noted that in the former convictions in the sexting cases, the prosecution
proved that the wrongdoer teen circulated the sexted image among his
friends with no ulterior motive or intention or even knowledge that it
may create permanent reputation damage for the original creator–sender
of the sexted message. However, revenge porn largely differs from this.

---

[24] See Leary, 2010, p. 491. Also see CUA Columbus School of Law Legal Studies
Research Paper No. 2010–31. Available at SSRN: http://ssrn.com/abstract=1657007

The wrongdoer knowingly circulates the sexted message or the stored images of his victim by breaking the promise of confidentiality to create harm to the victim. Probably, this is the core reason that revenge porn by teens aided by victim-supported material(s) needs a special legal treatment which may stand apart from regular sexting cases or even child pornography cases; and in such cases, we refuse to accept the US trend of categorising the offending teen as a 'sex offender'[25] as has been done in previous cases, where teens got involved in creating or distributing images showing sexual organs or performing sexual activities. The issue needs to be dealt with from the perspective of privacy and confidentiality and the responsibility of the teens in upholding the inherent philosophy of the fourteenth amendment essentially, coupled with abuse of First Amendment Guarantees. This is especially so because the Unites States may set a universal trend to deal with such cases which are generally followed by other countries including India.

In India, the very first reported case of teen revenge in the cyber space came out in 2001[26] when a 16 year Delhi school boy created a porn website and posted porn images of girls of his own class and of the teachers with lewd remarks, publishing in detail about their sexual preferences. The reports suggest that he did this as revenge to these girls who used to taunt him. The boy was arrested under Section 67 of the erstwhile IT Act[27] for charges of obscenity in the cyber space and later was released on bail by the juvenile court. The extreme punishment came when he was rusticated

[25] Miller Vs. California, 413, U.S. 15(1973).

[26] See Times Internet Network. Confusion prevails over tackling cyber crime. Published in *Times of India* on 22 May 2001. Available at http://timesofindia.indiatimes.com/city/pune/Confusion-prevails-over-tackling-cyber-crime/articleshow/409953300.cms

[27] This provision stated that

> Whoever publishes or transmits or causes to be published in the electronic form, any material which is lascivious or appeals to the prurient interest or if its effect is such as to tend to deprave and corrupt persons who are likely, having regard to all relevant circumstances, to read, see or hear the matter contained or embodied in it.

The adjacent part of the provision prescribed punishment which would be imprisonment for a term which may extend to five years and with fine which may extend to ₹1 lakh and in the event of second or subsequent conviction with imprisonment of either description for a term which may extend to 10 years and also with fine which may extend to ₹2 lakh. However, the IT Act was

from the school. This case drew huge attention of the media, the public, the law researchers and also the police as this was the first-ever case of teen revenge through cyber space in India.

The generation of web 2.0 had literally outsmarted the older generation and created this peculiar trend which was later followed by many adults to execute their revenge. This is evident from the search results on the internet with key words as 'revenge porn', 'Porn India', 'India teen porn' and so on. The numerous results may also include various porn websites created under categories such as 'Indian Desi Girl', 'South Indian Mallu' and so on apart from YouTube videos with similar tag words. Nonetheless, the case sets precedence for many other teens to execute their revenge through various websites which can be accessed by teens below 16 years, predominantly by the popular social networking sites. However, before discussing the legal treatment of these issues, an analysis on the Indian socio-economic condition with regard to sexting is essential here.

Sexting or consensually digital capturing of the private moments of two teens of different sexes, or sending pictures of oneself with scanty attires through video chats and so on are new age behaviours for Indian teens. The social culture of average Indian societies predominantly barred the parents to allow the children to wear revealing 'western dresses' which may show too much of the skin. However, the situation rapidly changed since the introduction of new age movies,[28] huge display of the usage of electronic devices like mobile phones, desktop as well as laptop computers in popular movies and TV serials meant for teens and young adults, and the gradual lowering of the prices and easy availability of these devices for household purposes and easily available broadband services. The web 2.0 era children are now used to seeing both parents occupied with their digital devices for their own professional as well as personal purposes. The internet accessibility changed the orthodox mindset of Indians and this resulted in change in the

---

subsequently amended and the amended version came into life in the later part of 2009. The amended version deals with child pornography under section 67B. The Act can be found at http://www.cyberpolicebangalore.nic.in/pdf/it_amend-ment_act2008.pdf

[28] This was suggested by one anonymous individual who made a comment to the lead author's blog, 'Be aware of online mischief mongers.' Available at http://debaraticyberspace.blogspot.com/2011/10/be-aware-of-online-mischief-mongers.html#comments

formal dress code to exclusive teen hangouts, even the approach towards sex education at homes and also at schools has changed.[29] This further encouraged the younger generation to ape the Western culture to dress 'sexily' to attract the opposite sex and even convey self-captured images to impress internet savvy high school sweethearts and dating partners, and also consensual capturing of the sexual performances (excluding penetration) with the partner by the partner himself or by automatic devices that would finally store the 'moments' in the partner's device.[30] Even though this new teen sexual behaviour has gained a highlight due to the infamous Delhi Public School (DPS) school case, where a 16 year old boy allegedly circulated a video clipping of his sexual acts along with his classmate, another 16 year old girl,[31] we could find no single Indian study with reference to the usage of such clipping for teen revenge and legal treatment of the same from the perspective of pornography and privacy laws. The reason could be highly attributed to the stringent juvenile justice laws prevailing in India which prevents detailed publishing of such ongoing cases involving minors as offenders and confused state of laws when it comes to victim aided offences in the cyber space like that of Delhi's DPS school case.

In this context, we need to analyse the general law in reference to the approach towards this issue in India. In 2001, when the 16 year old student of Air Force Bal Bharti School created a porn website with the pictures of his female classmates and teachers; unlike the Unites States, the police did not arrest the accused.[32] The case was handled by the juvenile welfare board after the father of one of the minor female victims lodged a complaint to the police. Even though the Indian parliament had passed the Information Technology Bill, 2000 which was heavily influenced by the model Law on electronic commerce adopted by the United Nations Commission on International Trade Law through the resolution

---

[29] We have discussed about the issue of sex education in schools in India in the later part of this Chapter.

[30] From the personal experiences as Directors of the Centre for Cyber victim Counseling (www.cybervictims.org), we have seen that this tendency is growing among the Indian teens.

[31] Express News Service. Sex scandal: Boy who shot MMS clip held. Published in *Express India* on 19 December 2004. Available at http://www.expressindia.com/news/fullstory.php?newsid=39787

[32] Basharat Peer. Student accused in porn website case secures Bail. Published on 30 April 2001. Available at http://www.rediff.com/news/2001/apr/30porn.htm (Accessed on 12 December 2015).

A/RES/51/162, dated 30th January 1997; the police was left much in awe of the nature of the crime as that was the first of its kind in India. The boy was released on bail by the Juvenile court, Delhi.[33] Justice Sanjay Agarwal, who granted bail to the accused, noted that this is an 'example of tech–graffiti' and it should 'not be taken seriously'.[34] But he was proved very wrong. Next, when the students of DPS were caught circulating the compromising position of their two classmates in 2004 by the school authorities, and the clipping was even found on the internet for a larger audience, the police immediately applied Section 67 of the IT Act along with sections 292 of the IPC to arrest the key person, a boy of 17, who had allegedly captured the sexual act along with the girl. The arrest was made after two more high profile arrests, involving the CEO of Baazee.com, Avinash Bajaj, who allegedly bought the clipping to circulate it through the website, and one Raviraj, a student of Indian Institute of Technology, Kharagpur, who allegedly sold the clippings to Baazee.com, an auction site. While Section 67 of the erstwhile IT Act, 2000 dealt with publishing, transmitting, causing to be published any obscene material in the electronic form; section 292 of the IPC prescribes punishment for selling, publishing, distributing, importing or exporting, making a monetary profit of, or advertising for obscene materials[35] and section 294 prescribes punishment for obscene acts and songs in public.[36] Even though the CEO of Baazee.com (which was later sold to eBay) challenged the Delhi High Court judgment[37] that quashed the Penal Code provision against him, but permitted prosecution under the Provisions of IT Act, on the ground of lack of clarity of section 67 in reference to his case and due diligence

[33] Presently, Juvenile court is substituted by Juvenile Justice Board after coming into effect of the Juvenile Justice (Care and Protection) Act, 2000. For more details, see http://delhicourts.nic.in/JUVENILE_JUSTICE_BOARD.htm

[34] Basharat Peer. Student accused in porn website case secures Bail. Published on 30 April 2001. Available at http://www.rediff.com/news/2001/apr/30porn.htm

[35] S.292 (2), IPC prescribes punishment with imprisonment of either description for a term which may extend to two years, and with fine which may extend to ₹2,000, and, in the event of a second or subsequent conviction, with imprisonment of either description for a term which may extend to five years, and also with fine which may extend to ₹5,000.

[36] S.294 of the IPC, 1860 prescribe punishment with imprisonment of either description for a term which may extend to three months, or with fine, or with both.

[37] See Avinash Bajaj v. State. Available at http://www.indiankanoon.org/doc/309722

of the website;[38] there was no further news about the prosecution or the post prosecution treatment of the main accused, the 17 year old student, except that he was suspended from the school.

As it could be seen, in both these cases, and especially in the latter case, the court highlighted the monetary gain for adults out of the clipping that was made depicting private sexual moments of two adolescent teens; and later focused its attention more on the issue of distributing pornography by an adult, i.e., Bajaj. In the former case, the judge waived off any 'seriousness' to the issue of the motive of the wrongdoer. Predominantly, that may have affected the legal treatment of the offender teen in the latter case. This can be largely attributed to the traditional Indian mindset towards the offence that could be done by the children, treatment of child offenders[39] and lack of constitutional guarantees towards privacy rights of the children. Since the independence, the Indian parliament has been busy in safeguarding the rights of the children in relation to basic education, food and shelter and health.[40] Through Juvenile Justice (Care and Protection) Act, 2000, this right has been broadened to cover abuse of children. Accordingly, the Indian laws have started to see the offences done by children more from the perspective of how and why they are being used for criminal gratifications of the adults. Misuse of digital knowledge by children had remained largely ignored by lawmakers until

[38] See DPS MMS scandal: SC stays proceedings against eBay, its chief. Published in Press Trust of India/New Delhi on 26 August 2008. Available at http://www.business-standard.com/india/news/dps-mms-scandal-sc-stays-proceedings-against-ebay-its-chief/332573

[39] The Juvenile Justice Act, 2000, which was subsequently amended in 2006, divided the category of children that could fall under two heads; namely, 'children in conflict with law', which is dealt by chapter II of the Act, and 'children in need of care and protection', which is dealt by Chapter III of the Act. Chapter II does not clarify separately as how the juvenile offender charged with offences under Indian Information Technology Act can be dealt with. The chapter however highlights the treatment of juvenile victims who may have been abused by adults by way of engaging the child for begging, employing the child for hazardous work, withholding the child's earnings and so on, or by negligence, abundance, or by giving intoxicating objects or psychotropic substances and so on, and the punishment of the adults who do these.

[40] National Commission for Protection of Child Rights (NCPCR), The Commissions for Protection of Child Rights Act, 2005 (No. 4 of 2006), The Right of Children to Free and Compulsory Education Act, 2009 (No. 35 of 2009) are the glaring examples.

the implementation of the IT Act, 2000 (as amended in 2008) and later the POCSO Act, 2012. But neither of these novel laws specifically focuses on the issue of revenge porn created and published by children.[41] Further, the Indian Constitution has expanded the scope of right to life[42] to right to privacy through the famous case Kharak Singh v. State of UP.[43] But this right has not been tested in reference to digital privacy of adults as well as children, other than hacking related cases.[44]

Furthermore, in India, unlike the Unites States, rarely any legal highlight has been focused on adolescent teen's sexual behaviours. Adolescent sexual behaviours like self-sexual gratification,[45] kissing or even dating opposite sex partners are still now considered as a taboo in many parts of India. However, at the same time, teens are turning to the internet for such apparently normal sexual habits at an alarming rate. This could be largely attributed to two factors: (a) on the internet, there is hardly any parental supervision, especially when teens use popular social networking sites (Halder & Jaishankar, 2011, pp. 5–6) and (b) the sites that teens favour to frequently visit, like the Facebook, Orkut and so on, have lowered the minimum age criteria to 13,[46] which encourages elder teens to experience something which in reality is forbidden. However, measures have been taken by the state governments to curb children's usage of digital devices, especially mobile phones inside the school premises since 2007 on the ground of health hazards and the supposed 'nuisances in the classrooms'[47] that may be created by such devices. Following this

[41] This point will be elaborated later.

[42] Right to life has been guaranteed vide Article 21 of the Indian Constitution which states, 'No person shall be deprived of his life or personal liberty except according to procedure established by law.'

[43] Kharak Singh v. State of UP ((1964) 1 SCR 332).

[44] See Vinod Kaushik & another v. Madhvika Joshi & Others, *Complaint no.2 of 2010, Before Sh Rajesh Aggarwal, Adjudicating officer, Information Technology Act, 2000. Government of Maharashtra, at Mantralaya, Mumbai-400032.* Available at http://catindia.gov.in/pdfFiles/Appeal_No_2.pdf (Accessed on 23 October 2011). Even though this present case does not primarily emphasize on the right to privacy in the digital space, it has highlighted the privacy factor through hacking and related issues.

[45] This may include masturbation, viewing adult porn sites, adult movies, reading adult sex stories and so on.

[46] See additional terms of service for Orkut. Available at http://www.orkut.co.in/html/en-US/additalterms.orkut.html; Also see, Registration and account security for Facebook. Available at http://www.facebook.com/terms.php?ref=pf

governmental policy, the governments of the states of Maharastra[48] and Gujarat[49] also issued orders to restrict mobile phones by minors under the age of 16. But, the most effective result could be seen in the notice issued by the Central Board of Secondary Education (CBSE) of India,[50] wherein CBSE had noted as follows:

> The use of Mobile Phones definitely needs to be restricted in school environments. The Board is of the opinion that all stakeholders connected with school education such as students, parents, teachers and heads of institutes need to arrive at a consensus on the use of mobile phones in their schools and restricting its entry in the school campus. This is because mobile phones can be a serious cause of distraction, lack of concentration, anxiety, fear and sometimes even misuse. Even if the mobiles are in silent mode they can be a source of disturbance within the classroom as students can make use of Short Messaging Service (SMS) during the class or even during an assignment. The cameras which are a common feature now in most mobile phones can also be misused. There have been enough lessons that have been learnt in the past regarding the use of mobile phones and the Board strongly recommends that students should be convinced about not carrying mobile phones to the school.

Presently, this order is effective in almost all the schools in India, and predominantly, this is the only measure to curb revengeful activities through digital devices by school-going teens. As the news reports suggest, if a teen is caught violating this rule, he could be severely warned, or fined or even rusticated depending upon the school's internal policies. We argue that this cannot be the solution for this problem. Since India has witnessed two incidents which probably had created huge effects on the teens, it cannot be ruled out that adolescent students will not fall upon safer platforms like

---

[47] Special correspondent, Karnataka bans mobiles for those under 16s. Published on 12 September 2007. Available at http://www.hindu.com/2007/09/12/stories/2007091262261200.htm

[48] Agencies. Mobile phones banned in schools in Maha. Published on 21 February 2009. Available at http://www.expressindia.com/latest-news/Mobile-phones-banned-in-schools-in-Maha/426462

[49] Press Trust of India. Gujarat government bans mobile phones in schools, colleges. Published on 2 August 2010. Available at http://articles.timesofindia.indiatimes.com/2010-08-02/india/28287399_1_mobile-phones-colleges-gujarat-government

[50] See CBSE circular of 2009. Restriction in the use of Mobile Phones in Schools. Available at http://cbse.nic.in/welcome.htm

that of the internet communication systems, including social networking sites. This is more so because these web platforms are guided by the US laws, which may help the child from India to execute his anger, frustration and revenge swiftly and not be caught under the legal tangle immediately, unless the authorities frame proper charges as per Indian standards.

The Unites States had set a tradition until the mid of 2011 to punish the wrongdoer teens by categorising them as 'sex offenders'.[51] Even though the term is grave for teens who may have exercised normal adolescent sexual behaviour; it must be noted that internet era teens have now become matured enough to abuse their rights of speech and expression. In India, S.67B of the IT Act (as amended in 2008) briefly touches on this issue. This provision extensively deals with online sexual crimes targeting children and it includes prohibitory measures against creation, publication or causing to be published any material depicting a child in sexually explicit conduct, collecting, seeking, browsing, advertising for material depicting children in obscene, indecent or sexually explicit act, online grooming of children for such purposes, facilitates abuse of children online, or records own abuse or other's abuse pertaining to sexually explicit act with children through five subclauses.[52]

The provision expands its scope with the opening words,

whoever—thus bringing the offending teens under its purview as well. Further, the 2012 regulation Protection of Children from Sexual Harassment Act, 2012 also braces the issue quite in the same line as Section 67B of the Information Technology Act 2000 (amended in 2008) did. It does not focus on revenge porn created by children or sexting aided by children exclusively. However, it addresses online sexual harassment and in S.11, it makes 'any person' guilty of sexual harassment if that person irrespective of gender makes the child show the body parts so that it can be seen by him/her or by others,[53] or shows material to child for pornographic purposes,[54] or threatens to use in any form of media the real or fabricated depiction through any electronic, film or digital or any other mode, the child's body parts or the involvement of the child in sexual acts that may be already stored with such person,[55] As it could be seen, this last provision briefly touches the issue of sexting and resultant revenge pornography.

---

[51] Miller vs. California, 413 U.S. 15 (1973).

[52] See S.67B of the IT Act, 2000 (amended in 2008). Available at http://www.cyberpolicebangalore.nic.in/pdf/it_amendment_act2008.pdf

[53] See S.11 (ii) of the POCSO Act, 2012.

[54] See S.11 (iii) of the POCSO Act, 2012.

[55] See S.11 (v) of the POCSO Act, 2012.

The law through S.12 also prescribes punishment for such types of sexual harassment which may include imprisonment for a term extended to three years, as well as pecuniary fines. But neither these provisions are properly used against any offending teen still now. As it could be seen, lawmakers may not have been ready yet to confer such serious punishment as has happened in the US, for wrong doer teens, but time has definitely ripened to think about punitive steps for wrong doer children which may safeguard the inherent essence of digital privacy and reputation of the victim, and at the same time upholding the constitution's core value to protect child rights, including sexual rights of adolescent teens. (pp. 96–104)

In this context, we need to mention that since 2013, there has been a positive improvement in introducing revenge porn laws in the United States. As of June, 2015, 23 states in the United States have passed laws criminalising unauthorised dissemination of private sexual images.[56] In India, even though we do not have any law titled 'anti-revenge porno law', the scope of S.354C of the IPC can be extended to cover revenge porn issues for adult women. But it needs to be remembered that this law is actually made to cover voyeurism and even though it does cover the aspect of privacy, it may not cover the aspect of revenge taking mentality. Hence, the lawmakers need to develop a focused law targeting revenge porn which may be beneficial for both adults and children. However, the police and the prosecution also needs to see the reach of the revenge porn content as well as any other sexually explicit material which may fall in the category of regulable porn. If the content is used for gross indecent representation of the victim, then the police must also consider bringing in provisions from Indecent Representation of Women (Prohibition) Act, especially S.4 (prohibition of publication or sending by post of books, pamphlets and so on; containing indecent representation of women) along with S.67A of the IT Act and S.354C of the IPC depending upon the facts of the case. However, we also need to note that too many laws may finally deter the main motive of the preventive jurisprudence framed by lawmakers especially when the law with maximum penalty may be given preference over the other, even if the same may not be a completely focused law on the issue. Hence, we feel that while the

---

[56] For more information on this issue, see Franks, M. (2015). How to defeat revenge porn: First recognize it's about privacy, not revenge. Published in *The Huffington Post* on 22 June 2015. Available at http://www.huffingtonpost.com/mary-anne-franks/how-to-defeat-revenge-porn_b_7624900.html?ir=India&ads SiteOverride=in

reporting agency (i.e., the police) needs to apply their mind to book the offence under correct laws, the lawmakers should also think about bringing more focused and comprehensive laws in this regard.

Child Pornography

While discussing about sexting and revenge pornography, we have shown how India's child pornography laws as enshrined in S.67B of the IT Act as well as in Ss.11 and 13 of the POCSO Act, 2012 can be utilised. It further needs to be pointed out that S.67B of the IT Act also criminalises collection, browsing, dissemination, advertising, seeking or creation of contents showing children in sexually explicit acts (S.67B(b)), grooming or enticing children for the purpose of creation of child pornography (S.67B(c)), with a punishment for a term which may extend to five years and with a fine which may extend to ₹10 lakh and in the event of second or subsequent conviction with imprisonment of either description for a term which may extend to seven years and also with fine which may extend to ₹10 lakh. Going by this provision, it may be seen that while criminalisation of watching adult porn by adults in private is possible or not is still being considered by the courts, the laws are crystal clear in this regard when it comes to browsing, downloading or seeking child porn materials. It may be necessary to point out here that of late, complaints regarding creation of child porno materials in the social media are growing in number. To tackle such crimes, states like Tamil Nadu have developed stringent laws such as Tamil Nadu Prevention of Dangerous Activities of Bootleggers, Drug Offenders, Forest Offenders, Goondas, Immoral Traffic Offenders, Sand Offenders, Slum-grabbers and Video Pirates Act, 1982 (popularly known as Goonda's Act), which has extended its scope to creation of offensive, derogatory materials on the internet, including child pornography. The recent arrest and detention of one Yadava Manikanta by the Tamil Nadu Police for creation of Facebook pages with paedophilic contents is noteworthy here. The police booked him under S.67B of the IT Act, the POCSO Act as well as the Goondas Act.[57] It is

---

[57] See The News Mint. (2015). Why the arrest of a man running paedophilic page on Facebook is significant. Published in *The News Mint* on 22 May 2015. Available at http://www.thenewsminute.com/article/why-arrest-man-running-paedophilic-page-facebook-significant

hoped that such examples would create positive effect on the society in bringing down crimes related to child pornography.

Cyber Obscenity

As we have already mentioned, when we speak about sexual offences on the internet targeting women and girls, we may see many instances where the concepts of cyber obscenity have overlapped the concept of cyber pornography. This is because in India, we have well developed legal provisions for curbing obscenity, including cyber obscenity. In our earlier research (Halder & Jaishankar, 2011) we have observed:

> The very first legal attempt to define obscenity was made in the landmark case of Miller v. California, which defined obscenity as 'hard core pornography'. The verdict also specified several activities which would amount to obscenity; these are: lewd caricature of sexual organs or sexual activities communicated by photography or graphic designs or even lascivious messages; comments or texts about the recipient's/sender's/body, sexual acts etc. We have noticed that often obscenity in the cyber space is linked with pornography and the trend leads to discussions about child pornography. While it is true that obscenity and pornography are interlinked, it is to be noted that pornography is one of the modes to express obscenity. Pornography is largely used to explain sexual activities with the help of graphics including movies and still photos. Obscenity can be expressed even by verbal written words not which may not include such images. In the cyber space, not only children but adult women are also targeted for obscenity attacks.

The question which arises at this point is: Which are the constituting elements that make obscenity a crime against women? We will analyse this question from two angles: first, from the behavioural aspect of the harasser and the victim and second, in the light of Miller's verdict.

When seen from the first aspect, i.e., the behavioural aspect, the constituting elements could be as follows.

- the concupiscent act of forcefully sending obscene, lewd messages about the victim's body or lustrous images of a female or male naked/semi-nude body depicting sexual organs in an indecent way to create unnecessary hatred or fear or uncomfortable feeling for the victim to look at the message, or

- sending to one's inbox the visual images depicting sexual activities portraying women as 'sex slaves', or
- creating stories in prurient language about sexual activities involving victim's name and/or photographs, cartoons, graphic images and so on floating in the web, which successfully portrays the victim as a perverted sex partner and generates huge despise against the victim among common people and not sympathy.

When seen from the second aspect, i.e., in the light of Miller v. California, the constituting elements would include the following logical deductions:

(a) Whether 'the average person, applying contemporary community standards' would find that the work, taken as a whole, appeals to the prurient interest,

(b) Whether the work depicts or describes, in a patently offensive way, sexual conduct specifically defined by the applicable state law, and

(c) Whether the work, taken as a whole, lacks serious literary, artistic, political or scientific value.

In short, the Miller verdict emphasises on the societal acceptance of the behaviours and social value systems when terming such activities as crime. Most of the countries that have developed their own internet laws, have accepted Miller's judgmental analysis in regard to obscenity. However, cyber obscenity targeting adult women is getting momentum due to ever improving digital tools (Halder & Jaishankar, 2011, pp. 28–29).

In India, obscenity was traditionally addressed by the IPC in S.292(1), which explains the scales of decency in any content that can be called as obscene by stating that,

... [A] book, pamphlet, paper, writing, drawing, painting, representation, figure or any other object, shall be deemed to be obscene if it is lascivious or appeals to the prurient interest or if its effect, or (where it comprises two or more distinct items) the effect of any one of its items, is, if taken as a whole, such as to tend to deprave and corrupt person, who are likely, having regard to all relevant circumstances, to read, see or hear the matter contained or embodied in it.

The provision also criminalised publication, dissemination and so on of obscene works or contents to others (S.292(2) of the IPC) as well as to children (S.293 of the IPC). Further, S.294 of the IPC prescribes punishment for obscene acts and reciting songs to annoyance of others. On the shadow of all these three provisions, S.67 was framed and amended in the IT Act, 2000 (amended in 2008) which says,

> Whoever publishes or transmits or causes to be published in the electronic form, any material which is lascivious or appeals to the prurient interest or if its effect is such as to tend to deprave and corrupt persons who are likely, having regard to all relevant circumstances, to read, see or hear the matter contained or embodied in it, shall be punished on first conviction with imprisonment of either description for a term which may extend to two three years and with fine which may extend to five lakh rupees and in the event of a second or subsequent conviction with imprisonment of either description for a term which may extend to five years and also with fine which may extend to ten lakh rupees.

In our previous research (Halder & Jaishankar, 2011), we have made specific observations in this regard:

> We may note that the draftsmen of this Act have carefully retained the hairline difference between the meaning of obscenity and sexually explicit materials. The core notions of obscenity and pornography are differentiated for legal understanding of the two in a fine language by Britton, Maguire, and Nathanson (1993) which is as follows:
>
> … Obscenity is sexual words and images which are not protected by Constitutional guarantees of free speech. To be illegally obscene, a work must appeal to the prurient interests, depict sex in a patently offensive way, and lack serious literary, artistic, political or scientific value. Pornography is material designed to arouse and has no legal or consistent definition. Each person's definition depends on her upbringing, sexual preference and viewing context. One woman's 'trash' may be another's treasure or boredom (Britton, Maguire, & Nathanson, 1993, para 3).
>
> Even though this differentiation was made in view of American constitutional guarantees on freedom of speech, the Indian laws hardly differentiate between the two. The Indian Supreme Court has adopted Cockburn's definition of obscenity, i.e., 'the test of obscenity is this, whether the tendency of the matter charged as obscene is to deprave and corrupt those whose minds are open to such immoral influences and into whose hands a publication of this sort may fall'.[58] The Indian Supreme Court addressed obscenity as a

---

[58] *The Indian Supreme Court has adopted Cockburn's definition of obscenity (as explained in* Cockburn, C.J., in Hicklin, (1868), LR 3 QB360, 371).

social crime in the case of Ranjit D. Udeshi vs. State of Maharashtra[59] and stated that 'when treatment of sex becomes offensive to public decency and morality as judged by the prevailing standards of morality in the society, then only the work may be regarded as an obscene production. (Halder & Jaishankar, 2011, pp. 122–123)

Thus, when a police officer needs to book a complaint regarding obscenity on the internet, he/she has to apply his/her mind to segregate the offence from the concept of pornography. There are many examples of lodging cases relating to obscene cinemas; the latest example of using S.67 of the IT Act on cyber obscenity may be that of slapping charges of obscenity on Sunny Leone for distributing obscene contents on the internet.[60] But we understand that segregating elements of obscenity from pornography for slapping correct provisions may become a herculean task since pornographic content may contain obscenity as well. Further, as we have mentioned, due to preference of heavy punishments, many police officers may tend to club up both the provisions of Ss.67 and 67A of the IT Act as well as S.292 IPC or S.67B of the IT Act and S.293 of the IPC. We feel to set a good example for handling offences related to pornography and obscenity, this tendency should be avoided by the police.

Conclusion

As can be seen from the previous discussions, India has laws to deal with sexual offences targeting women and girls. But these laws are still half baked laws. Consider the case of Yadava Manikanta again; the convict could create offensive Facebook pages because primarily he could photograph young girls in public places. Similarly, we (Halder & Jaishankar, 2014a) have shown how lack of public photography regulation laws as well as lack of proper privacy laws on the internet as well as in the real life can victimise women including tribal women when their images are

[59] Ranjit. D. Udeshi (1965) 1SCR65 SC.

[60] The news report does not mention about the application of S.67 of the IT Act, 2000. But as the report suggests, we feel S.67 could have been pulled in. For details, see Press Trust of India. (2015). Sunny Leone charged with obscenity. Published in *The Hindu* on 15 May 2015. Available at http://www.thehindu. com/entertainment/sunny-leone-charged-with-obscenity/article7210308.ece (Accessed on 9 June 2015).

uploaded as porn contents in the social media or adult sites with xxx movie tags. It needs to be understood that images so misused may create fake avatars which may stay on the internet for a long time.[61] This may motivate the victims to take extreme steps such as resorting to irrational coping methods[62] or even committing suicide. We feel that the criminal justice machinery has the primary responsibility to make the victims feel confident that there are proper legal mechanism to address the situation and that the perpetrators can be punished when the victims cooperate properly with police and the courts. Not only this, the victims must also be given the confidence that objectionable images can be taken off the internet, if they cooperate. Obviously in removing the contents, the websites play major roles,[63] and for this, the web companies must also cooperate with the victim and the police and prosecution. If the victims gain such confidence, we feel the problem may be tackled easily.

References

Bartow, A. (2008). Pornography, coercion, and copyright law 2.0. *Vanderbilt Journal of Entertainment and Technology Law, 10*(4), 101–142. Available at http://works.bepress.com/cgi/viewcontent.cgi?article=1030&context= ann_bartow (Accessed on 10 February 2016).

Citron, D. (2014). *Hate crimes in cyber space.* Harvard: Harvard University Press.

Dworkin, A., & MacKinnon, C. A. (1988). Pornography and civil rights: A new day for women's equality. Published & Distributed by Organizing against Pornography: A resource centre for education and action. Minneapolis, Minnesota.

George, C. E., & Scerri, J. (2007). *Web 2.0 and user-generated content: Legal challenges in the new frontier. Journal of Information, Law and Technology, 2.* Available at http://ssrn.com/abstract=1290715 (Accessed on 10 February 2016).

Halder, D., & Jaishankar, K. (June 2011). *Cyber crime and the victimization of women: Laws, rights, and regulations.* Hershey, PA: IGI Global.

Halder, D., & Jaishankar, K. (2013). Revenge porn by teens in the United States and India: A socio-legal analysis. *International Annals of Criminology, 51*(1–2), 85–111.

---

[61] See previous chapter for detailed discussion on this.

[62] Detailed discussion regarding this has been done in later chapters.

[63] See detailed discussions on this in later chapters.

Halder, D., & Jaishankar, K. (July/August, 2014b). Teen sexting: A critical analysis on the criminalization vis-à-vis victimization conundrums. *The Virtual Forum Against Cybercrime (VFAC) Review,* Korean Institute of Criminology, *1*(6), 26–43.

———. (2014a). Online victimization of Andaman Jarawa tribal women: An analysis of the 'human safari' YouTube videos (2012) and its effects. *British Journal of Criminology, 54*(4), 673–688.

Leary, M. (2010). Sexting or self-produced child pornography? The dialogue continues—Structured prosecutorial discretion within a multidisciplinary response. *Virginia Journal of Social Policy and the Law, 17*(3), 487–566.

Malamuth, N. (1999). Pornography. Encyclopedia of violence, peace and conflict (vol. 3. pp. 77–89). Available at http://www.sscnet.ucla.edu/comm/malamuth/pdf/99evpc3.pdf (Accessed on 15 May 2015).

Sunstein, C. (1986). Pornography and the First Amendment. *DUKE Law Journal, 1986*(4), 589–627. Available at http://scholarship.law.duke.edu/cgi/viewcontent.cgi?article=2951&context=dlj. (Accessed on 2 January 2015).

7

Right to be Forgotten:
Liability of the Service Providers

The biggest fear a woman may develop due to online harassment including online misogyny is that her social reputation can be destroyed due to the harm done to her modesty, morality and chastity. Women often fear that this may lead to numerous other problems, including killing. In India, since time immemorial, morality and chastity of women have been considered as important factors to judge a woman's character. Consider the epic tale of Ramayana where Sita had to go through *agni parikhsha* (trial by fire) to prove her chastity to her husband Rama because she had stayed in Lanka in Ravan's captivity. In modern India, there is no law that has actually defined the meaning of morality and chastity, and as such, compelling women to prove their morality or chastity by such inhuman ways has been condemned by courts. But the orthodox social mindset in many occasions defied the legal rules and women, whose morality and chastity would have been questioned, were subjected to extreme violation of basic human rights; there are plenty of examples available in the society including putting burning coal on the palm to prove the morality and chastity of women, sticking label on the forehead of women calling them names, socially ostracising and even killing the woman in the name of honour killing. A typical linguistic definition of chastity may show three basic criteria for fitting into the meaning of 'chastity', purity, self-control and incorruptibility (Mahalingam, 2007).

Morality, on the other hand, implies certain principles set by the society itself that distinguishes between the right and wrong behaviour. For women in the Indian society, chastity and morality are used almost always synonymous with sexual purity. Morality and chastity, if taken in this meaning, may also be clubbed with 'modesty', a term which like the earlier two was never defined by the laws in India. But the term modesty has been used in S.354 (assault or criminal force to woman with intent to outrage her modesty) and S.509 (words, gesture and so on used to harm the modesty of women); both the provisions have made the modesty of women as subjects to penalise physical force as well as gesture or words (verbal, pictorial or written) which attack the modesty of women. The term modesty has been interpreted by the courts in the same linguistic meaning as has been provided by the Oxford English Dictionaries, which explains the term as 'womanly propriety of behaviour: scrupulous chastity of thought speech and conduct.'[1] The term modesty had earlier been interpreted as an 'attribute of woman's sex'[2] and the courts have tended to rely on the test laid down by the State of Punjab v. Major Singh (AIR 1967 S. 63), which is 'the action of the offender such as could be perceived as one which is capable of shocking the sense of decency of woman'. In the cyber space, the morality, chastity and modesty of a woman may be harmed with a simple 'bad talk', a 'fake avatar' or a defamatory post targeting the woman and all these can be done without directly applying physical force to the woman concerned or making her see and hear offensive gestures or words. This is mainly because Internet provides a wider platform for showcasing the thoughts of the individual, even if the same is offensive.

But we need to remember that the level of morality, chastity and modesty (especially in regard to women) differs from society to society (Miller v. California, 1973).[3] Given the fact that most of the internet companies are hosted in the Unites States, the factors which may decide the levels of speech, images or write-ups to be categorised as 'offensive' may be settled as per the laws of the hosting nation. In such a case, what may be perceived as 'offensive' in India may not be perceived so according to the rules and policies followed and created by internet companies based in the Unites States. Similarly, internet companies as well as email or digital telecommunication service providers hosted in India may also have their own rules and policies, and they may also have their own levels of understanding in regard to categorising speech or thought or images as offensive or non-offensive. It may be worthy to note that all internet companies and service providers are liable to safeguard the interest of

[1] See Mrs Rupan Deol Bajaj and Anr v. Kanwar Pal Singh Gill and Anr on 12 October 1995. Equivalent citations: 1996 AIR 309, 1995 SCC (6) 194.

[2] See State of Punjab v. Major Singh (AIR 1967 S.63).

[3] Miller v. California, 413 U.S. 15 (1973).

all the subscribers, irrespective of their intent or motive with which they use the services. It is because of this very reason that the private information of the subscribers with which one creates an account, including the geolocation, original name, social identification number, phone numbers and Internet Protocol (IP) addresses are not revealed by internet companies and service providers unless the subscriber himself/herself reveals this information in their own profile page or messages. The liability of internet companies and service providers also include answering distress calls from the subscribers as well as non-subscribers, who may have been offended by the activities of any subscriber. But oftener than not, this particular liability is seen as more controversial by the stakeholders when compared to the liability to maintain secrecy regarding the private information of the subscribers. This is especially so because the liability that arise due to complaints made by victims, especially women victims, in most cases cover victim's right to be 'forgotten' in the particular web portal from the image that may have been created by the harasser. This concept of the 'right to be forgotten' which would be discussed in the light of the 'right to be forgotten' that is now being debated by the European Union (EU) against the broad understanding of the freedom of speech by the US based internet companies, slightly differs from the latter in the narrower sense since we would emphasise more on female victim's rights to claim a complete deletion of offensive posts or images. We would rather lean on the second and third categories of rights to 'oblivion' as has been stated by Peter Fleischer, Chief Privacy Counsel of Google,[4] for this reason.

Liability: What? Why and for Whom?

As can be understood from the discussions in the earlier chapters, the internet provides a platform for people to express their minds and interact with people for various reasons. Similarly, digital telecommunication system also provides a channel to interact with people either only by way of oral communication or by oral communication as well as generating messages (including text which may or may not be accompanied by

---

[4] See for more details, Fleischer. (2011). Foggy thinking about the Right to Oblivion. Published in Peter Fleischer: Privacy...? on 9 March 2011. Available at http://peterfleischer.blogspot.in/2011/03/foggy-thinking-about-right-to-oblivion.html (Accessed on 2 July 2015).

photographs or graphic images). While the creator of the speech, text or post may have primary liability for the speech, it needs to be understood that the career or channel or platform through which such speech, thought or message reaches the receiver also has certain liabilities. Such a channel or platform is provided by the internet and it has its own rules, liabilities and policies which may decide which speech may not be withdrawn curtailing the rights of the content creator and which speech may stay and be delivered to the target recipient, irrespective of the content of the post, message or mail and so on.

The situation can best be described in the following words:

> What many consider the largest public space in human history is not public at all. Paradoxically, the Internet—a content-agnostic communication network available to anyone with access to a computer—contains no true 'public forum.' It embraces no public commons upon which a citizen is free to stand on his or her virtual soapbox and regale the public. It is layered on privately owned [w]eb sites, privately owned servers, privately owned routers, and privately owned backbones. Without the acquiescence of these intermediaries, the public would have no access to speak or to be heard. (Ardia, 2010, p. 377)

This platform, which helps individuals to communicate through cyber space and digital technology, is known as 'intermediary'. In India, the term 'intermediary' has been defined by S.2 (1) (w) of the IT Act, 2000 (amended in 2008). This section defines the term as:

> [A]ny person who on behalf of another person receives stores or transmits that record or provides any service with respect to that record. Further, the definition of intermediary includes telecom service providers, network service providers, internet service providers, web-hosting service providers, search engines, online payment sites, online-auction sites, online-market places, and cyber cafes.

It may be pertinent to note that the concept of intermediary, which is defined in S.2 (1) (w) of the IT Act, 2000 (amended in 2008), is heavily influenced by the US concepts of 'interactive computer services'[5] and

---

[5] The term 'interactive computer service' means any information service, system or access software provider that provides or enables computer access by multiple users to a computer server, including specifically a service that provides access to the internet and such systems operated or services offered by libraries and educational institutions. (See S.47 USC, S.230(e)(2) of the CDA).

'information content provider.'[6] Both these terms are defined by S.230 (e) (2) and (3) of the CD Act, 1996. Since most of the intermediaries including internet companies like Google, Yahoo, Facebook, Twitter, e-commerce sites, other networking sites including adult dating sites and also adult entertainment sites which host adult porn materials are hosted in the Unites States, they are guided by the US laws and regulations regarding intermediary liability. Hence, we need to first understand the liability that are imposed upon the intermediaries and the immunity that are available for the immunities from the US perspectives.

Categories of Intermediaries and Types of their Liabilities

The primary liability of the intermediaries may include providing a subscriber a platform to express his opinion or connecting the subscriber to another. On the basis of this very understanding, intermediaries have been classified into three groups by Ardia (2010), which are (a) communication conduits, (b) content hosts and (c) search/application providers. Analysing the definition of intermediaries as provided in S.2 (1) (w) of the IT Act, 2000 (amended in 2008), it may be seen that Ardia's classification may be expanded to include two more classification based on the nature of the purpose of the intermediary; these may include e-commerce sites and cyber cafes. But considering the fact that e-commerce sites can be included in the category of content hosts, we limit the classification into four groups, namely, communication conduits, content hosts, search/application sites and cyber cafes. The groups of intermediaries and their liabilities are explained as follows.

1. Communication Conduits

These intermediaries are entrusted with the liability of physically transporting the data, enabling the subscriber to access the content on the internet and so on. Ardia (2011) simplifies the explanation by examples

---

[6] 'Information content provider' is defined as 'any person or entity that is responsible, in whole or in part, for the creation or development of information provided through the internet or any other interactive computer service.' (See S.47 USC S.230(e)(3) CDA).

of such intermediaries which include telephone companies, cable companies and so on. In the Indian context, the term 'communication conduits' may include telecom and network service providers; the best examples of such intermediaries, therefore, could be Bharat Sanchar Nigam Limited (BSNL), Mahanagar Telephone Nigam Limited (MTNL) and so on which are used by subscribers to get connected to the World Wide Web. As Ardia (2011) stated, these intermediaries have restricted liability limited only to data transaction from point to point and they have no knowledge about the content of the data. However, in case such communication conduit serves as source and destination internet service providers (ISPs), they may have contractual relationship with 'end users', that is, the users who send the data and the users who receive the data through the same intermediary. As the function of the communication conduits is limited to delivering the data, it may be seen that such intermediaries may have limited liability towards the subscribers. These liabilities may include providing uninterrupted services to the subscriber; verifying the personal information details as per the laws of the land before providing the services and preserving the personal information, call logs and so on of the subscriber; to protect the privacy of the subscriber and not to divulge the personal information and the call log records to anyone other than for police or court cases; to take action to restore the services if the services are interrupted for technical reasons; to take action against a defaulter and also against persons who had misused the services and who had been reported against by the subscriber, empowered with a police or court notice; to provide all details about the personal information, call log details and so on when required by law enforcement agencies.

2. Content Hosts

Intermediaries who fall in this category typically do the work of storing, cacheing or providing space to host third party contents and have access to the same (Ardia, 2011). Such intermediaries may include internet companies including Google or Facebook, which may work not only as content hosts, but may also provide platforms for interactive communication; such intermediaries may also include Wordpress.com, GoDaddy.com, which may provide space to create a website or a blogsite, or e-commerce sites like Criaglist, OLX.in and so on. When compared with communication conduits, content hosts have greater liability towards subscribers and towards non-subscribers as well. Almost all of these liabilities stem

from DMCA, especially S.512 (C) which speaks about safe harbour policies; the US First Amendment guarantees free speech and expression;
and the US Fourth amendment guarantees on privacy. These liabilities
may include the following:

- To provide uninterrupted services to the subscriber.
- To host contents which are uploaded by the subscriber and make it
  accessible for others.
- To provide adequate measures for the subscribers to protect his/
  her private information which are provided to the hosting site as
  necessary information for creating the account as well as those
  information which the subscriber wishes to exhibit through the
  intermediary.
- To provide free platform for the subscriber to express his/her
  thoughts and opinions without interrupting, except when required
  by their own policy guidelines or by the laws (this and the liability
  turns the subscriber into a data controller himself).
- However, while the subscriber as a primary data controller may
  have the freedom to exhibit data as he wishes, the intermediaries
  as the secondary data controller may have bigger liability when the
  primary data controller cannot cope with the violative behaviour
  of the perpetrator.
- To develop policy guidelines in line with the laws and to monitor
  illegal contents.
- To notify grievance redressal forum, officer or office and to take
  note of the complaints made by the subscriber/s.
- To cooperate with the law enforcement agencies.
- To take action against subscribers who may have misused the
  services.
- To not host anything that depicts child pornography.
- To take down contents when reported against either for copyright
  violation or for violating any other terms and policies developed
  by the said Internet Company or any other law of the country from
  where the victims may have brought any court order or police
  request.

As may be seen from the discussions, content hosts may be considered as store houses of information of various types, especially when
considered from the perspective of private user, who may use content
hosts for their personal blogs, social networking sites or communication

through mails, messages or image sharing. Content hosts, therefore, are also called information warehouses. Content hosts, however, may not be considered as 'publishers of the opinions' of the users, but they can be treated as physical space libraries or book stores, who may be liable to remove offensive contents if complained by the third party on the basis of complaints ranging from copyright violation to defamatory materials to privacy infringement. It needs to be remembered that when seen from the perspective of cyber crimes against women, content hosts play a great role in both positive as well as negative sense. In the negative sense, content hosts are the prime targets to upload and showcase defamatory materials, obscene or sexually explicit, morphed or original images, hate speech including speech amounting to offensive, defamatory, harassing, threatening, intimidating, bullying or trolling messages, creation and circulation of fake avatars targeting women and so on.

Content hosts are also targeted to carrying on cyber stalking and resultant harassment to victims, by vandalising profiles and damaging reputation and so on. Content hosts are also used to create and use materials for grooming for the purpose of all sorts of online victimisation targeting women and girls including paedophilia, phishing, cheating, sexual offences, consensual pornography, revenge porn and so on. In the positive sense, content hosts, if used properly, can make the users able to spread positive messages seeking information and may even help in police investigation. Saying this, it needs to be mentioned again that content hosts may be considered as prime guardians for securing user's private information. Often users tend to overlook subtle loopholes in the user agreements with the content hosts whereby the user agrees to let the content hosts use their private information for various research activities or building up marketing strategies by the latter. Facebook's usage of users' data attracted attention of millions of privacy advocates in the past year when it was seen that Facebook was using emoticons to know the moods of the users for their own research.[7] There are also loads of literatures discussing how content hosts like Google and Facebook are using user's private information for their own marketing strategies.[8] Twitter, on the other hand, encourages users to use hashtags since long. This practice

---

[7] Booth, R. (2014). Facebook reveals news feed experiment to control emotions. Published in The Guardian on 30 June 2014. Available at http://www.theguardian.com/technology/2014/jun/29/facebook-users-emotions-news-feeds (Accessed on 2 February 2015).

[8] Ibid.

was recently adopted by Facebook also. While hashtags may attract maximum views for the said posts or threads, keywords or words along with hash tags create metadata which may be used to contribute to the big data of information storehouses and obviously, users using hash tags cannot escape the 'publicity lime light' because they may have already agreed with such policies for privacy loopholes with the content hosts. However, in this procedure, the positive liability of the content hosts, especially social media sites cannot be overlooked.

Consider the devastating Nepal earthquake in mid-2015. Google deployed 'person-finder' app through people finder interchange format (PFIF), an open data standard for gathering and sharing information about missing or displaced people and this person finder is basically built upon cloud computing mechanism.[9] While Google's person finder app was already in use since 2010 Haiti earthquake, Instagram was also being used to share the information. Facebook also came up with similar ideas in 2015 whereby 'safety check tool' was used by Facebook to find out about survivors or missing persons using the geolocations provided in the profiles of the users and also other relevant information uploaded by the user regarding the place in question.[10] It is expected that content hosts like Google or Facebook may thus help women survivors as well in similar mechanism in case they are in distress due to domestic violence. It may be noted that there are many safety apps available to people in India like SafetyPin[11] which helps people, especially women, to get connected to their families when they are travelling. This app made by Safetypin.com also provides a database of unsafe, dim lighted areas where crime can be apprehended. However, this again brings the concern about privacy of the users, especially because the users may share their geolocations and perpetrators who may unauthorisedly access the profile or the content host as a whole may prove dangerous to the society.

---

[9] Crilly, R. (2015). Google 'person finder' tool deployed to help relatives find loved ones in Nepal. Published in *The Telegraph* on 25 April 2015. Available http://www.telegraph.co.uk/news/worldnews/asia/nepal/11563157/Google-person-finder-tool-deployed-to-help-relatives-find-loved-ones-in-Nepal.html (Accessed on 4 May 2015).

[10] Clark, L. (2015). Facebook and Google launch people finder tools for Nepal quake. Published in Wired.co.uk on 27 April 2015. Available at http://www.wired.co.uk/news/archive/2015-04/27/facebook-google-nepal-earthquake-emergency-response (Accessed on 2 July 2015).

[11] See about this app at http://safetipin.com.

Content hosts also play a major role in getting users connected with the 'big data' or the information super highway by way of connecting the contents or the users to the search engines. Content hosts play the 'provider' of information to the search engines. However, in such cases, the liability of the content hosts as companies and individual users as 'data controller' may differ. Content hosts as companies or legal entities may provide information to the search engines, especially in relation to user's privately generated contents only when the user agrees for the same. In cases when the content host is a web host for which the user would have paid some amount for uploading some content, the user may expect that the content host would in its turn link the content to the search engines for better publicity. This may be an implied condition in the agreement between the content host and the user. In other cases, when the user uses content hosts which provide the user to create or generate any content free of charge, (e.g., social networking sites or video uploading sites like YouTube), adult entertainment sites, porn sites and so on), depending upon the privacy settings opted for by the user primarily and also the public sharing policy of the content, the content host may provide the content for listing in the search engines (Ardia, 2011).

As can be seen, the user may therefore play an important role as 'data controller' of his/her content. This group of data controller can be called as group-1 data controllers whereas content hosts can be called as group-2 data controllers. With the every content the host gives the user/subscriber, it also gives him/her the opportunity to control the audience who can view his/her information as well as publication. When it is the email service providers, if they are seen from the perspective of content hosts, it may be seen that the users can get three distinct options as data controller: (a) block the unwanted people from sending mails to them; (b) stop conveying the message in the midway if the sender feels that the particular message is erroneous or going to the wrong receiver and (c) reveal or hide personal or professional designation in the message text as signatory, hide the availability status in the chat box and reveal or hide profile pictures in the side bar to make the receivers able to see the images of the user. It may be seen that similar opportunities are given to users in the social networking sites, blogging sites or video uploading sites. Users as data controllers, therefore, need to have a better understanding about their own liabilities for posting or sending offensive, defamatory or risky contents which may push them to be targets of online perpetrators. As such, group-2 data controllers, namely, the content hosts, may provide those information/content to the search engines for which the group-1 data controllers have authorised the earlier, either by simply indicating that such contents may be made 'searchable' on the internet or by paying charges for making the contents available on search engines.

However, when considered from the perspective of online victimisation of women, a very recent development on the issue of the liability of the content host must be mentioned here. In the United States, some law professors and activists had started working with the government to make revenge porn a punishable offence (Citron, 2014). Given the fact that social media like the Facebook and Twitter are the most chosen platforms for creating and circulating revenge porn materials, in 2015, Twitter took note of using it as a platform for revenge porn and started taking action on monitoring metadata which mentions about revenge porn; Facebook soon followed.[12] However, as both Facebook and Twitter had repeatedly mentioned that extensive monitoring of the contents by them is not possible because of the huge inflow of the data, it needs to be mentioned that both Facebook and Twitter as well as Google had started taking commendable steps in monitoring extreme hardcore porn, revenge porn, child porn, violent videos and so on with the help of content moderators who are engaged by these companies on outsourcing basis.[13] Even though this may have helped in blocking of publication of such contents to a certain extent, unfortunately, these sites continue to be used as chosen platforms for publishing contents for harming the rights of individuals, especially women, children and people from lesbian, gay, bisexual and transgender (LGBT) community.

3. Search Engines

World Wide Web has now become unthinkable without search engines. According to Grimmelmann (2007), 'a search engine is a service that helps its users locate content on the Internet'. It needs to be understood that search engines are not independent entities like the communication

---

[12] Price, R. (2015). Facebook has banned revenge porn. Published on Business Insider on 16 March 2015. Available at http://www.businessinsider.in/Facebook-has-banned-revenge-porn/articleshow/46585337.cms (Accessed on 2 April 2015).

[13] See for more details about this in Chaudhury. P., Chatterjee, A., & Verma, V. (2014). Guardians of the Internet. Published in The Telegraph on 7 December 2014. Available at http://www.telegraphindia.com/1141207/jsp/7days/story_2412.jsp (Accessed on 8 December 2014).

conduits or the content hosts. They live upon three basic factors: (a) indexing of the available information/contents by the search engines, which the search engines need to work upon by using software like spiders, crawlers, robots and so on; (b) user queries, which actually motivate search engines to produce effective results and thereby remain active and (c) results, which the search engines produce in the form of lists of web pages or web links with the accurate contents that were being searched for by the users. The popularity of search engines depends on how faster they can produce accurate results. This can be done by various indexing mechanisms which may be query dependant or query independent. Google, for example, uses the latter method by way of 'Page Rank'. This is basically an algorithm used by Google search to rank websites according to their popularity in their search engine results. According to Google:

> 'PageRank works by counting the number and quality of links to a page to determine a rough estimate of how important the website is. The underlying assumption is that more important websites are likely to receive more links from other websites'.[14]

It needs to be remembered that content hosts or users as data controllers also play an important role in bringing up their websites in the top most list of the result. Many content hosts or websites may have their own business terms to improve their ranks by way of advertisements in the search list by paying the search engines. Such advertisements may be just one or two line texts or a few words with hyperlinks indicating the websites. These advertisements may automatically come up when a user starts searching any particular content with keywords. It may be noted that many e-commerce websites and also porn websites may use such business models to come up in the list.

The liability of search engines is much of a grey area when compared to that of the content hosts or communication conduits. Legal debates on search engine laws are diverted more towards the three actors, that is, the content providers (including the group 1 and 2 data controllers), the users who use the search engines for effective results and the third party who may gain a tremendous profit or face extreme damage due to search results. Analysing from this perspective, it may be seen that the liabilities of the search engines are quite similar to that of the content hosts and

---

[14] See for more information at http://web.archive.org/web/20111104131332/ http://www.google.com/competition/howgooglesearchworks.html (Accessed on 2 March 2015).

they majorly flow from S.512 (c) of the DMCA and the First Amendment of the US constitution; these may include the followings:

- Proper indexing of the contents.
- Responding to queries of the searcher.
- Providing proper accurate results.
- Effectively dealing with 'click frauds'.
- Not to disclose the private information or browsing history of the searcher unless the searcher has provided the search engine the right to do so by various implied or even camouflaged terms in the agreements.
- To take down particular content from the index and the search results when the same is complained about by third parties through DMCA take-down mechanisms or through private legal complaints.
- Not to index or produce any content depicting child pornography.
- To indicate the grievance officer's details in the homepage.

However, it needs to be mentioned that similar to that of communication conduits and content hosts, search engines do not extensively monitor the contents that are flowed in for indexing and outflow of the result. It is for this very reason that search engines may indicate 'click fraud' contents, but do not restrict the outflow of information on defamatory or harmful or reputation damageable contents or even copyright infringing materials unless they are informed about such issues by the third parties, namely those who may be harmed by such contents.

'Right to be Forgotten': How Far the Intermediaries are Liable in the Indian Context?

Since 2010 onwards, the 'right to be forgotten' is being considered as an extended right within the meaning of EU privacy protection laws (Bennet, 2012). In 2012, the EU commission formally proposed a new law to introduce the 'right to be forgotten' for individuals who can ask internet companies or intermediaries to delete unwanted data about themselves.[15] The proposed law which was first formally discussed in

[15] See BBC. (2012). EU proposes 'right to be forgotten' by internet firms. Published on 8 March 2012. Available at http://www.bbc.com/news/technology-16677370 (Accessed on 2 February 2015).

detail by Viviane Reding, the EU Justice Commissioner,[16] is now being considered as a great blow to the understanding of privacy laws as per the US First and Fourth Amendment as well as the safe harbour policies for the intermediaries. The 'right to be forgotten' is essentially a right to erase the past unwanted history of the 'data subject' from the intermediaries including search engines and the social media (Ambrose, 2012; Bennett, 2012). But as Peter Fleischer of Google rightly pointed out in 2011, data in relation to the 'right to be forgotten' may imply four types of data; these may include: (a) content posted by the user himself/herself about himself/herself and which he/she may have the control to delete from the particular website but may not find it easy to delete from the search engines, if the intermediary is exhibiting cached copies; (b) content posted by the user which is reposted by some other user in the same or other website and when the original user wishes to delete those contents, the procedure may include involving the second poster's right to expression, the website's own policy for take-down notices and the original user's right to privacy; (c) contents involving information about the claimant posted by someone. In such cases, Fleischer comments:

> Traditional law has mechanisms, like defamation and libel law, to allow a person to seek redress against someone who publishes untrue information about him. Granted, the mechanisms are time-consuming and expensive, but the legal standards are long-standing and fairly clear. But a privacy claim is not based on untruth. I cannot see how such a right could be introduced without severely infringing on freedom of speech.[17]

And (d) contents which involve the personal identifiable information and which are retained or transmitted by the web platforms (Voss, 2014).

As may be seen, these classifications of the data may indicate different types of data controllers and they may have different types of mechanisms or policies to restrict the outflow of the data, reducing the burden of the intermediaries as the prime liable subject for erasing unwanted data. But the EU commission considered the issue of non-compliance of privacy norms (as per the EU regulations) by the US based intermediaries when they refused to take down unwanted, which may or may not have become viral and which may prove detrimental to the 'data subject'.

[16] Ibid.
[17] See Fleischer, P. (2011). Foggy thinking about right to oblivion. Available at http://peterfleischer.blogspot.in/2011/03/foggy-thinking-about-right-to-oblivion.html (Accessed on 20 January 2016).

The 'right to be forgotten' was upheld by the EU commission for justice in Google Spain SL and Google Inc. v. Agencia Española de Protección de Datos (AEPD) and Costeja Gonzalez whereby it was finally held that considering the fact that the information published attracted the 'sensitivity for the data subject's private life' and that it was no more needed for public interest after a long gap, the data subject can have the right to claim for removal of such data from the web platforms which were making those data accessible by others (Voss, 2014). Google accordingly took steps to include new online forms which are to be used by data subjects indicating the links to the unwanted contents, and which (the forms) must be accompanied by valid reasons and photo identification of the data subjects (Voss, 2014).

The Indian position: The 'right to be forgotten' is still a very much European right which has not been extended to other continents other than the US because of the involvement of US based intermediaries in the same. While explaining the necessity for the 'right to be forgotten' for a data subject, Ambrose (2012) showed four distinct reasons; these are intellectual property restrictions, contractual obligations, defamation and privacy torts. Ambrose further expanded the scope of privacy torts by adding four factors, namely, 'intrusion upon seclusion', 'public disclosure of private facts', 'misappropriation' and 'false light'. When seen from the perspective of victimisation of women in the cyber space, all these may seem to be appropriate for applying similar rights of the 'data subject' like that of the 'right to be forgotten' in India. Consider Kharak Singh v. State of UP (1963) case which is considered as a landmark judgment for establishing the concept of privacy rights in India, especially the concept of 'leave alone'. The 'right to be forgotten' can be enforced in similar lines in India. Of late, there are numerous instances of circulating rape videos or images of fake avatars created by perpetrators by social media users who may feel such circulation may actually benefit the rape victim herself or the victims of fake avatars or other categories of cyber crimes as discussed in this book, as well as the criminal justice machinery in identifying the perpetrator.

Consider the Andaman Jarawa women's dance videos or the rape videos, or the derogatory, obscene, lewd comments about women journalists, activists, celebrities or even ordinary women posted by people who may not like the particular person in question; these posts or news items may remain in the World Wide Web for a prolonged time enabling friends, acquaintances, prospective employers, students and even the children of the concerned women to view them when they grow up matured enough to understand the meaning of such derogatory posts and why they are still there. It may be seen that a rape victim may feel extremely uncomfortable to find the images of the rape scene even if she is not fully shown in the images, floating of fake avatars have been proved extremely detrimental for women and girl students as well as job seekers and home makers. Some of such women had repeatedly sent take-down notices, tried to contact the websites by phone or emails asking them to remove the content; some had been successful, some got frustrating replies and some got to see cached copies of the objectionable data still available in the search results when searched by herself or others in search engines.

Laws such as the 'right to be forgotten' may redress the grievances of such women against the websites who refused to comply with the requests of such women. As may have been mentioned by many US based researchers, intermediary liabilities as enshrined in the safe harbour policies or DMCA rules as well as policy guidelines of internet companies or websites impliedly carried the essence of the 'right to be forgotten' and there were no need to bring an extra law for enforcing the right of the data subject over that of the intermediaries. When seen from the perspectives of the victimisation of women in the cyber space, the liabilities of the intermediaries must be designed to show more concern towards the causes of women victims and by especially keeping in mind the cultural aspects of the country of the data subject. Given the fact that liabilities as well as immunities of the intermediaries are primarily concerned with the freedom of speech of the users, concern about privacy of the individuals, especially women (who may or may not be users of the internet and digital communication technology) must also be considered. However, it is interesting to note about the recent case on 'right to be forgotten' that has been preferred by a Delhi based petitioner against websites including India Kanoon, Google and so on.[18] The media report suggested that the petitioner's plea was based on the issue that the search engine continues to bring up information regarding his marital dispute which was resolved amicably in the past. Since such information, which contained his name along with the names of his family members, not only infringes his privacy but may also damage his reputation, he sought the reference of the European Union Case of Google Spain SL, Google Inc. v AEPD, Mario

[18] For more information see Garg. A (2016) |Delhi banker seeks 'right to be forgotten' online. Published on 1 May 2016 in Times of India. Available at http://timesofindia.indiatimes.com/india/Delhi-banker-seeks-right-to-be-forgotten-online/articleshow/52060003.cms. (Accessed on 20 June 2016).

Costeja González (2014) to apply the principle of 'right to be forgotten' online to delete the information related to the criminal case involving him. The Delhi High Court has sought the response of the Central government, Google and the India Kanoon website authorities as whether this can be brought within the broader scope of right to privacy to settle the issues. The outcome of this case is yet to be seen, as this may establish a landmark example for many other individuals including women victims of online harassment.

Indian laws regarding liability of the intermediaries: Intermediary liability and the immunity clauses are dealt with under the IT Act, 2000 (amended in 2008). It needs to be mentioned that there are no specific chapters in the main Act which deals with this issue. S.79 of the Act and the Information Technology (Intermediary guidelines) Rules, 2011 are the main resources for dealing with intermediary liability and immunities. However, the main principles followed in these provisions flow from the US laws on due diligence and safe harbour policies as mentioned earlier. Liabilities of the intermediaries as per the IT Act and Rules can be discussed in two segments. These are discussed as under:

1. General liabilities of the intermediaries: Information Technology (Intermediary guidelines) Rules, 2011 provides a set of liabilities in Rule 3 under the name 'due diligence'. These liabilities are to be followed by all intermediaries hosted in India and also by virtue of S.75 of the IT Act, 2000 (amended in 2008), which extends the scope of the law to any offence or contravention committed outside India by any person irrespective of his nationality, the liabilities may also be extended to intermediaries hosted outside India. These general liabilities may be further grouped into three categories as has been specified by Rule 3 of the Information Technology (Intermediary guidelines) Rules, 2011. These are as follows:

   i. Liability to develop policy guidelines, maintain the principles with impartiality and follow the provisions of the Act. The rules following under this category are:

      (a) The intermediary shall publish the rules and regulations, privacy policy and user agreement for accessor usage of the intermediary's computer resource by any person. (Rule 3(1)).

      (b) The Intermediary shall inform its users that in case of non-compliance with rules and regulations, user agreement and privacy policy for access or usage of intermediary computer resource, the Intermediary has the right to immediately terminate the access or usage rights of the users to the computer resource of Intermediary and remove non-compliant information. (Rule 3(5)).

(c) The intermediary shall strictly follow the provisions of the Act or any other laws for the time being in force. (Rule 3(6)).

(d) When required by lawful order, the intermediary shall provide information or any such assistance to Government Agencies who are lawfully authorised for investigative, protective, cyber security activity. The information or any such assistance shall be provided for the purpose of verification of identity, or for prevention, detection, investigation, prosecution, cyber security incidents and punishment of offences under any law for the time being in force, on a request in writing stating clearly the purpose of seeking such information or any such assistance. (Rule 3(7)).

(e) The intermediary shall report cyber security incidents and also share cyber security incidents related information with the Indian Computer Emergency Response Team. (Rule 3(9)).

(f) The intermediary shall not knowingly deploy or install or modify the technical configuration of computer resource or become party to any such act which may change or has the potential to change the normal course of operation of the computer resource than what it is supposed to 'perform thereby circumventing any law for the time being in force: provided that the intermediary may develop, produce, distribute or employ technological means for the sole purpose of performing the acts of securing the computer resource and information contained therein'. (Rule 3(10)).

(g) The intermediary shall publish on its website the name of the Grievance Officer and his contact details as well as mechanism by which users or any victim who suffers as a result of access or usage of computer resource by any person in violation of rule 3 can notify their complaints against such access or usage of computer resource of the intermediary or other matters pertaining to the computer resources made available by it. The Grievance Officer shall redress the complaints within one month from the date of receipt of complaint. (Rule 3(11)).

ii. Liability to categorise the types of contents that may be removed and declaration of policy towards removal of such contents. These liabilities are as follows:

(a) Informing the users of computer resource not to host, display, upload, modify, publish, transmit, update or share any information that (a) belongs to another person and to which the user does not have any right to; (b) is grossly harmful, harassing, blasphemous defamatory, obscene, pornographic, paedophilic, libellous, invasive of another's privacy, hateful, or racially, ethnically objectionable, disparaging, relating or encouraging money laundering or gambling, or otherwise unlawful in any manner whatever; (c) harm minors in any way; (d) infringes any patent, trademark, copyright or other proprietary rights; (e) violates any law for the time being in force; (f) deceives or misleads the addressee about the origin of such messages or communicates any information which is grossly offensive or menacing in nature; (g) impersonate another person; (h) contains software viruses or any other computer code, files or programs designed to interrupt, destroy or limit the functionality of any computer resource and (i) threatens the unity, integrity, defence, security or sovereignty of India, friendly relations with foreign states, or public order or causes incitement to the commission of any cognisable offence or prevents investigation of any offence or is insulting any other nation. (Rule 3(2)).

(b) The intermediary shall not knowingly host or publish any information or shall not initiate the transmission, select the receiver of transmission, and select or modify the information contained in the transmission as specified in sub-rule (2), provided that the following actions by an intermediary shall not amount to hosing, publishing, editing or storing of any such information as specified in sub-rule (2)—(a) temporary or transient or intermediate storage of information automatically within the computer resource as an intrinsic feature of such computer resource, involving no exercise of any human editorial control, for onward transmission or communication to another computer resource; (b) removal of access to any information, data or communication link by an intermediary after such information, data or communication link comes to the actual knowledge of a person authorised by the intermediary pursuant to any order or direction as per the provisions of the Act. (Rule 3(3)).

(c) The intermediary, on whose computer system the information is stored or hosted or published, upon obtaining knowledge by itself or been brought to actual knowledge by an affected person in writing or through email signed with electronic signature about any such information as mentioned in sub-rule (2), shall act within 36 hours and where applicable, work with user or owner of such information to disable such information that is in contravention of sub-rule (2). Further, the intermediary shall preserve such information and associated records for at least 90 days for investigation purposes. (Rule 3(4)).

(d) The intermediary shall inform its users that in case of non-compliance with rules and regulations, user agreement and privacy policy for access or usage of intermediary computer resource, the Intermediary has the right to immediately terminate the access or usage lights of the users to the computer resource of Intermediary and remove non-compliant information. (Rule 3(5)).

iii. Liability towards protection of privacy: This liability for the intermediaries may be further discussed under two segments: the first one being the intermediary's liability to protect private information. Even though this provision does not explicitly mention the term 'users', it may be implied that this provision targets the privacy of the users. Hence, as may be seen, Rule 3(8) of the Information Technology (Intermediary guidelines) Rules, 2011 states that 'the intermediary shall take all reasonable measures to secure its computer resource and information contained therein following the reasonable security practices and procedures as prescribed in the Information Technology (Reasonable security practices and procedures and sensitive personal Information) Rules, 2011'. It may be interesting to note that by virtue of this provision, the intermediaries become liable to protect the 'privacy' of the users and such 'privacy' has been explained as 'sensitive personal information' by the same. These sensitive personal information may include 'password, financial information such as Bank account or credit card or debit card or other payment instrument details, physical, physiological and mental health condition; sexual orientation; medical records and history; Biometric information; any detail relating to the above clauses as provided to body corporate for providing service; and any of the information received under above clauses by body corporate for processing, stored or processed under lawful contract or otherwise'. (Rule 3(3) of the Information Technology; Reasonable security practices and procedures and sensitive personal information; Rules, 2011)

The second liability in the course of protection of privacy is the liability to follow proper procedure for obtaining such private information and providing policy guidelines whereby users may be made to know what sorts of information are collected and what would be done with them. These liabilities are mentioned in Rules 4 to 8 of the Information Technology (Reasonable security practices and procedures and sensitive personal information) Rules, 2011, which are as follows:

Rule 4: Body corporate to provide policy for privacy and disclosure of information.—(1) The body corporate or any person who on behalf of body corporate collects, receives, possess, stores, deals or handles information of provider of information, shall provide a privacy policy for handling of or dealing in personal information including sensitive personal data or information and ensure that the same are available for view by such providers of information who has provided such information under lawful contract. Such policy shall be published on website of body corporate or any person on its behalf and shall provide for—

(a) Clear and easily accessible statements of its practices and policies;
(b) Type of personal or sensitive personal data or information collected under Rule 3;
(c) Purpose of collection and usage of such information;
(d) Disclosure of information including sensitive personal data or information as provided in Rule 6 and
(e) Reasonable security practices and procedures as provided under Rule 8.

Rule 5: Collection of information.—(1) Body corporate or any person on its behalf shall obtain consent in writing through letter or Fax or email from the provider of the sensitive personal data or information regarding purpose of usage before collection of such information.

(2) Body corporate or any person on its behalf shall not collect sensitive personal data or information unless—(a) the information is collected for a lawful purpose connected with a function or activity of the body corporate or any person on its behalf; and (b) the collection of the sensitive personal data or information is considered necessary for that purpose.

(3) While collecting information directly from the person concerned, the body corporate or any person on its behalf snail take such steps as are, in the circumstances, reasonable to ensure that the person concerned is having the knowledge of—

(a) the fact that the information is being collected;
(b) the purpose for which the information is being collected;
(c) the intended recipients of the information; and
(d) the name and address of—

    (i) the agency that is collecting the information; and
    (ii) the agency that will retain the information.

(4) Body corporate or any person on its behalf holding sensitive personal data or information shall not retain that information for longer than is required for the purposes for which the information may lawfully be used or is otherwise required under any other law for the time being in force.

(5) The information collected shall be used for the purpose for which it has been collected.

(6) Body corporate or any person on its behalf permit the providers of information, as and when requested by them, to review the information they had provided and ensure that any personal information or sensitive personal data or information found to be inaccurate or deficient shall be corrected or amended as feasible. The permission to review the given provided that a body corporate shall not be responsible for the authenticity of the personal information or sensitive personal data or information supplied by the provider of information to such body corporate or any other person acting on behalf of such body corporate.

(7) Body corporate or any person on its behalf shall, prior to the collection of information including sensitive personal data or information, provide an option to the provider of the information to not provide the data or information sought to be collected. The provider of information shall, at any time while availing the services or otherwise, also have an option to withdraw its consent given earlier to the body corporate. Such withdrawal of the consent shall be sent in writing to the body corporate. In the case of provider of information not providing or later on withdrawing his consent, the body corporate shall have the option not to provide goods or services for which the said information was sought.

(8) Body corporate or any person on its behalf shall keep the information secure as provided in Rule 8.

(9) Body corporate shall address any discrepancies and grievances of their provider of the information with respect to processing of information in a time bound manner. For this purpose, the body corporate shall designate a Grievance Officer and publish his name and contact details on its website. The Grievance Officer shall redress the grievances of the provider of information expeditiously but within one month from the date of receipt of grievance.

Rule 6: Disclosure of information.—(1) Disclosure of sensitive personal data or information by body corporate to any third party shall require prior permission from the provider of such information, who has provided such information under lawful contract or otherwise, unless such disclosure has been agreed to in the contract between the body corporate and the provider of information, or where the disclosure is necessary for compliance of a legal obligation. This permission is sought provided that the information shall be shared, without obtaining prior consent from the provider of information, with Government agencies mandated under the law to obtain information including sensitive personal data or information for the purpose of verification of identity, or for prevention, detection, investigation including cyber incidents, prosecution and punishment of offences. The Government agency shall send a request in writing to the body corporate possessing the sensitive personal data or information stating clearly the purpose of seeking such information. The Government agency shall also state that the information so obtained shall not be published or shared with any other person.

(2) Notwithstanding anything contain in sub-rule (1), any sensitive personal data or Information shall be disclosed to any third party by an order under the law for the time being in force.

(3) The body corporate or any person on its behalf shall not publish the sensitive personal data or information.

(4) The third party receiving the sensitive personal data or information from body corporate or any person on its behalf under sub-rule (1) shall not disclose it further.

Rule 7: Transfer of information.—A body corporate or any person on its behalf may transfer sensitive personal data or information including any information, to any other body corporate or a person in India, or located in any other country, that ensures the same level of data protection that is adhered to by the body corporate as provided for under these Rules. The transfer may be allowed only if it is necessary for the performance of the lawful contract between the body corporate or any person on its behalf and provider of information or where such person has consented to data transfer.

Rule 8: Reasonable Security Practices and Procedures.—(1) A body corporate or a person on its behalf shall be considered to have complied with reasonable security practices and procedures, if they have implemented such security practices and standards and have a comprehensive documented information security programme and information security policies that contain managerial, technical, operational and physical security control measures that are commensurate with the information assets being protected with the nature of business. In the event of an information security breach, the body corporate or a person on its behalf shall be required to demonstrate, as and when called upon to do so by the agency mandated under the law, that they have implemented security control measures as per their documented information security programme and information security policies.

(2) The International Standard IS/ISO/IEC 27001 on 'Information Technology–Security Techniques—Information Security Management System—Requirements' is one such standard referred to in sub-rule (1).

(3) Any industry association or an entity formed by such an association, whose members are self-regulating by following other than IS/ISO/IEC codes of best practices for data protection as per sub-rule (1), shall get its codes of best practices duly approved and notified by the Central Government for effective implementation.

(4) The body corporate or a person on its behalf who has implemented either IS/ISO/IEC 27001 standard or the codes of best practices for data protection as approved and notified under sub-rule (3) shall be deemed to have complied with reasonable security practices and procedures provided that such standard or the codes of best practices have been certified or audited on a regular basis by entities through independent auditor, duly approved by the Central Government. The audit of reasonable security practices and procedures shall be carried out by an auditor at least once a year or as and when the body corporate or a person on its behalf undertakes significant upgradation of its process and computer resource.

When the intermediary or the 'body corporate' fails to protect the privacy of the users by way of breaching these liabilities, they may be liable for punishment either by way of civil tortuous liability or by way of criminal penal liability. The earlier is available through S.43A of the IT Act, 2000 (amended in 2008), which speaks about Compensation for failure to protect data and states that,

[W]here a body corporate, possessing, dealing or handling any sensitive personal data or information in a computer resource which it owns, controls or operates, is negligent in implementing and maintaining reasonable security practices and procedures and thereby causes wrongful loss or wrongful gain to any person, such body corporate shall be liable to pay damages by way of compensation, not exceeding five crore rupees, to the person so affected.[19]

The latter is available through S.72A of the IT Act, 2000, (amended in 2008), which speaks about punishment for disclosure of information in breach of lawful contract and states that,

> Save as otherwise provided in this Act or any other law for the time being in force, any person including an intermediary who, while providing services under the terms of lawful contract, has secured access to any material containing personal information about another person, with the intent to cause or knowing that he is likely to cause wrongful loss or wrongful gain discloses, without the consent of the person concerned, or in breach of a lawful contract, such material to any other person shall be punished with imprisonment for a term which may extend to three years, or with a fine which may extend to five lakh rupees, or with both.

A perusal of the liabilities may show two important issues when seen from the perspective of cyber crimes against women; the liabilities include prohibition of publication of any information which may be detrimental to the reputation of women or security of women and considering sexual orientation among other factors as 'sensitive personal information'. While the former attracts our information more because this may be immensely helpful for women to bring charge against the intermediary, especially

[19] Explanation attached to this Section states,

> For the purposes of this section (i) 'body corporate' means any company and includes a firm, sole proprietorship or other association of individuals engaged in commercial or professional activities (ii) 'reasonable security practices and procedures' means security practices and procedures designed to protect such information from unauthorised access, damage, use, modification, disclosure or impairment, as may be specified in an agreement between the parties or as may be specified in any law for the time being in force and in the absence of such agreement or any law, such reasonable security practices and procedures, as may be prescribed by the Central Government in consultation with such professional bodies or associations as it may deem fit. (iii) 'sensitive personal data or information' means such personal information as may be prescribed by the Central Government in consultation with such professional bodies or associations as it may deem fit.

the social media sites and communication message services like the WhatsApp when they refuse to consider monitoring such information as out of the scope of their liability, this provision as enshrined in Rule 3(4) of the Information Technology (Intermediary guidelines) Rules, 2011 attracted attention of the free speech advocates as this contains the shadow of S.66A which was scrapped off by the Supreme Court in Shreya Singhal's case in 2015 for being vague. The latter factor, that is, the consideration of 'sexual orientation' as sensitive personal information which the intermediary is liable to protect, further attracts our attention as this may be helpful for women belonging to LGBT community. Even though, many such women are now disclosing their sexual orientation in the social media in India, we get to see mounting rate of victimisation targeting the sexual orientation of the women. In such case, intermediaries must take their liabilities in the line of the first issue, that is, prohibition of certain categories of information, with more concern.

The Immunities from Liabilities

When we speak about internet intermediary liabilities, the exemptions from the same are an obvious observation for all stakeholders. In case of cyber crimes against women, we often get to see that women are continuously harassed by unwanted phone calls or missed calls from unknown numbers, lewd or intimidating SMSs, or unwanted adding up by strangers on WhatsApp or other mobile phone communication services, or floating of offensive images, defamatory texts, videos and so on in various content hosts including the social media and spreading of the same through search engines. Victims often complain about lacklustre attitude of the service providers or intermediaries when they complained about such harassing content. In majority of cases, service providers' answers towards the victims are extremely frustrating when the former refuse to take any action on the complaints referred by the latter. The question which is asked often is, if the intermediaries have their liabilities as set up by the laws and their own policy guidelines, why don't they exercise the same when victims refer complaints? The answer is that the intermediaries enjoy immunities which make them not liable to take action on each and every complaint referred by the third party, namely, the victims. Typically, the immunity for the service providers from the liabilities discussed flows from several principles and legal provisions of the US laws; these include due diligence principle, safe harbour principles, S.230 of the CDA and DMCA, Part II.

Discussions about the immunities would obviously pull up the discussions about the policy guidelines developed by the service providers as well. Service providers including Google, Facebook, Twitter and so on adhere to Safe Harbour policies of the United States for claiming immunity from third party liabilities.[20] This Safe Harbour policies are developed on the principles of the EU Data Directives on protection of individual privacy on data flow which was based on Organisation for Economic Co-operation and Development (OECD) Guidelines.[21] Typically, internet service providers and domain hosts can avail two types of immunities, namely, (a) immunity from all sorts of liabilities including third party liability from defamation under section 230(c) of the CDA, codified at 47 USC,[22] and (b) immunity from liabilities regarding copyright infringement under DMCA Title 512, provided the service providers follow principles of due diligence, which includes that they had not intentionally and knowingly hosted such infringing materials, have not knowing and intentionally received any monetary benefits out of the infringed materials and have taken down the objectionable materials on notifying. The earlier provision, that is, S.230(c) of the CDA also exempts the service providers to be categorised as publishers of any defamatory,

[20] See Google. (February 26, 2011). Self regulatory frameworks. Available at http://www.google.com/policies/privacy/frameworks; See Facebook. (February 26, 2011). Clause VI of data use policy. Available at https://www.facebook.com/full_data_use_policy; Also see Twitter. (February 26, 2011). Clause on EU Safe harbor frame work. Available at http://twitter.com/privacy; See Google. (February 26, 2011). Policies and principles: Terms of service. Available at http://www.google.com/intl/en/policies/terms/; Facebook. (February 26, 2011). Statement of rights and responsibilities. Available at http://www.facebook.com/legal/terms; Twitter. (February 26, 2011). Terms of service. Available at http://twitter.com/tos

[21] OECD. (April 21, 2012). Guidelines on the protection of privacy and transborder flows of personal data. Available at http://www.oecd.org/document/18/0,3343,en_2649_34255_1815186_1_1_1_1,00.html. Also see Schild, R. (April 16, 2010). Does the safe harbor programme adequately address third parties online? The Center for Internet and Society. Available at http://cis-india.org/internet-governance/blog/does-the-safe-harbor-program-adequately-address-third-parties-online (Accessed on 21 April 2012).

[22] See Digital Media Law Project. (April 21, 2012). Immunity for online publishers under the Communications Decency Act. Berkman Centre for Internet and Society. Available at http://www.citmedialaw.org/legal-guide/immunity-online-publishers-under-communications-decency-act

harassing content; it also immunes services providers and hosts from any civil and criminal liability for actions taken in good faith towards removing any contents.[23] Further, as it was held in the case of Doe v. MySpace, 474 F.Supp.2d 843 (W.D. Tex. 2007), the immunity available to the service providers may also be used for users as well as non users who may have been affected by any publication on the websites concerned. As such, all service providers following the above mentioned provisions need to prepare their policy guidelines including policies regarding removing of offensive contents. As it was held in the case of Barnes v. Yahoo! Inc., 570 F.3d 1096 (9th Cir. 2009),[24] the service provider may not avail the benefits of immunity for failure of promissory estoppels if he has failed in his promise to remove the contents (that may have been notified in his policy guidelines) after receiving the necessary notice from the concerned victim. Presently all the service providers have in their terms and conditions specified specific types of contents including nudity and sexually explicit contents, malicious contents which indicates causing harm, injury to reputation and so on, bullying, threatening and harassing, hate speech, impersonation and so on, which may be liable to be removed once reported.

But in reality, many victims may still fail to get any positive response from the service providers in spite of such notification apparently because such offensive contents must pass the test of "offensiveness" as per the particular service provider's policy standards and not necessarily as per the victim's understanding, even though the terms and conditions of all the foreign-based service providers indicate about "choice of law" and agree to respect the local laws.[25] The service providers can still claim immunity from any liabilities because of the laws related to the freedom of speech and expression of the US standard, which is much broader than the Indian standards and understandings. This is evident from the case of Vinay Rai v. Facebook India and Ors, No. 136/11, in the Court of Metropolitan Magistrate, New Delhi,[26] In this case, the petitioner filed

---

[23] For more information, see clause for 'Protection for "Good Samaritan" Blocking and Screening of Offensive Material under S.230 (c) of the CDA'.

[24] Ibid.

[25] For example, see column 16 in Facebook Statement of rights and responsibilities. Available at https://www.facebook.com/legal/terms; also see 'about these terms'. Available at https://www.google.co.in/intl/en/policies/terms/regional.html

[26] For more information about this case, see NDTV Correspondent. (16 January 2012). Delhi High Court to hear Google–Facebook's petition today. NDTV.com. Available at http://www.ndtv.com/article/india/delhi-high-court-to-hear-google-facebooks-petition-today-167302?slider (Accessed on 21 April 2012).

against the 21 websites including Google, Facebook, Orkut, Yahoo and so on, praying for suitable action against them for hosting objectionable materials, namely, depiction of religious figures in obscene, derogatory fashion, that are posted there. The petitioner's claim that such contents can create religious unrest that the service providers failed to take note of despite their claim in their policy guidelines to remove such contents. Noticeably, the petitioner based his claim majorly on the traditional penal laws including sections 153-A (promoting enmity between different groups on grounds of religion, race, place of birth and so on and doing acts prejudicial to maintenance of harmony etc), 153-B (imputations, assertions prejudicial to nation's harmony), 292 (sale of obscene books and so on), 293 (sale and so on of obscene objects to young person's etc), 295(A) (deliberate and malicious acts intended to outrage religious feelings of any class by insulting its religion or religious beliefs), 298 (uttering words and so on with deliberate intent to wound religious feelings), 109 (punishment of abetment if the act abetted is committed in consequence and where no express provision is made for its punishment), 500 (punishment for defamation) and 120-B (punishment for criminal conspiracy) of the IPC. As the present updates in this case suggests, the service providers including Google Inc., Facebook and so on were issued summons and they had removed the contents after being notified by the courts. But still now we have not come across any such case preferred by women victims on website liability as a publisher/host for offensive contents especially when the said victim may have not received any positive response from the service provider after reporting the contents which may fall within the categories of prohibited contents as per their policy guidelines.

Indian Laws Regarding Intermediary Immunity

Immunities from the liabilities: While the above mentioned laws discuss about the liabilities of the intermediaries, the immunities from the liabilities are discussed in S.79 of the IT Act, 2000 (amended in 2008). It says as follows:

> (1) Notwithstanding anything contained in any law for the time being in force but subject to the provisions of sub-sections (2) and (3), an intermediary shall not be liable for any third party information, data, or communication link hosted by him.

(2) The provisions of sub-section (1) shall apply if—(a) the function of the intermediary is limited to providing access to a communication system over which information made available by third parties is transmitted or temporarily stored; or (b) the intermediary does not—(i) initiate the transmission, (ii) select the receiver of the transmission, and (iii) select or modify the information contained in the transmission (c) the intermediary observes due diligence while discharging his duties under this Act and also observes such other guidelines as the Central Government may prescribe in this behalf.

(3) The provisions of sub-section (1) shall not apply if—(a) the intermediary has conspired or abetted or aided or induced whether by threats or promise or otherwise in the commission of the unlawful act (ITAA 2008); (b) upon receiving actual knowledge, or on being notified by the appropriate Government or its agency that any information, data or communication link residing in or connected to a computer resource controlled by the intermediary is being used to commit the unlawful act, the intermediary fails to expeditiously remove or disable access to that material on that resource without vitiating the evidence in any manner.

Explanation attached to this section states for the purpose of this section, the expression 'third party information' means any information dealt with by an intermediary in his capacity as an intermediary.

As may be seen from this section, the intermediaries can claim liabilities only on two factors: (a) when they practiced due diligence for offensive contents and (b) when they do not gain any financial profit for any information uploaded by any third party. But, along with these, there are some other factors which may further immune the intermediaries from the liabilities as has been mentioned. As such, intermediaries cannot be made liable for any information about any individual or organisation which is already available for public knowledge. Such information may also include information in government websites or available through Right to Information Act, 2005. But intermediaries may not claim immunities for information that are published by users which the latter had received through viral circulation on the internet or gossip columns. It is for this very reason that sharing of obscene images of women, fake avatars or defamatory information about women or even trolling or bullying comments targeting specific women may make the group-1 data controller (i.e., the user who shares the same in the intermediary) primarily responsible for publishing the same, and group-2 data controller (i.e., the intermediary) secondarily responsible if they fail to take note of the 'take down' complaints.

These liabilities and immunities are provided by the laws specifically to delegate the restorative procedure to the intermediaries in cases of harms caused due to misuse of information digital technology by others. This is a measure to bring down the volume of direct suits preferred to the courts directly against the intermediaries. It may be mentioned that when the Delhi High Court considered the defence preferred by Yahoo in Vinay Rai's case as mentioned, this factor was narrowly touched over and the court set aside the order of the magistrate in the 2011 case.

Conclusion

The discussions may show that intermediaries may claim immunities from their liabilities on the ground of user's use or misuse of the intermediary as a platform and their own no-profit, unaware involvement in the same. In practice, we have seen that intermediary liability when in the case of women victims, turn much towards erasing the unwanted data and help the concerned women to be 'forgotten' for those data which are irrelevant or dangerous for her. But this happens rarely. The liabilities indicate filling up of forms, contacting the intermediaries and taking note of the report by acknowledging the receipt of the report. However, the liabilities also indicate forming their own policy guidelines to consider content as fit to be removed from or to stay in the data warehouse. Furthermore, even if the data is erased from the concerned websites, the data may still be there in the search engines, and they may not be as cooperative as the primary websites where the information was first published. The woman victim therefore cannot gain full benefits of the implied right to claim to be forgotten as is promised by the websites. In India, women largely do not prefer to seek police help or that of the courts fearing infringement of privacy and risks for their own as well as family's security. In such situations, even if the 'right to be forgotten' is introduced as a separate law in the same line as has been done in the EU countries, it may remain underused and may even turn a subject to be misused as had happened in the case of S.66A of the IT Act, which was scrapped off by the Supreme Court due to its vagueness and constant misuse by others. Furthermore, it must also not be forgotten that as the effect of the Gonzales case on the 'right to be forgotten', Google had taken effective steps to enable affected data subjects to contact them; but they did not guarantee for withdrawal of the contents from the search engines in other continents. In India,

Google is considered as the 'search giant', followed by Bing, Yahoo and so on and all of them are US entities. The biggest problem they, as internet companies as well as the criminal justice machinery, are facing as of 2015 is the absence of their servers in India or unwillingness to disclose the contact persons to the concerned affected parties. Enforcement of rights such as the 'right to be forgotten', therefore, may take its own time and process within which, the victim may lose interest in the law and may avail on the irrational coping mechanism to remove the links faster than the rational methods (Halder & Jaishankar, 2015). It is for these reasons that we prefer to attract the attention of the intermediaries to build up policy guidelines which would enable the women victims to avail the 'right to be forgotten' through the effective reporting mechanism itself. However, the introduction of separate right in the light of 'right to leave alone', which may have the essence of the 'right to be forgotten', may definitely be always helpful for women victims of online crimes.

References

Ambrose, M. L. (2012). It's about time: Privacy, information lifecycles, and the right to be forgotten. *Stanford Technology Law Review, 16*(2), 369–422. Available at SSRN: http://ssrn.com/abstract=2154374 (Accessed on 2 April 2015).

Ardia, D. S. (16 June 2010). Free speech savior or shield for scoundrels: An empirical study of intermediary immunity under section 230 of the Communications Decency Act. *Loyola of Los Angeles Law Review, 43*(2), 373–506. Available at SSRN: http://ssrn.com/abstract=1625820. (Accessed on 7 May 2015).

Bennett, S. C. (2012). The 'right to be forgotten': Reconciling EU and US perspectives. *Berkeley Journal of International Law, 30*, 161. Available at: http://scholarship.law.berkeley.edu/bjil/vol30/iss1/4 (Accessed on 5 May 2015).

Citron, D. K. (2014). *Hate crimes in cyber space*. Harvard: Harvard University Press.

Fleischer, P. (2011). Foggy thinking about right to oblivion. Available at http://peterfleischer.blogspot.in/2011/03/foggy-thinking-about-right-to-oblivion.html (Accessed on 20 January 2016).

Grimmelmann, J. (2007). The structure of search engine law. *Iowa Law Review, 93*(1). NYLS Legal Studies Research Paper No. 06/07-23. Available at SSRN: http://ssrn.com/abstract=979568 (Accessed on 31 March 2016).

Halder, D., & Jaishankar, K. (2015). Irrational coping theory and positive criminology: A framework to protect victims of cyber crime. In N. Ronel and D. Segev (eds), *Positive criminology* (pp. 276–291). Abingdon, Oxon: Routledge.

Mahalingam, R. (2007). Beliefs about chastity, machismo, and caste identity: A cultural psychology of gender. *Sex Roles*, 56(3–4): 239–49. DOI10.1007/ s11199-006-9168-y (Accessed on 02 May 2015).

Voss, W. G. (July 2014). The right to be forgotten in the European Union: Enforcement in the court of justice and amendment to the proposed general data protection regulation. *Journal of Internet Law, 18*(1). Available at SSRN: http://ssrn.com/abstract=2567626 (Accessed on 2 April 2015).

8

Procedural Practices for Investigation, Prosecution, Arrest and Detention

Cyber crimes in general need a special procedure for investigation and prosecution due to the intangible data involved in it. It needs to be remembered that when a crime is repo.⁻ᵗᵈd, the police first needs to assert what sort of victim they are going to deal with: the government? A corporate house? An individual victim? Since, in this book, we are concentrating on individual victims, let us see what types of categorisation can be made in this issue: When a cyber crime is reported when the victim is an individual, there can be three types of cases: (a) cases of interpersonal harassment; (b) financial crimes where the victim is targeted with phishing, job scam types of attacks or his/her ATM/debit/credit card is unauthorisedly scanned or accessed and used and (c) online harassment including cyber assisted offline crimes. In all these cases, the procedure for filing the report, investigation, collection of evidences, storing the evidences and so on may be quite similar to general procedural practices as are followed in other cyber crime cases including website hacking, phishing attack or even cyber terrorism cases; for example, the police needs to look for the chain of custody, time stamp, digital data, source code, communication transactions and so on in the similar way for interpersonal crimes as it is done for other crimes. But, when it comes to women including teenager girls as victims, the entire procedure takes a different turn due to privacy issues of the victims.

There are some research reports including 'Cyber victimization in India: A baseline survey report' (Halder & Jaishankar, 2010), 2013

National crime records Bureau report and so on, which would show that cyber crimes targeting women and girl children are alarmingly growing in India. But, unfortunately, reporting of such crimes to the criminal justice machinery is comparatively less. There can be three specific reasons for the same: (a) fear of social taboo in the minds of the victims (Halder & Jaishankar, 2011a, 2011b), (b) absence of properly trained police officers and proper infrastructure to assist the victims (Halder & Jaishankar, 2011a; Jewkes, 2010) as well as nonchalant attitude of the intermediaries to respond to the reports filed by the victims, especially women (Halder & Jaishankar, 2011a, 2011b) and (c) rise of ethical and amateur hackers groups in whom the victims can have a quick confidence for taking irrational coping methods (Halder & Jaishankar, 2015). All of the three reasons are interconnected with each other. Given the fact that India is majorly a patriarchal orthodox society, women are often bound by societal norms which are customary in nature; for example, when in a marriage, a woman may not adopt a child without the consent of her husband or may not be permitted to avail a passport for her children without the signature of her spouse. The criminal laws in India also recognise male dominance in Indian families. Consider the laws for maintenance or matrimonial alimony or even the property rights of women (Halder & Jaishankar, 2008), even though the modern sociological developments have been able to change judicial perspectives in this regard to a certain extent, women are still considered as vulnerable units in a family and society at large.

As such, women are often discouraged from reporting crimes to the criminal justice machinery, thinking that such reporting may not only let the police, lawyers and the judges know about the 'shameful situation' in which they would have pulled their families in, but the police inquiry and subsequent court cases may also drag on years after years which may make the families a laughing stocks for neighbours as well as the society as a whole. We have seen that many families also discourage women from reporting due to the fear that the police may visit the house of the victim/s and, thereby, neighbours may start feeling that either the victim herself or any other member of the family would have done some heinous social crimes; such a feeling further leads to the fear of social ostracising. Furthermore, some victims may also feel that reporting to the police may lead to the leaking of the issue to the media and through media a wider audience may come to know about the plight of the woman as well as her family. Given the fact that the majority of women victims of cyber crimes may be victimised by offences which are either sexual in nature (e.g., creating 'fake avatars' in the social media, posting obscene, offensive remarks or sexting and revenge pornography) or the offence may be caused due to their own involvement (e.g., online grooming, sexting, responding to phishing mails and getting victimised) or may face victimisation which lowers the morals in front of huge internet audience (e.g., bullying or trolling and so on). Victims may feel that reporting to the police might bring secondary traumatisation when the police start questioning them. Victims, especially teenagers and young adult women, would not prefer to discuss the matter with their family members as well thinking that this may attract unnecessary problems, curtailing of freedoms and even honour killing in cases when the families are extremely orthodox.[1] Even when they do, parents or other guardians or even their husbands try to hush up the matter by either ceasing the electronics communication devices from the girls and women and destroying the SIM cards or alienating them from computers, laptops, iPads and so on, or may threaten the victims to not contact the perpetrator or in that case any stranger. In certain cases, the victims or their guardians or families may take up irrational coping methods (Halder & Jaishankar, 2015) which would be discussed later. This, in our experience, escalates the problems even further.

Victims or their local guardians (especially when they are from rural or semi-rural backgrounds where internet penetration and literacy is not as high as in metro cities or when the victims are the first generation information communication technology (ICT) users and their parents or guardians are not aware of cyber issues) may never understand the mobile nature of the data. It may travel from one computer to another, from one mobile phone to another mobile phone or tablet or iPad and may finally land in websites which may make money out of them by circulating the same on the World Wide Web or on social media where the perpetrator would be unknowingly sharing the personal information with millions of people which may bring further harassment to the victim.

However, in cases when the victims or their families or peers understand the nature of mobility of the data and the offences that may be generated from illegal and unauthorised sharing of such personal data with ulterior motives, they may prefer to lodge complaints with the police and report to the websites or data hosts where such data has been shared. But not all victims are successful in getting due justice from the criminal justice machinery as well as the websites. Let us now see why there is an

---

[1] This is from the personal experiences of the lead author.

increasing frustration regarding reporting cases to the police. As we have mentioned in (Halder & Jaishankar, 2015, pp. 279–280):[2]

> Often several forms of interpersonal cyber crimes including online harassments such as trolling, bullying, creation of *fake avatars* etc., do not find any specific legal restriction in many jurisdictions (Citron, 2009; Halder & Jaishankar, 2011a). While harassments like cyber stalking or online defamation are recognised in several jurisdictions like the US, UK or India, often victims are refused any police help due to non understanding of the issue (Halder & Jaishankar, 2011b) or trivialising of the issue by the police (Citron, 2009). Further, given the fact that in cases of defamatory crimes or sexual crimes or privacy infringement crimes, the internet service providers (ISPs) may or may not respond to the victim's pleas (Halder & Jaishankar, 2011b) and anonymous character of the harasser may help him/her to escalate the victimisation, the victims start losing trust in the 'report abuse' sections of the ISPs. This is evident from the statistics shown by Working to Halt Online Abuse (WHOA), a volunteer organization in the USA founded in 1997 to fight online harassment.[3] In their statistics for 2013, it was shown that among 256 cases that were handled by them, 75% of the victims reported the harassment before coming to WHOA. As the statistics shows, 35% victims reported to the ISPs (including Facebook, Email service providers, YouTube, Twitter etc.), 37% reported to the police, 14% sought the help from the lawyers and 14% reported the matter to the Websites. But not all of them were satisfied with results of such reporting and 68% cases were solved by WHOA itself.[4]

In India, S.80 of the IT Act, 2000 (amended in 2008) states that notwithstanding anything contained in the CrPc 1973, any police officer not below the rank of an inspector or any other officer of the central government or a state government authorised by the central government in this behalf may enter any public place and search and arrest without warrant any person found therein who is reasonably suspected of having committed or of committing or of being about to commit any offence under this Act.[5] It may be

---

[2] The paragraphs are reproduced with the permission of editors of the book *Positive Criminology*, where this chapter was published.

[3] The lead author was the Vice President of WHOA.

[4] See http://www.haltabuse.org/resources/stats/2013Statistics.pdf (Accessed on 7 May 2014).

[5] Explanation added to S.80 states, that

> (1) For the purposes of this subsection, the expression 'Public Place' includes any public conveyance, any hotel, any shop or any other place intended for use by, or accessible to the public.

noted that this provision specifically speaks about cognisable offences and as per S.77B of the IT Act, any offence which is punishable with imprisonment for a period of three years and above is a cognisable offence. The Act itself does not mention about any special police station where the victim can report the crimes. A plain reading of this section may say that the crimes can be reported to the police in the same procedure as has been mentioned in the CrPc S.154, which speaks about information in cognisable cases and says in subsection (1):

> [E]very information relating to the commission of a cognizable offence, if given orally to an officer in charge of a police station, shall be reduced to writing by him or under his direction, and be read Over to the informant; and every such information, whether given in writing or reduced to writing as aforesaid, shall be signed by the person giving it, and the substance thereof shall be entered in a book to be kept by such officer in such form as the State Government may prescribe in this behalf.

The Criminal Law Amendment Act, 2013 amended S.154 of the CrPc by adding some new provisions after this paragraph and the first of these new provision states,

> [P]rovided that if the information is given by the women against whom an offence under section 326A, section 326B, Sections 354, 354A, 354B, 354C, 354D, sections 376, 376 A, 376B, 376C, 376D, 376E, or section 509 of the Indian Penal Code is alleged to have been committed or attempted, then such information such information shall be recorded by a woman police officer, or any woman officer.

The second provision that has been inserted in S.154 of the CrPc states,

> [P]rovided further that (a) in the event that the person against whom an offence under section 326A, section 326B, Sections 354, 354A, 354B, 354C, 354D, sections 376, 376 A, 376B, 376C, 376D, 376E, or section 509 of the Indian penal code is alleged to have been committed or attempted, is temporarily or permanently mentally or physically disabled, then such information

---

(2) Where any person is arrested under subsection (1) by an officer other than a police officer, such officer shall, without unnecessary delay, take or send the person arrested before a magistrate having jurisdiction in the case or before the officer-in-charge of a police station.

(3) The provisions of the Code of Criminal Procedure, 1973 shall, subject to the provisions of this section, apply, so far as may be, in relation to any entry, search or arrest, made under this section.

shall be recorded by the police officer at the residence of the person seeking to report such offence or at a convenient place of such person's choice, in the presence of an interpreter or a special educator as the case may be; (b) the recording of such information shall be videographed; (c) and the police officer shall get the statement of the person recorded by a judicial magistrate under clause (a) of Subsection 5A of section 164 as soon as possible.

S.154 of the CrPc further states that a copy of the information as recorded under subsection (1) shall be given forthwith, free of cost, to the informant.

As such, a woman may prefer her complaint of cyber victimisation to her local police station either herself or through the male members of her family as S.160 of the CrPc provides respite for women witnesses and complainants from being physically present in the police station.[6] It may be noted that almost all the metro cities in India have police headquarters with their own websites, and each of them have separate category for offences against women and also for cyber crimes where some details about cyber crimes are given.[7] Apart from this, several metro cities, including Chennai, Bangalore, Delhi and Kolkata, have their own cyber crime cells. Victims of cyber crimes may contact the police headquarters through the phone numbers provided on these websites or the emails provided therein. In non-metro cities, the police headquarters are responsible to look after cyber crime cases. Apart from this, each police station in every village, district or city must have a separate cell to take care of cyber crime cases. But in reality, many victims have reported that even when they contact cyber crime cells, they are asked to report the matter to their local police station as the local police station is the first responsible organisation to register the crime information.

Victims often face trouble in making the officer in charge understand the nature of the crime. Many police officers are not properly trained in handling digital crimes and evidences and as such, they may never

---

[6] Proviso to Subsection (1) of S.160 CrPc states that

Provided that no male person 'under the age of fifteen years or above the age of sixty-five years or a woman or a mentally or physically disabled person' shall be required to attend at any place other than the place in which such male person or woman resides.

Subsection (2) stated that the state government may, by rules made in this behalf, provide for the payment by the police officer of the reasonable expenses of every person, attending under subsection (1) at any place other than his residence.

[7] For more detail, see the police websites of various states.

understand who has victimised the woman concerned, how it caused such devastating effect and what may be the result if it is not taken care of. In many rural or semi-urban areas, where women prefer to lodge complaint with the women police officers, the story may be the same or even more horrific. Victims have complained regarding reluctance of the police officers to even enter the case details in the diary as is required by the law. Also, there are cases where the police may have taken excessive time to send the details to the cyber crime cell or there may be no response from the cyber crime cell as well. Victims have also complained about they are being blamed by the police. Even though provisions like S.160 of the CrPc provides a solace by stating that the victim may directly contact the superior officers with all the details or the victims may also prefer to lodge complaint with the courts in this regard, unfortunately, the first impression with the police may prove disastrous and victims may be demotivated to take up further action. This leads the victims to take up irrational coping mechanism whereby the victims may themselves reverse attack the perpetrators to make the problem even more critical or may rely upon ethical and armature hackers. This can be explained best through our observation (Halder & Jaishankar, 2015, p. 283), where we stated,

> [T]he presence of and accessibility to the tools to counter victimisation may motivate the victims to take up irrational coping mechanisms to deal with online victimisation, which, the victims may perceive as rational for reasons mentioned above, but in the long run may prove to be irrational. The tools of counter victimisation may include (i) numerous internet reading materials and videos on tricks of hacking, (ii) personal email and chat options to talk to the harasser back, (iii) availability of platforms like blogs and social media profiles to speak about the harasser and harassment done by him/her, (iv) social media provided 'tagging' opportunities whereby a user can tag the name or photograph of another and showcase the name of the tagged individual through his/her profiles, and (v) social media specifically made for writing about the frustration regarding a particular organisation or individual.[8]

We have seen that majority of women and girls who may have faced online victimisation had preferred to contact the hackers to track the origin of the harassing contents and remove the same quickly. But, it

---

[8] For example, there are many web platforms which provide opportunity to vent out frustration and so on.

must be understood that besides the fact that hacking or unauthorisedly accessing any computer, computer resources, documents and network is considered as a penal offence both under S.43 and S.66 of the IT Act. Relying on hackers may bring a different kind of problem, which was explained by the lead author in her blog titled 'Ethical Hacking: How Far it is Ethical and Safe?'[9] As such, when the victim contacts the ethical hacker to save her, the whole operation is carried out basically on 'trust'. Indeed, there are many ethical hackers who really keep up with the ethics. They do use this tricky technology to help and not to destroy. But there may be situations when the same 'ethical hacker' may turn unethical if the victim in distress could not 'pay' him as promised or refused to do some other activities in lieu of 'hacking back' the hacked contents. It would then turn up as again contacting another ethical hacker to prevent the earlier one from playing with the victim's emotions and distresses, and then the cycle of working with irrational coping methods may go on pulling the victim into a deeper trouble. Also, it needs to be noted that being 'ethical' sometimes may not help the hacker to get away from the legal proceedings unless the person in charge of such activities is acting as and under the law and justice machinery. Ethical hacker may balm the disaster faster and without any legal hassle but in other way, pulls the victim more towards the legal hassle in case he/she is caught in relation to other hacking activities and the present victim is 'exhibited' as one of those who 'encouraged' the (ethical) hacker to play more tricks.[10]

Collection of Evidence and Admissibility of the Same and Preparation of Charge Sheet

Victims' responsibilities: As we have been discussing in the other chapters as well as in the above paragraphs in this book, cyber crimes targeting individuals may consist of offensive messages, images, audio–visual contents and so on sent to the victim's email or social media account or may be created in one's own blog, other websites and so on. Once the victim comes to know of the harassment or receives the same, he/she must

---

[9] See Halder, D. (April 2010). Ethical hacking: How far it is ethical and safe? Available at http://cybervictims.blogspot.in/2010/04/ethical-hacking-how-far-safe.html (Accessed on 3 March 2015).

[10] Ibid.

preserve the evidences in the form of data[11] and/or any information[12] for reporting the matter to the criminal justice machinery and also to the website concerned. It may be seen that the websites of cyber crime cells, like the Bangalore cyber crime cell or any other websites of police head-quarters in India, may provide several e-safety tips and among these tips, the police may often tell people to save harassing comments, contents or images, links and so on which have been created to harass the particular victim. Even if the nature of the harassment is extremely disturbing or embarrassing, victims, especially women and girls, must save the harassing contents either in their own devices or save it in some storage devices or take out hardcopies like printouts and so on. There are simple tools available in the computers or even smartphones to save the pages or contents or images and the victim/s must use the same to save the harassing contents along with copying the full header (in case of emails or messages), links (in case of website contents) and so on. This is necessary because not only the contents may verify as what sort of offence has been committed by the harasser, the links, headers, phone number/s, account information and so on may also help the police to investigate as to who did it, using which computer or device and from which jurisdiction. All these may be vital evidences to bring charges against the harasser.[13] Along with this, the victims must also remember to save the reports that may have been lodged with the websites concerned or the Internet Service Providers (ISPs) or the

[11] According to S.2 (o) of the IT Act, 2000, the word 'data' is defined as follows: 'Data' means a representation of information, knowledge, facts, concepts or instructions which are being prepared or have been prepared in a formalised manner, and is intended to be processed, is being processed or has been processed in a computer system or computer network, and may be in any form (including computer printouts magnetic or optical storage media, punched cards, punched tapes) or stored internally in the memory of the computer.

[12] According to S.2 (v) of the IT Act, 2000, defines the term 'information' as follows: 'Information includes data, message, text, images, sound, voice, codes, computer programmes, software and databases or micro film or computer generated micro fiche'.

[13] S.65B of the Indian Evidence Act speaks about the admissibility of electronic records and states,

> (1) Notwithstanding anything contained in this Act, any information contained in an electronic record which is printed on a paper, stored, recorded or copied in optical or magnetic media produced by a computer (hereinafter referred to as the computer output) shall be deemed to be also a document, if the conditions mentioned in this section are satisfied in relation to the information and computer in question and

digital communication service providers. In certain cases, website operators, ISPs or the digital communication service providers may have secondary liability, especially when they allow the harassing content to stay in the sites or get spread to other sites in spite of the reports made by the victims. As has been discussed in the previous chapter, the liability of the websites or the service providers regarding the protection of privacy is ensured by Information Technology (intermediary guidelines) Rules, 2011 and the service providers must exercise their due diligence as has been provided in S.79 of the IT Act. Additional information regarding victim's report to the websites or ISPs and their reply or nonchalant attitude may help the police and the courts to bring formal charges against the later and

---

shall be admissible in any proceedings, without further proof or production of the original, as evidence of any contents of the original or of any fact stated therein or which direct evidence would be admissible.

(2) The conditions referred to in subsection (1) in respect of a computer output shall be the following, namely, (a) the computer output containing the information was produced by the computer during the period over which the computer was used regularly to store or process information for the purposes of any activities regularly carried on over that period by the person having lawful control over the use of the computer, (b) During the said period, information of the kind contained in the electronic record or of the kind from which the information so contained is derived was regularly fed into the computer in the ordinary course of the said activities, (c) Throughout the material part of the said period, the computer was operating properly or, if not, then in respect of any period in which it was not operating properly or was out of operation during that part of the period, was not such as to affect the electronic record or the accuracy of its contents and (d) the information contained in the electronic record reproduces or is derived from such information fed into the computer in the ordinary course of the said activities.

(3) Where, over any period, the functions of storing or processing information for the purposes of any activities of regularly carried on over that period as mentioned in clause (a) of subsection (2) was regularly performed by computer, whether (a) by a combination of computers operating over that period or (b) by different computers operating in succession over that period or (c) by different combinations of computers operating in succession over that period or (d) in any other manner involving the successive operation over that period, in whatever order, of one or more computers and one or more combinations of computers. All the computers used for that purpose during that period shall be treated for the purposes of this section as constituting a single computer; and references in this section to a computer shall be construed accordingly.

may create wonderful precedence regarding intermediary liability towards curbing violence and victimisation of women in the cyber space. It might also be noted that even when the harasser causes victimisation due to the lapse of the reasonable security process of any company or body corporate that is entrusted to protect the data of the victim. The said body corporate or the company is liable to pay compensation for the damages to the victim.[14] In such cases, this may generate a civil remedy.

---

(4) In any proceedings where it is desired to give a statement in evidence by virtue of this section, a certificate doing any of the following things, that is to say, (a) identifying the electronic record containing the statement and describing the manner in which it was produced, (b) giving such particulars of any device involved in the production of that electronic record as may be appropriate for the purpose of showing that the electronic record was produced by a computer, (c) dealing with any of the matters to which the conditions mentioned in subsection (2) relate and purporting to be signed by a person occupying a responsible official position in relation to the operation of the relevant device or the management of the relevant activities (whichever is appropriate) shall be evidence of any matter stated in the certificate; and for the purpose of this subsection, it shall be sufficient for a matter to be stated to the best of the knowledge and belief of the person stating it.

(5) For the purposes of this section, (a) information shall be taken to be supplied to a computer if it is supplied thereto in any appropriate form and whether it is so supplied directly or (with or without human intervention) by means of any appropriate equipment, (b) whether in the course of activities carried on by any official, information is supplied with a view to its being stored or processed for the purposes of those activities by a computer operated otherwise than in the course of those activities, that information, if duly supplied to that computer, shall be taken to be supplied to it in the course of those activities, (c) a computer output shall be taken to have been produced by a computer whether it was produced by it directly or (with or without human intervention) by means of any appropriate equipment. Explanation, for the purposes of this section any reference to information being derived from other information shall be a reference to its being derived there from by calculation, comparison or any other process.

[14] S.43A of the IT Act, 2000 speaks about compensation for failure to protect data and states that where a body corporate, possessing, dealing or handling any sensitive personal data or information in a computer resource which it owns, controls or operates, is negligent in implementing and maintaining reasonable security practices and procedures and thereby causes wrongful loss or wrongful gain to any person; such body corporate shall be liable to pay damages by way of compensation, not exceeding 5 crore rupees, to the person so affected (Change vide ITAA, 2008).

It needs to be remembered that victim or her family members (in case the victim is not fully digitally literate) should take up the first responsibility to collect as much evidence as possible. Digital contents are erasable in nature, and it has been seen many times that the perpetrator, after creating the offensive contents to cause harm to the victim, may subsequently withdraw the same along with the digital identity that was created to or availed by the harasser to cause the victimisation. It is for this very reason that the victim must save the harassing contents. But at the same time, it must also be ensured that in case the victim is unable to report crimes to the police or the courts, any other person who may be willing to help the victim must be properly authorised by the victim to lodge the report to the police. It may be understood that there are several legal provisions, including POCSO, Juvenile Justice Care and Protection Act, Sexual Harassment of Women at Workplace (Protection, Prevention, and Redressal) Act, 2013, Indecent Representation of Women (Prohibition) Act, 1986, and the concerned Rules and so on which provide confidentiality to the victims whereby the victim may anonymously lodge complaint or may take help of her family members or friends to lodge the complaint and the names of the victims cannot be published by any reporting or investigating agency or body. But, all these legal provisions as well as Indian Evidence Act also provide that the burden of proof of victimisation lies on the complainant/victim.[15]

Explanation—for the purposes of this section,

(i) 'Body corporate' means any company and includes a firm, sole proprietorship or other association of individuals engaged in commercial or professional activities.

(ii) 'Reasonable security practices and procedures' means security practices and procedures designed to protect such information from unauthorised access, damage, use, modification, disclosure or impairment, as may be specified in an agreement between the parties or as may be specified in any law for the time being in force and in the absence of such agreement or any law, such reasonable security practices and procedures, as may be prescribed by the Central Government in consultation with such professional bodies or associations as it may deem fit.

(iii) 'Sensitive personal data or information' means such personal information as may be prescribed by the Central Government in consultation with such professional bodies or associations as it may deem fit.

[15] S.101 of the Indian Evidence Act says,

Whoever desires any Court to give judgment as to any legal right or liability dependent on the existence of facts which he asserts, must prove that those facts exist. When a person is bound to prove the existence of any fact, it is said that the burden of proof lies on that person.

As such, lodging reports regarding victimisation by a third party complainant (i.e. cyber bystander), who may not be primary victim, but may lodge the complaint just because he/she may presume that the offensive content targeting a particular victim was generated by the harasser, may prove to be extremely risky for the third party complainant. This is because he may be pushed to unwanted legal trouble.[16] This is because the supposed 'harasser' may also be the target of the real perpetrator. Furthermore, the real perpetrator may create fake identities impersonating the supposed harasser or may be in nexus with the victim for pulling the supposed harasser to trouble by creating offensive contents against the victim through impersonating identity of the harasser. If the real perpetrator wishes to escape the legal liabilities, he may thus invite cyber bystanders to frame false evidence unknowingly.[17]

The other factor that the victim/complainant needs to remember is not to publicise the victimisation in other public forums, if she determines to register a complaint with the police and the courts. This may not only escalate the problem more by attracting more anger from the actual harasser as well as trolls who may start trolling on this issue, it may also weaken the case for the victim/complainant. The harasser may claim that the victim had unnecessarily brought in more 'pressure' on him and provoked him/her to attack the victim in a more grievous manner; the harasser may also claim that he was exercising his right to speech which the victim unnecessarily attacked. In sum, such activities may corrupt the actual evidences as the offensive content may be removed, modified or edited and then may get republished in a completely different form. In such a case, the victim herself or her friends or the compassionate cyber bystanders may be held liable for

---

[16] Ibid.

[17] S.192 of the IPC speaks about fabricating false evidences and states that whoever causes any circumstance to exist or makes any false entry in any book or record, or electronic record or makes any document or electronic record containing a false statement, intending that such circumstance, false entry or false statement may appear in evidence in a judicial proceeding, or in a proceeding taken by law before a public servant as such, or before an arbitrator, and that such circumstance, false entry or false statement, so appearing in evidence, may cause any person who in such proceeding is to form an opinion upon the evidence, to entertain an erroneous opinion touching any point material to the result of such proceeding, is said 'to fabricate false evidence'.

the destruction of the document or electronic records as has been provided in S.204 of IPC.[18]

Furthermore, it is also very much necessary to note that circulation of offensive messages or videos for a wide publicity of the issue may attract S.67 (punishment for publishing or transmitting material containing obscene acts and so on in the electronic form), 67A (punishment for publishing or transmitting material containing sexual explicit acts in the electronic form), 67B (punishment for publishing or transmitting material depicting children in explicit acts and so on in the electronic form), of the IT Act, 2000, S.354C (voyeurism and punishment for the same) of the IPC and Ss. 11(iii) (sexual harassment), 12 (punishment for sexual harassment), 13 (use of child for pornographic purposes) and 14 (punishment for using children for pornographic purposes) of the POCSO Act. Such activities may also destroy the chain of custody in case the victim has already given the harassing contents to the police, and the police have started the initial investigation. Furthermore, such publicising may also attract blame game from the police as well, especially when the police officer concerned is not well aware about the issues of internet crimes.

Once the victim has all the proofs ready, she may decide to register the complaint with the police with all the evidences she has. Often there is confusion such as where to lodge the complaint. S.78 of the IT Act, 2000 notwithstanding anything contained in the CrPc, 1973, a police officer not below the rank of Inspector shall investigate any offence under this Act. As such, if the offence is in the nature of any offence which are described in Chapter XI of the IT Act or any offence in the nature of cyber stalking or voyeurism or creation/distribution of rape videos and so on, the victim may contact the inspector in charge of the local police station first. In case of the latter, as S.154 of the CrPc, a woman police officer

---

[18] S.204 IPC speaks about destruction of document or electronic record to prevent its production as evidence and states that whoever secretes or destroys any document or electronic record which he may be lawfully compelled to produce as evidence in a Court of Justice, or in any proceeding lawfully held before a public servant as such, or obliterates or renders illegible the whole with the intention of preventing the same from being produced or used as evidence before such court or public servant as aforesaid or after he shall have been lawfully summoned or required to produce the same for that purpose, shall be punished with imprisonment of either description for a term which may extend to two years or with fine or with both.

should record the statement of the victim/complainant.[19] If the concerned officer refuses to take her statement, she can directly contact the superior officer like Superintendent of Police and so on.[20] Presently, the police in many cities have created digital complaint registering systems, including through schemes like 'Alert 306'[21] and 'Hello police' scheme, whereby people can lodge complaints through CAN and even WhatsApp.

Apart from that, as has been stated previously, the victims can also send emails to specific police headquarters or call the given phone numbers to contact the police in such cases. However, in all these cases, the

[19] Proviso added to S.154(1) CrPc states that

Provided that if the information is given by the woman against whom an offence under section 326A, section 3268, section 354, section 354A, section 3548, section, 354C, section 3540, section 376, section 376A, section 3768, section 376C, section 45 of 1860. 3760, section 376E or section 509 of the Indian Penal Code is alleged to have been committed or attempted, then such information shall be recorded, by a woman police officer or any woman officer:

Provided further that (a) in the event that the person against whom an offence under section 354, section 354A, section 354B, section 354C, section 3540, section 376, section 376A, section 3768, section 376C, section 3760, section 376E or section 509 of the Indian 45 of 1860. Penal Code is alleged to have been committed or attempted, is temporarily or permanently mentally or physically disabled, then such information shall be recorded by a police officer, at the residence of the person seeking to report such offence or at a convenient place of such person's choice, in the presence of an interpreter or a special educator, as the case may be, (b) the recording of such information shall be video graphed (c) the police officer shall get the statement of the person recorded by a Judicial Magistrate under clause (a) of subsection (5A) of section 164 as soon as possible.

[20] See S.154 (3) of the CrPc which states that

Any person aggrieved by a refusal on the part of an officer in charge of a police station to record the information referred to in subsection (1) may send the substance of such information, in writing and by post, to the Superintendent of Police concerned who, if satisfied that such information discloses the commission of a cognizable offence, shall either investigate the case himself or direct an investigation to be made by any police officer subordinate to him, in the manner provided by this Code, and such officer shall have all the powers of an officer in charge of the police station in relation to that offence.

[21] See PTI (2015), Alert 306 facility introduced by police for public, published in The Economics Times on Mar 19, 2015, http://articles.economictimes.india-times.com/2015-03-19/news/60286858_1_police-officers-alert-police-network (Accessed on 4 May 2015).

subsequent proceedings may take as per Ss.154 of the CrPc and 78 of the IT Act. Apart from registering complaints with the police, the victims may also consider filing cases directly with any magistrate. S.190 (1) of the CrPc speaks in this regard and states that subject to the provisions of this Chapter. Any Magistrate of the first class and/or the second class, specially empowered in this behalf under subsection (2), may take cognisance of any offence—(a) upon receiving a complaint of facts which constitute such offence, (b) upon a police report of such facts, and (c) upon information received from any person other than a police officer, or upon his own knowledge, that such offence has been committed. Furthermore, if the case is of the nature of defamation as has been defined by S.499 of the IPC, coupled with online victimisation, and the victim is frustrated with the police apathy, then she may also consider filing a case directly to the court under S.199 (1) of the CrPc[22] read with S.190 of the CrPc. It may be noted that S.199 (1) of the CrPc provides privacy to the women victims and exempts them from appearing in public for any prosecution procedures if the circumstances so need.[23] S.200 of the CrPc states about the subsequent prosecutional procedure in this regard by stating,

[A] magistrate taking cognizance of an offence on complaint shall examine upon oath the complainant and the witnesses present, if any, and the substance of such examination shall be reduced to writing and shall be signed by the complainant and the witnesses, and also by the Magistrate.[24]

---

[22] S.199 (1) of the CrPc states that no court shall take cognisance of an offence punishable under Chapter XXI of the Indian Penal Code (45 of 1860) except upon a complaint made by some person aggrieved by the offence:

Provided that where such person is under the age of eighteen years, or is an idiot or a lunatic, or is from sickness or infirmity unable to make a complaint, or is a woman who, according to the local customs and manners, ought not to be compelled to appear in public, some other person may, with the leave of the Court, make a complaint on his or her behalf.

[23] See Ibid.

[24] Proviso added to this Section states that

Provided that, when the complaint is made in writing, the Magistrate need not examine the complainant and the witnesses-(a) if a public servant acting or purporting to act in the discharge of his official duties or a Court has made the complainant; or(b) if the Magistrate makes over the case for inquiry or trial to another Magistrate under section 192:Provided further that if the Magistrate makes over the case to another Magistrate under section 192 after examining the complainant and the witnesses, the latter Magistrate need not re-examine them.

However, since some of the types of cyber crimes against women that are discussed in this book are recognised as offences under the IT Act and also the IPC, and both these laws along with POCSO and so on direct that such offences must be investigated by the police officers generally not below the rank of inspectors; we strongly suggest that victims must first exhaust their right to seek help from the police. In case the police do not help, they may also consider filing writ petitions to the High Courts or the Supreme Court, if necessary, under Articles 32[25] or 226[26] or to get an order in nature of mandamus for directing the police to take necessary action.

---

[25] Article 32 of the Indian constitution speaks about Remedies for enforcement of rights conferred by Part III of the constitution and states that

(1) The right to move the Supreme Court by appropriate proceedings for the enforcement of the rights conferred by this Part is guaranteed.

(2) The Supreme Court shall have power to issue directions or orders or writs, including writs in the nature of habeas corpus, mandamus, prohibition, quo warranto and certiorari, whichever may be appropriate, for the enforcement of any of the rights conferred by this Part.

(3) Without prejudice to the powers conferred on the Supreme Court by clause (1) and (2), Parliament may by law empower any other court to exercise within the local limits of its jurisdiction all or any of the powers exercisable by the Supreme Court under clause (2) (4) The right guaranteed by this article shall not be suspended except as otherwise provided for by this Constitution.

[26] Article 226 of the constitution of India speaks about power of High Courts to issue certain writs and states that

(1) Notwithstanding anything in Article 32 every High Court shall have powers, throughout the territories in relation to which it exercise jurisdiction, to issue to any person or authority, including in appropriate cases, any Government, within those territories directions, orders or writs, including writs in the nature of habeas corpus, mandamus, prohibitions, quo warranto and certiorari, or any of them, for the enforcement of any of the rights conferred by Part III and for any other purpose.

(2) The power conferred by clause (1) to issue directions, orders or writs to any Government, authority or person may also be exercised by any High Court exercising jurisdiction in relation to the territories within which the cause of action, wholly or in part, arises for the exercise of such power, notwithstanding that the seat of such Government or authority or the residence of such person is not within those territories.

The Role of the Police

When an officer is intimated about any sort of cyber crimes committed against any woman, he/she must assure that the victim/complainant feels comfortable to share each and every detail with the officer concerned even if the said officer is not well versed with computer and cyber crimes. As has been stated above, officers not below the rank of inspectors can investigate the offences in this regard. As such, it must be ensured that the victim can directly talk with the inspector when she wishes to lodge the complaint. It needs to be remembered that cyber crimes against women may not always be sexual in nature, but may have enough power to destroy the reputation of the victim or push the victim to take extreme steps like committing suicide due to shame. It may happen that the victim takes some preliminary preventive steps like complaining to the website concerned or blocking the phone number and so on. The concerned police officer must ensure that the victim reveals each of such activities and has the proof of the facts. The procedural practices that need to be followed in this stage are similar to any other criminal cases that are tried on the basis of CrPc along with the special laws and the traditional IPC designated for handling special types of

---

(3) Where any party against whom an interim order, whether by way of injunction or stay or in any other manner, is made on, or in any proceedings relating to, a petition under clause (1), without (a) furnishing to such party copies of such petition and all documents in support of the plea for such interim order; and (b) giving such party an opportunity of being heard, makes an application to the High Court for the vacation of such order and furnishes a copy of such application to the party in whose favour such order has been made or the counsel of such party, the High Court shall dispose of the application within a period of two weeks from the date on which it is received or from the date on which the copy of such application is so furnished, whichever is later, or where the High Court is closed on the last day of that period, before the expiry of the next day afterwards on which the High Court is open; and if the application is not so disposed of, the interim order shall, on the expiry of that period, or, as the case may be, the expiry of the aid next day, stand vacated.

(4) The power conferred on a High Court by this article shall not be in derogation of the power conferred on the Supreme court by clause (2) of Article 32.

offences. The procedural practices in cases of cyber crimes against women can therefore be summed up as below:

1. Who may be approached and what are the powers entrusted upon him/her?

S.78 of the IT Act empowers any police officer not below the rank of an Inspector to investigate the offences mentioned under chapter XI of the Act. Further, S.75 provides extraterritorial jurisdiction to this Act. In subsection (1) it states that the provisions of this Act shall apply to any offence or contravention committed outside India by any person irrespective of his nationality. Subsection (2) further states that this section will apply to any offence committed outside India by anyone if the act or conduct constituting the offence or contravention involves a computer, computer system, or computer network located in India. Section 80 of IT Act further speaks about power of the police officer and other officers to enter, search and so on. These proceedings should follow the regular CrPc.

2. The pre-trial stage:

Pre-trial stage includes gathering information about incidence of crime by the police officer. At this stage, the officer concerned needs to ascertain whether the offence concerned is a cognisable offence or a noncognisable offence. At this stage, S.77B of the IT Act, 2000 (amended in 2008) must also be considered, which states that 'Notwithstanding anything contained in Criminal Procedure Code 1973, the offence punishable with imprisonment of three years and above shall be cognizable and the offence punishable with imprisonment of three years shall be bailable.' However, if the officer concerned needs to apply traditional penal law from IPC, then he/she must also consider the First Schedule of the CrPc, 1973. In case of cognisable offence, the officer concerned must initiate the proceedings as per S.156 CrPc (which prescribes police officer's power to investigate cognisable offences)[27]. In case of a

---

[27] S.156 CrPc states that

(1) Any officer in charge of a police station may, without the order of a Magistrate, investigate any cognizable case which a court having jurisdiction over the local area within the limits of such station would have power to inquire into or try under the provisions of Chapter XIII.

(2) No proceeding of a police officer in any such case shall at any stage be called in question on the ground that the case was one which such officer was not empowered under this section to investigate.

(3) Any Magistrate empowered under section 190 may order such an investigation as above- mentioned.

non-cogniszable offence, the officer concerned must initiate the proceedings under S.155 CrPc.[28] As such, in the pre-trial stage, the police officer must follow the CBI guidelines for investigating cyber crimes.[29] But it needs to be remembered that in most of the complaints related to cyber crimes against women (especially those that are discussed in this book), the investigating officer (IO) needs to look more for onsite data that may have been published by the harasser targeting the victim. As paragraph 18.15 of the CBI guidelines states,

> [B]efore conducting the search, the Investigator will need to decide whether to seize data on site, or seize hardware for examination at a Computer Forensic Laboratory. While on-site data seizure has the advantage, that one does not have to transport much hardware, one may need services of a Computer Forensic Expert to download data for analysis and preserve data for presenting it in the Court. When in doubt, make use of a Computer Forensics Specialist at the scene, if possible, to determine whether one needs to seize data or seize hardware. In case, a specialist is not available, it is recommended that one seizes everything.

But when the nature of the offence involves circulating images or audio–visual clippings, and if the victim/complainant provides reliable information about the origin of such data (e.g., in cases of interpersonal crimes like sexting, revenge porn, cyber stalking, creation of fake avatar

---

[28] S.155 CrPc states that

(1) When information is given to an officer in charge of a police station of the commission within the limits of such station of a non-cognizable offence, he shall enter or cause to be entered the substance of the information in a book to be kept by such officer in such form as the State Government may prescribe in this behalf, and refer the informant to the Magistrate.

(2) No police officer shall investigate a non-cognizable case without the order of a Magistrate having power to try such case or commit the case for trial.

(3) Any police officer receiving such order may exercise the same powers in respect of the investigation (except the power to arrest without warrant) as an officer in charge of a police station may exercise in a cognizable case.

(4) Where a case relates to two or more offences of which at least one is cognizable, the case shall be deemed to be a cognizable case, notwithstanding that the other offences are non-cognizable.

[29] Available at http://cbi.nic.in/aboutus/manuals/Chapter_18.pdf (Accessed on 20 March 2016).

and so on, the victim may be aware that the concerned data has been stored in the devices of the harasser, who may be an ex-boyfriend or ex-husband or any other known person with whom the victim would have exchanged information earlier) or even when the crime consists of hacking and unauthorised access to data or creation, distribution of sexually explicit materials and so on, the investigator must also cease the devices as well.

In all these cases, whenever the victim/complainant provides any information, the officer in charge after recording the statements and providing case/diary number to the case, if needed, may contact intermediary through their 'legal channel' to get the information about the IP address of the harasser and his/her information in detail with which he/she may have created his/her digital identity to carry out the harassment. It may be noted that all the intermediaries have special contact addresses for law enforcement officers whereby the officer in charge, either through governmental channels or directly, may ask for data about particular accused persons. In general, if the IO is unable to contact any intermediary on his own, he may take help of cyber crime cells to contact the intermediary. The information that can be gathered from such investigation are the subscriber registration information, geolocation, IP address, phone number, exact content that had been uploaded to harass the victim, associated time stamps, header of the mail, telephone billing information, call logs, voice mail content and so on.[30] IO may need to take extra care when the case relates to viral porn/obscene/rape videos of MMSs targeting women and children. In such case, the nature of the offence may become inclusive of an aggravated or penetrative sexual assault with that of violation of privacy and voyeurism. The victim must be given complete privacy in such cases as may happen when it is a case of rape under section 376 of the IPC or penetrative sexual assault under S.3 or sexual assault under S.7 or S.11 or 13 of the POCSO Act and so on. In such cases, the IO must refer to S.69 of the IT Act, which speaks about power to issue directions for interception or monitoring or decryption of any information through any computer resource and may subsequently refer to S.69A which speaks about power to issue directions for blocking the public access of any information through any computer resource and so on. Once IO avails entire onsite data, he/she may proceed to cease the devices. For search and seizure of the devices, IO has to follow the

[30] See for information: http://www.google.com/transparencyreport/userdata-requests/legalprocess/#what_is_a_mutual_legal (Accessed on 20 March 2016).

CBI guidelines step by step. The excerpts from the CBI guidelines in this regard under the title 'Search and Seizure of Digital Evidence' as has been mentioned are:

1. Some precautionary issues that the investigator must remember while planning for search:

    i. Intangible data can be stored in any jurisdiction in any networked computer/s and the perpetrators can access these data with dial-in-access from anywhere in the world. The quantity of information misused or amount of damage to the data or even the viral nature of the content may be controlled by the speed of the network and the equipment that the criminal is using.

    ii. It is always advisable to contact computer forensic scientists of a forensic science laboratory and ask them to accompany the search team to the places where the investigator suspects that the computer or computer networks or any other electronic memory devices are likely to be found.

    iii. In case, it is not possible, the investigator must remember to collect information including the type, make, model, operating system, network architecture, type and location of data storage, remote access possibilities and so on, which can be passed on to forensic experts that would help making necessary preparation to collect and preserve evidence.

    iv. When on some occasions, it may not be possible to remove the computer system physically and data may have to be copied at the scene of crime/place of search, the investigator or expert must carry necessary media, software and other specialised items as well as special packing materials which can prevent loss of data as data of magnetic media can be destroyed by dust, jerks, and electrostatic environment.

2. Precautions at the search site that must be taken by the investigator:

    i. Suspect or an accused should be not allowed to touch any part of the computer or accessory attached to it either by physical means or through wireless.

    ii. Physical networks such as fibre optic, cables, telephones or on Wi-Fi or Wi-max wireless networks or even through a mobile phone having a wireless communication port and so on must not be allowed to be touched or switched on by any one on the site including the accused. Since the data may be corrupted or wiped out even by remote controlling by different devices.

iii. Investigator must take similar precaution for small devices or removable storage devices, which have the capacity of storing huge amount of data.

iv. In case, the data reside at a remote location even in a different country or jurisdiction, the investigator needs to find out the storage location and take action accordingly. In such case, the investigator must consider to alert the Interpol and take necessary follow up steps to issue letters rogatory under the provisions of Section 166A CrPc.

v. When the investigator finds networked computers, he/she should not disconnect the computer if networks or mainframes are involved since pulling a computer from a network may damage the network, and cause harm to the company's operations.

vi. The CBI guidelines say that it is generally not practical to seize a mainframe because it requires disconnecting all the computers that are attached to it. Hardware seizure with computers on a network can be very complicated. If the investigator is not well versed, he/she should take the help of a computer forensics specialist in these cases.

vii. Steps should be followed in such search and seizure as the CBI guidelines state in para 18.17 to 18.20.

viii. The investigator should carry (a) disks or cartridges for storing copies from the files, (b) labels to label various devices, parts of the devices and so on, (c) screwdrivers and other tools used to dismantle the hardware for seizure, (d) gloves, (e) packing materials, (f) camera equipment for video-graphing, and (g) chain of custody report sheets and other paper to inventories seized evidence.

3. Once the steps to be followed as per para 18.19 are onsite, the investigator must survey the equipment and take precautionary steps as described above. Next, he will need to document the way the system is connected together and take the following steps:

i. Labelling and photographing the set-up: Labelling and photographing everything prior to dismantling the system is an important first step. Take some general photographs of the search site to document its pre-search condition for legal purposes, and to serve as a reference during investigation. This documentation on how the system was configured may prove essential when the system is reconnected in the forensic laboratory. As the IO is taking the pictures, he should make sure to get close-ups of the front and back of all equipment and the way it is connected. He should pay special attention to DIP switches on the back of certain equipment that must be in a certain configuration. These switch settings could accidentally be moved in transport creating problems for the examiner.

ii. Label all Parts: IO should label each part before he starts dismantling any of the equipment. He should remember to label all the connectors and plugs at both ends and on the computer so that reassembly is easy and accurate. A good way to do this is to label each item its own letter. For example, a power cord may be marked 'A' on the end and a corresponding label marked 'A' on the computer port where this plug is to be inserted.

iii. Power system down: As a rule, if a computer is off, it should not be turned on. Hackers can make their computers erase data if a certain disk is not in the drive when the machine is booted up or if a certain password is not entered. Likewise, if the machine is on, one should check it before turning it off otherwise it may destroy data. Keep in mind that a computer may look powered down but actually, it may be in 'sleep' mode. Hackers can set their computers to erase data if not properly awakened from the 'sleep' mode; so, one may be required to pull the plug or remove the battery from a laptop in these cases. IO may need to shut the machine down through the operating system rather than just 'pulling the plug'. If, however, he does need to 'pull the plug', he should disconnect it from the back of the machine rather than at the wall, because if the machine is plugged into a back-up power supply, it may initiate a shutdown procedure that could alter files.

iv. Dismantle the system: Once the system is labelled and powered down, it can be dismantled into separate components for transportation. If a computer is at a business location and a part of a network, proper procedure should be followed to properly disconnect the computer from the network.

v. Seize documentation: Seize all manuals for the computer, its peripheral devices, and especially the software and operating system. The examiners at a forensic laboratory need to refer to a manual to determine the kind of hardware and its technicalities. Seizing other documentation at the site like notes, passwords, and journals may prove very useful. Sticky notes, or other pieces of paper around the computer systems that may have passwords or login ID's written on them, should also be seized from the spot.

4. As para 18.20 instructs regarding handling evidence and computer hardware, the IO needs to follow the following steps:

i. Protecting data: IO should also write/protect disks or cartridges he finds at the site of search in order to protect the data. Most disks and cartridges have a small sliding tab that prevents changing the disk content when set correctly. Placing a blank disk in the hard drive of computer system will keep them from booting up from the hard drive if they are accidentally turned on.

ii. Packaging for transport: Once IO or the expert has dismantled the computer, it is ready to be packaged for transportation to the forensic laboratory. Computers parts being sensitive are easily damaged and the hard drives that usually store data have delicate mechanisms, so they should be handled carefully. One should not wrap the computer components using Styrofoam because small particles can break off and get inside the computer causing it to malfunction. Anti-static plastic bubble/wrap is preferred.

iii. Keep system components together: Keep the components of each computer system together. This small organisational step can save lots of time when the examiners are trying to reconstruct the system.

iv. Single machine, single seizing agent: If one person handles the seizure of a computer, that same person can authenticate the evidence at a trial. This simple consideration can avoid confusion later.

v. How to transport and store the system: Do not put the computer in the trunk of a police vehicle. The computer system should be secured in a way that reduces vibrations that may shake a part loose. IOP should store the computer in a secure, cool dry place away from any generators or other devices that emit electromagnetic signals.

Even though the guidelines mentioned here are provided mainly for economic crimes, hacking and so on, and there are no separate guidelines for cyber crimes against women, these guidelines may be followed for the latter as well and the police officer must carry on the search as per S.165 of the CrPc which speaks about search by police officer within the local jurisdiction.[31] But the investigating officer must remember that in each step that the confidentiality and privacy of the victim must be preserved, and he/she must assure the victim that proper steps are being followed for investigating. This will raise the faith in the victim to cooperate with the police and prosecution in the later stages. However, at this stage, it is important to find out the jurisdiction as to where the harasser resides, the devices are situated and the intermediary server is located. In case the police officer needs to conduct enquiry in the jurisdiction of another police station, he/she must refer to S.166 of the CrPc as well as Ss.1(2)[32] and 75

[31] S.165 CrPc states,

(1) Whenever an officer in charge of police station or a police officer making an investigation has reasonable grounds for believing that anything necessary for the purposes of an investigation into any offence which he is authorised to investigate may be found in any place within the limits of the police station of which he is in charge, or to which he is attached, and that such thing cannot in his opinion be otherwise obtained without undue delay, such officer may, after recording in writing the grounds of his belief and specifying in such writing, so far as possible the thing for which search is to be made, search, or cause search to be made, for such thing in any place within the limits of such station.

(2) A police officer proceeding under subsection (1), shall, if practicable, conduct the search in person.

(3) If he is unable to conduct the search in person, and there is no other person competent to make the search present at the time, he may, after recording in writing his reasons for so doing, require any officer subordinate to him to make the search, and he shall deliver to such subordinate officer an order in writing, specifying the place to be searched, and so far as possible, the thing for which search is to be made; and such subordinate officer may thereupon search for such thing in such place.

(4) The provisions of this Code as to search warrants and the general provisions as to searches contained in section 100 shall, so far as may be, apply to a search made under this section.

(5) Copies of any record made under subsection (1) or subsection (3) shall forth- with be sent to the nearest Magistrate empowered to take cognisance to the offence, and the owner or occupier of the place searched shall, on application, be furnished, free of cost, with a copy of the same by the Magistrate.

[32] S.1(2) of the IT Act, 2000 (amended in 2008) states that It shall extend to the whole of India and, save as otherwise provided in this Act, it applies also to any offence or contravention hereunder committed outside India by any person.

of the IT Act, which speaks about extraterritorial jurisdictional scope of the Act.[33]

However, it is necessary to remember, especially in cases of cyber crimes against women, that if the victim contacts the police even for issues which the officer in charge may feel very trivial, he/she may still carry on his/her investigation after fulfilling the initial requirements as has been mentioned in S.154 of the CrPc (information in cognisable cases).[34] During the gathering of the information from the victim/complainant, the police officer

[33] S.75 of the IT Act states

(1) Subject to the provisions of sub-section (2), the provisions of this Act shall apply also to any offence or contravention committed outside India by any person irrespective of his nationality.

(2) For the purposes of sub-section (1), this Act shall apply to an offence or contravention committed outside India by any person if the act or conduct constituting the offence or contravention involves a computer, computer system or computer network located in India.

[34] S.154 CrPc states,

(1) Every information relating to the commission of a cognizable offence, if given orally to an officer in charge of a police station, shall be reduced to writing by him or under his direction, and be read over to the informant; and every such information, whether given in writing or reduced to writing as aforesaid, shall be signed by the person giving it and the substance thereof shall be entered in a book to be kept by such officer in such form as the State Government may prescribe in this behalf.

(2) A copy of the information as recorded under subsection (1) shall be given forthwith, free of cost, to the informant.

(3) Any person, aggrieved by a refusal on the part of an officer in charge of a police station to record the information referred to in subsection (1) may send the substance of such information, in writing and by post, to the Superintendent of Police concerned who, if satisfied that such information discloses the commission of a cognizable offence, shall either investigate the case himself or direct an investigation to be made by any police officer Subordinate to him, in the manner provided by this Code, and such officer shall have all the powers of an officer in charge of the police station in relation to that offence.

Provided that if the information is given by the woman against whom an offence under Section 326A, Section 326B, Section 354, Section 354A, Section 354B, Section 354C, Section 354D, Section 376, Section 376A, Section 376B, Section 376C, Section 376D, Section 376E or Section 509 of the Indian Penal Code is

must abide by the proviso especially meant for women victims. It may be necessary to note that these types of 'trivial' cases may include bullying or trolling (which are not recognised as separate offences either as per the IT Act or as per the IPC still now), cyber stalking (both by persistent calling over phone or monitoring online activities through emails/social media/WhatsApp and so on) or creation of fake avatar and so on. These may seem trivial at the onset, but they may yield devastating results if not monitored properly. However, in all cases, the police officer must abide by S.160 of the CrPc (police officer's power to require attendance of witnesses), especially the proviso, which says,

> [P]rovided that no male person under the age of fifteen years or above the age of sixty-five years or a woman or a mentally or physically disabled person shall be required to attend at any place other than the place in which such male person or woman resides.

And S.161 of the CrPc (examination of the witnesses), especially the proviso, which states,

> [P]rovided further that the statement of a woman against whom an offence under section 354, section 354A, section 354B, section 354C, section 354D, section 376, section 376A, section 376B, section 376C, section 376D, section 376E or section 509 of the Indian Penal Code is alleged to have been committed or attempted shall be recorded, by a woman police officer or any woman officer.

The police officers must also follow general rules in this regard that are stated in S.162 (statements to police not to be signed) and also in S.163

---

alleged to have been committed or attempted, then such information shall be recorded, by a woman police officer or any woman officer.

Provided further that (a) in the event that the person against whom an offence under section 354, section 354A, section 354B, section 354C, section 354D, section 376, section 376A, section 376B, section 376C, section 376D, section 376E or section 509 of the Indian Penal Code is alleged to have been committed or attempted, is temporarily or permanently mentally or physically disabled, then such information shall be recorded by a police officer, at the residence of the person seeking to report such offence or at a convenient place of such person's choice, in the presence of an interpreter or a special educator, as the case may be; (b) the recording of such information shall be video-graphed (c) the police officer shall get the statement of the person recorded by a Judicial Magistrate under clause (a) of sub-section (5A) of section 164 as soon as possible.

(no inducement to be offered). In case it is a rape video and the officer in charge combines the physical and virtual offences for investigation, he/ she must also see that proper medical tests have been done for the victim and the accused.

Preparation of charge sheet: Immediately after the information is received and investigation is over, the officer concerned must start preparing the charge sheet as per the procedure laid down under S.173 CrPc (report on completion of investigation).[35] However, it needs to be noted that there may be several issues at this stage which may delay the preparation of charge sheet. But, it is important to mention about the 'advisory

[35] S.173 CrPc states that
   (1) Every investigation under this Chapter shall be completed without unnecessary delay.
   (2) (i) As soon as it is completed, the officer in charge of the police station shall forward to a Magistrate empowered to take cognizance of the offence on a police report, a report in the form prescribed by the State Government, stating-
      (a) the names of the parties;
      (b) the nature of the information;
      (c) the names of the persons who appear to be acquainted with the circumstances of the case;
      (d) whether any offence appears to have been committed and, if so, by whom;
      (e) whether the accused has been arrested;
      (f) whether he has been released on his bond and, if so, weather with or without sureties;
      (g) whether he has been forwarded in custody under section 170.

      (ii) The officer shall also communicate, in such manner as may be prescribed by the State Government, the action taken by him, to the person, if any, by whom the information relating to the commission of the offence was first given.

   (3) Where a superior officer of police has been appointed under section 158, the report shall, in any case in which the State Government by general or special order so directs, be submitted through that officer, and he may, pending the orders of the Magistrate, direct the officer in charge of the police station to make further investigation,
   (4) Whenever it appears from a report forwarded under this section that the accused has been released on his bond, the Magistrate shall make such order-for the discharge of such bond or otherwise as he thinks fit.

on crime against women' issued by Ministry of Home affairs to all the police headquarters in 2009[36] and which was later followed up by adding guidelines set forth in Court in its own motion v. State of Punjab and others (Civil writ petition No. 26229 of 2012, in the High court of Punjab and Haryana).[37] In this advisory, it was mentioned that crime against women includes all sorts of crimes targeting women including stalking, voyeurism, cyber crimes, misusing the electronic media and so on, as well as words and gestures that harm the modesty of women as has

(5) When such report is in respect of a case to which section 170 applies, the police officer shall forward to the Magistrate alongwith the report-

    (a) all documents or relevant extracts thereof on which the prosecution proposes to rely other than those already sent to the Magistrate during investigation;

    (b) The statements-recorded under section 161 of all the persons whom the prosecution proposes to examine as its witnesses.

(6) If the police officer is of opinion that any part of any such statement is not relevant to the subject-matter of the proceedings or that its disclosure to the accused is not essential in the interests of justice and is inexpedient in the public interest, he shall indicate that part of the statement and append a note requesting the Magistrate to exclude that part from the copies to be granted to the accused and stating his reasons for making such request.

(7) Where the police officer investigating the case finds it convenient so to do, he may furnish to the accused copies of all or any of the documents referred to in sub-section (5).

(8) Nothing in this section shall be deemed to preclude further investigation in respect of an offence after a report under sub- section (2) has been for warded to the Magistrate and, where upon such investigation, the officer in charge of the police station obtains further evidence, oral or documentary, he shall forward to the Magistrate a further report or reports regarding such evidence in the form prescribed; and the provisions of sub-sections (2) to (6) shall, as far as may be, apply in relation to such report or reports as they apply in relation to a report forwarded under sub-section (2).

[36] 'Advisory on crime against women' issued by Ministry of Home affairs. F. NO.15011/48/2009-SC/ST-W Government of India/Bharat Sarkar Ministry of New Delhi/CS DIVISION New Delhi, issued on 4 September, 2009. Available at http://ncw.nic.in/pdfFiles/AdvisoryCrimeAgnstWomen170909.pdf (Accessed on 2 March, 2015).

[37] See for full judgement at http://indiankanoon.org/doc/158287429/ (Accessed on 2 May 2015).

been mentioned in S.509 of the IPC. It was further mentioned that all such crimes targeting women and girls must be given priority, information must be recorded accordingly in all cases and the investigation must be finished in due time to prevent unnecessary delay that may facilitate for bail application for the accused. We feel that these guidelines must be followed by every police officer who is dealing with cyber crimes against women.

Questions of bail/mediation: It needs to be understood that in cases of cyber crimes against women, the major problem that the criminal justice system, especially the police may face is, unwillingness of the victims to carry on with further process once they have approached the police and the harasser has been identified. In case the harasser has been taken in custody after complying with the laws mentioned above including S.88A of the Indian Evidence Act,[38] the accused should not be denied the right to bail under S.436 CrPc.[39] But, in case the accused has been thus released, the police officer should not retrieve from his duty to further

---

[38] S.88A of the Indian Evidence Act (Presumption as to electronic messages) states that

> The Court may presume that an electronic message, forwarded by the originator through an electronic mail server to the addressee to whom the message purports to be addressed corresponds with the message as fed into his computer for transmission; but the Court shall not make any presumption as to the person by whom such message was sent. S. 88A. Presumption as to electronic messages.—The Court may presume that an electronic message, forwarded by the originator through an electronic mail server to the addressee to whom the message purports to be addressed corresponds with the message as fed into his computer for transmission; but the Court shall not make any presumption as to the person by whom such message was sent. Explanation. — For the purposes of this section, the expressions 'addressee' and 'originator' shall have the same meanings respectively assigned to them in clauses (b) and (za) of sub-section.

[39] S.436 CrPc states that

> (1) When any person other than a person accused of a non-bailable offence is arrested or detained without warrant by an officer in charge of a police station, or appears or is brought before a Court, and is prepared at any time while in the custody of such officer or at any stage of the proceeding before such Court to give bail, such person shall be released on bail: Provided that such officer or Court, if he or it thinks fit, may, instead of taking bail from such person, discharge him on his executing a bond without sureties for his appearance as hereinafter provided: Provided

render help to the victim in case she complaints of repeat victimisation. It is especially so because the harasser may still come back with anonymous identity. Similarly, in case the victim does not want to proceed with registering of the FIR or any other judicial process, the police should not send the accused back with a simple warning. The officer concerned must make it sure that the mediation is effective and all the devices have been detected, offensive contents have been successfully removed not only from the devices but also from the social media profiles and other websites. This can be and should be done by the harasser under the instruction of the concerned officer. However, at this stage, it becomes important for the police to try to convince the victim to take the case forward so that she gets justice, at the same time, courts may get opportunities to effectively interpret and execute the laws for the benefit of the society as a whole.

The Prosecution

The IT Act, 2000 (amended in 2008) unlike the POCSO Act does not establish any special court, especially for offences categorised under chapter XI of the IT Act. In such a case, the Provisions of CrPc must be followed to take the case to concerned courts as designated therein. The prosecution at this stage must go according to provisions including Ss.177 (ordinary place of jurisdiction and trial), 178 (place of inquiry or trial), 179 (offence triable where act is done or consequences ensues), 180 (place of trial where act is an offence by reason of relation to the other offence), 181(place of trial in case of certain offences), 182 (offences committed by letters etc.), 183 (offence committed on journey of voyage), 184 (place of trial for offences triable together), 187 (power to issue summons or warrant for offence committed beyond local jurisdiction),

---

further that nothing in this section shall be deemed to affect the provisions of sub-section (3) of section 116 or section 446A1.

(2) Notwithstanding anything contained in sub- section (1), where a person has failed to comply with the conditions of the bail-bond as regards the time and place of attendance, the Court may refuse to release him on bail, when on a subsequent occasion in the same case he appears before the Court or is brought in custody and any such refusal shall be without prejudice to the powers of the Court to call upon any person bound by such bond to pay the penalty thereof under section 446.

188 (offences committed outside India) of the CrPc along with S.75 of the IT Act, whichever is/are suitable to the particular case depending upon the facts of the case. S.75 of the IT Act speaks about extraterritorial jurisdiction of the courts by stating that

(1) Subject to the provisions of sub-section (2), the provisions of this Act shall apply also to any offence or contravention committed outside India by any person irrespective of his nationality.

(2) For the purposes of sub-section (1), this Act shall apply to an offence or contravention committed outside India by any person if the act or conduct constituting the offence or contravention involves a computer, computer system or computer network located in India.

In cases where the victim has approached the police, she may be represented by the government pleaders. But it has been seen by these authors that in many cases where the victim (especially women victims of sexual assault) is represented by the police and the government pleader, he/she may not get due justice due to lacklastering attitude of the pleaders. She may have to suffer victim blaming at many stages of prosecution. It needs to be noted that many women in India do not prefer to cooperate with the police or prefer to withdraw the complaints at the initial stages when the case is admitted in the courts. Even though many state governments as well as the courts are engaging lawyers who have specialised in cyber laws as government pleaders, it depends upon the effective understanding of the whole case and counselling by the pleaders to the victims to have a successful restitution of justice in cases of cyber crimes against women.

At the prosecution stage, the courts and the prosecutors must also consider to let the victim know about the liabilities of the service providers in case the services providers had not taken action on 'take down' reports preferred by the victims. There are several examples of seeking civil remedies through permanent injunction in copyright infringement cases like Super Cassette Industries Ltd. V. MySpace Inc,[40] and in cyber defamation cases like Nirmaljit Singh Narula V. Indijobs at Hubpages.com[41] and so on, where victims could successfully benefitted by laws related to intermediary liabilities. We suggest that in cases of cyber crimes against women, which may involve copyright violation and cyber defamation as well, the courts must take initiatives to approach the intermediaries as

[40] 2011(48), PTC 49, Del.
[41] 2012(50)PTC 320(Del)

had been in the case of Vinay Rai that has been discussed above and guide the victims accordingly. This is especially so because S.81 of IT Act 2000 (amended in 2008) empowers the affected persons to seek help of other provisions by stating that

> The provisions of this Act shall have effect notwithstanding anything inconsistent therewith contained in any other law for the time being in force. Provided that nothing contained in this Act shall restrict any person from exercising any right conferred under the Copyright Act 1957 or the Patents Act 1970.

Similarly, it must also be ensured that complete confidentiality to the identity of the victim is maintained through out pre-trial, prosecution and sentencing stages. In case the victim is a minor girl, the prosecution must follow relevant provisions from POCSO Act, especially as has been stated in Chapters VI (procedure for recording statement of the child), VII (provisions for special courts) and VIII (procedure and powers of the special courts in recording evidence and other matters in prosecution). Along with it, both the police and courts must give total consideration to S.23 of the POCSO Act which speaks about the procedure for media along with S.228A of the IPC (disclosure of the identity of the victim of certain offences and so on).[42]

While the discussion speaks about criminal prosecution, the victim may also avail civil remedy as has been stated in Chapter IX in the IT Act. S.43 of the IT Act speaks about penalty and compensation for damage to the computer, computer system, network, data and so on. A minute analysis of this section may show that if any victim suffers any

---

[42] S.228(A) IPC says,

(1) Whoever prints or publishes the name or any matter which may make known the identity of any person against whom an offence under section 376, section 376A, section 376B, section 376C or section 376D is alleged or found to have been committed (hereafter in this section referred to as the victim) shall be punished with imprisonment of either description for a term which may extend to two years and shall also be liable to fine.

(2) Nothing in subsection (1) extends to any printing or publication of the name or any matter which may make known the identity of the victim if such printing or publication is,

(a) by or under the order in writing of the officer-in-charge of the police station or the police officer making the investigation into

sort of victimisation due to illegal and unauthorised access to data, as may happen in cases of email hacking, social media profile hacking, computer or smartphone, tablet and so on devices hacking and misuse of the data stored therein, including personal information, sensitive personal information, personal photos, videos and so on. The victim can avail this provision for filing a case before the adjudicating officer.[43] It needs to be remembered that while availing this provision, the victim/complainant steps into the shoes of the civil suit litigator and may expect compensation for the damages but not any criminal proceedings against the harasser unless the adjudicator so decides or the case situation so demands. As S.46 of the IT Act states any official of the

---

such offence acting in good faith for the purposes of such investigation; or
- (b) by, or with the authorisation in writing of, the victim; or
- (c) where the victim is dead or minor or of unsound mind, by, or with the authorisation in writing of, the next of kin of the victim: Provided that no such authorisation shall be given by the next of kin to anybody other than the chairman or the secretary, by whatever name called, of any recognised welfare institution or organisation. Explanation—for the purposes of this subsection, 'recognised welfare institution or organisation' means a social welfare institution or organisation recognised in this behalf by the Central or State Government.

(3) Whoever prints or publishes any matter in relation to any proceeding before a court with respect to an offence referred to in subsection (1) without the previous permission of such Court shall be punished with imprisonment of either description for a term which may extend to two years and shall also be liable to fine. Explanation—the printing or publication of the judgment of any High Court or the Supreme Court does not amount to an offence within the meaning of this section.

[43] S.46 of the IT Act, 2000 (amended in 2008) speaks about adjudicating officer. The section titled as 'power to adjudicate' states as (1) For the purpose of adjudging under this Chapter whether any person has committed a contravention of any of the provisions of this Act or of any rule, regulation, direction or order made there under which renders him liable to pay penalty or compensation, the Central Government shall, subject to the provisions of subsection (3), appoint any officer not below the rank of a Director to the Government of India or an equivalent officer of a State Government to be an adjudicating officer for holding an inquiry in the manner prescribed by the Central Government (amended vide ITAA 2008).

rank of director, including the state IT secretary, may also be appointed as adjudicator.[44] Nonetheless, there are several instances of very good judgements by the adjudicating officers, especially regarding infringing of privacy. The most mentionable are those of Vinod Kaushik v. Madhvi Joshi, and Nirmalkumar Bagherwal v. Minal Bagherwal, both decided by Shri Rajesh Aggarwal, Adjudicating Officer, ex-officio Secretary, IT Government of Maharashtra on 10 October 2011 and 26 August 2013 respectively. Both these cases involved privacy infringement by the respondent women by way of unauthorisedly accessing emails, chat sessions, bank documents and so on for separate cases of matrimonial cases. Both these cases were decided in the favour of petitioners, setting

(1A) The adjudicating officer appointed under subsection (1) shall exercise jurisdiction to adjudicate matters in which the claim for injury or damage does not exceed rupees five crore. Provided that the jurisdiction in respect of claim for injury or damage exceeding rupees five crore shall vest with the competent court (inserted Vide ITAA 2008).

(2) The adjudicating officer shall, after giving the person referred to in subsection (1) a reasonable opportunity for making representation in the matter and if, on such inquiry, he is satisfied that the person has committed the contravention, he may impose such penalty as he thinks fit in accordance with the provisions of that section.

(3) No person shall be appointed as an adjudicating officer unless he possesses such experience in the field of Information Technology and Legal or Judicial experience as may be prescribed by the Central Government.

(4) Where more than one adjudicating officers are appointed, the Central Government shall specify by order the matters and places with respect to which such officers shall exercise their jurisdiction.

(5) Every adjudicating officer shall have the powers of a civil court which are conferred on the Cyber Appellate Tribunal under subsection (2) of section 58, and

(a) All proceedings before it shall be deemed to be judicial proceedings within the meaning of sections 193 and 228 of the Indian Penal Code;

(b) Shall be deemed to be a civil court for the purposes of sections 345 and 346 of the Code of Criminal Procedure, 1973.

(c) Shall be deemed to be a Civil Court for purposes of order XXI of the Civil Procedure Code, 1908.

[44] See https://it.maharashtra.gov.in/1130/Filing-Complaints-under-IT-Act

up landmark judgements in regard to spouse's right to infringe the digital privacy of the other spouse.[45]

It may be pointed out that in the United States, academicians, lawyers and activists are working on 'cyber civil rights'[46] especially for cases of online defamation, revenge porn, harassment and so on targeting women. According to Professor Danielle Citron, one of the foremost advocates for cyber civil rights, if women victims avail this opportunity, they may not only forego exhausting, time-consuming criminal prosecutions but can also avail compensation for their reputation damage, which may have been caused by vandalising their reputation in the cyber space. She opines that due to reputation damage, many women may face the loss of the job or unwanted disciplinary actions by the educational or work institutes. Compensation availed from cyber civil right cases may help the victim to not only heal the psychological trauma but also regain lost monetary position to a certain extent. While preparing this manuscript, we did not find any information regarding any case filed by women victims under Chapter IX of the IT Act which deals with the penalty, compensation and adjudication related issues. It is further necessary to point out that the victim can not only bring cases against the harasser but also against companies or body corporates who are contractually or ethically liable to secure personal information of the victim as per S.43A of the IT Act.[47] The adjudicating officer when dealing with cases under this chapter, can exercise his power for damages up to ₹50,000,000 as per S.46 of the Act, and he has to consider three main factors for decision-making including (a) the amount of gain of unfair advantage, wherever quantifiable, made as a result of the default; (b) the amount of loss caused to any person as a result of the default and (c) the repetitive nature of the default

---

[45] Detailed discussions about these judgments may be found at Bhairav Acharya (2013), 'An Analysis of the Cases Filed under Section 46 of the Information Technology Act, 2000 for Adjudication in the State of Maharashtra', published on 30 September 2013. Available at http://cis-india.org/internet-governance/blog/analysis-of-cases-filed-under-sec-48-it-act-for-adjudication-maharashtra (Accessed on 02 February 2015).

[46] See Citron (2014), Hate crimes in the cyber space.

[47] 43A. Compensation for failure to protect data: Where a body corporate, possessing, dealing or handling any sensitive personal data or information in a computer resource which it owns, controls or operates, is negligent in implementing and maintaining reasonable security practices and procedures and thereby causes wrongful loss or wrongful gain to any person, such body corporate shall be liable to pay damages by way of compensation, not exceeding five crore rupees, to the person so affected. (Change vide ITAA 2008)

(S.47 of the IT Act). However, S.45 provides another solace to prospective victims by stating that

> [W]hoever contravenes any rules or regulations made under this Act, for the contravention of which no penalty has been separately provided, shall be liable to pay a compensation not exceeding twenty-five thousand rupees to the person affected by such contravention or a penalty not exceeding twenty-five thousand rupees.

This actually extends the provision for all offences that are recognised under Chapter XI as well. Hence, we feel that women victims who are victimised due to hacking and harassment or circulation of derogatory information sort of offences may be benefited by this chapter. We strongly support initiation of similar movement like that of cyber civil rights in the United States for women in India.

Conclusion

It needs to be noted that both the victim and the criminal justice machinery needs to take immediate note of the victimisation. This is because the intermediaries may retain the information regarding session logs and so on for a fixed period only. In this regard, S.69C of the IT Act (preservation and retention of information by intermediaries) states that intermediary shall preserve and retain such information as may be specified for such

---

Explanation: For the purposes of this section:

(i) 'body corporate' means any company and includes a firm, sole proprietorship or other association of individuals engaged in commercial or professional activities

(ii) 'reasonable security practices and procedures' means security practices and procedures designed to protect such information from unauthorised access, damage, use, modification, disclosure or impairment, as may be specified in an agreement between the parties or as may be specified in any law for the time being in force and in the absence of such agreement or any law, such reasonable security practices and procedures, as may be prescribed by the Central Government in consultation with such professional bodies or associations as it may deem fit.

(iii) 'sensitive personal data or information' means such personal information as may be prescribed by the Central Government in consultation with such professional bodies or associations as it may deem fit.

duration and in such manner and format as the Central Government may prescribe. Subsection (2) states any intermediary who intentionally or knowingly contravenes the provisions of subsection (1) shall be punished with an imprisonment for a term which may extend to three years and shall also be liable to fine. In practice, we have seen that if the victim delays the reporting or the police delays in their initial investigation, the intermediaries may not cooperate owing to the delay in time. It is only when police approaches the intermediaries within a time period (in general one week to three months), that this provision can be attracted to attach liability to the intermediary. But how far these theoretical provisions are actually beneficial to women victims in practice? It must be remembered that unless there is a general sensitisation about the gravity of the issues and availability of the legal remedial measures, no victim, especially women and their families, may feel confident about reporting the cases. Victims, police, lawyers and judges must also be aware of the utility and scope of S.77A of the IT Act, 2000 (amended in 2008) which speaks about compounding of offences. This provision states that

(1) A Court of competent jurisdiction may compound offences other than offences for which the punishment for life or imprisonment for a term exceeding three years has been provided under this Act. Provided that the Court shall not compound such offence where the accused is by reason of his previous conviction, liable to either enhanced punishment or to a punishment of a different kind. Provided further that the Court shall not compound any offence where such offence affects the socio-economic conditions of the country or has been committed against a child below the age of 18 years or a woman.

(2) The person accused of an offence under this act may file an application for compounding in the court in which offence is pending for trial and the provisions of section 265 B and 265 C of Code of Criminal Procedures, 1973 shall apply.

The modern understanding of plea bargaining may start with the application of this provision. But the courts must assure that victim gets due justice and simultaneously the accused understands his mistake and participates in restorating justice for the victim by effective sentencing method which may include payment of compensation or any other sentencing as per the traditional penal laws as well as S.77 of the IT Act, including directing the accused to take efforts to undo the wrong by approaching each website himself and removing the contents and thereby repairing harm caused to the reputation of the victim. S.77 of the

IT Act speaks about compensation, penalties, confiscation and so on and states that, 'No compensation awarded, penalty imposed or confiscation made under this Act shall prevent the award of compensation or imposition of any other penalty or punishment under any other law for the time being in force.'

We feel if these observations are taken note of by the government and the courts, victims may be benefited immensely.

References

Citron, K. D. (2009a). Cyber civil rights. *Boston University Law Review, 89*(61), 69–75.

———. (2009b). Law's expressive value in combating cyber gender harassment. *Michigan Law Review, 108*, 373–415.

Citron, K. D. (2014). *Hate crimes in cyber space.* Harvard University Press.

Halder, D., & Jaishankar K. (2008). Cyber crimes against women in India: Problems, perspectives and solutions. *TMC Academy Journal, 3*(1), 48–62.

———. (2010). Cyber victimization in India: A baseline survey report. Tirunelveli, India: Centre for Cyber Victim Counselling. Available at http://www.cybervictims.org/CCVCresearchreport2010.pdf (Accessed on 12 February 2016).

———. (2011a). Cyber gender harassment and secondary victimization: A comparative analysis of US, UK and India. *Victims and Offenders, 6*(4), 386–398.

———. (June 2011b). *Cyber crime and the victimization of women: Laws, rights, and regulations.* Hershey, PA: IGI Global.

———. (2015). Irrational coping theory and positive criminology: A frame work to protect victims of cyber crime. In N. Ronel & D. Segev (Eds), *Positive criminology* (pp. 276–291). Abingdon, Oxon: Routledge.

Jewkes, Y. (2010). Public policing and internet crime. In Y. Jewkes & M. Yar (Eds.), *Handbook of Internet crime* (pp. 525–545). Cullompton: Willan Publishers.

9

Combating of the Offences

When we speak about offences, discussions on combating the offences becomes necessary. In cases of cyber crimes targeting women and girls, it becomes even more necessary since in India neither the victims nor the criminal justice machinery, especially the police, may be fully aware about the nature of the offences or ways to deal with it or guiding the victims for justice. Combating of cyber crimes targeting women, transgender women and girls can be done in three different ways.

Sensitisation

We are aware of the fact that many schools, colleges and universities are regularly conducting awareness programmes on cyber crimes targeting individuals especially women and girls. While this initiative is welcome, we feel such initiatives must be encouraged further. Teachers, parents, students and stakeholders dealing with cyber crimes, including lawyers, police and NGOs, must come forward to create a massive awareness in this regard. In such sensitisation programmes, district legal service authorities (DLSA) and national legal service authorities (NALSA) must also be included.[1] Given the fact that organisations such as DLSAs and NALSA

---

[1] The lead author as a former panel advocate to DLSA, Tirunelveli regularly took part in awareness meetings arranged by DLSA Tirunelveli to spread awareness about cyber crimes among students, youth and individuals in urban and rural areas.

may have more authority to initiate widespread awareness through legal aid camps, we feel such organisations must be utilised for this cause. Further, sensitisation programmes must be differently planned according to the maturity of the groups to whom the awareness programme is targeted. The lead author has proposed unique model policy guidelines (Halder, 2015a). This proposed model policy guideline is as follows.

Model Policy Guidelines for Directing Students for Positive Use of Internet Including Social Networking Sites and WhatsApp

Objectives and missions of the policy guidelines: To protect children from the adversities of internet and educating them on the positive use of internet and social networking sites.

Scope of the policy guidelines: It may be used to educate children from Standard I to Class XII. It may also be used to provide guidance for teachers and counsellors to help children for positive usage of internet and social networking sites.

The guidelines:

1. Every school must encourage children to participate in debates or discussions on internet rights and positive and negative effects of the same. This may be made as a part of the subject of computer science, or as a part of co-curricular activities.
2. Junior students (from the age group of 4 to 8) must be encouraged to take part in awareness building sessions. In such sessions, the students may be shown how to handle the devices properly and why not to switch on devices without parent's supervision or permission. For this purpose the schools can consider making small skits with the help of older children and the teachers, or use movie clippings or other audio-visual learning materials.
3. Students from the age group of 8 to 13 must be encouraged to attend awareness sessions where they may be taught how to use the internet for positive gain. Given the fact that many study materials and books provide internet links or pages on specific subjects, the students must be encouraged to open such sites in the presence of the teachers. Parent–teacher–student sessions must be organised to sensitise parents about the positive use of internet and digital communication technology. Students may be

introduced to issues such as grooming by paedophiles, values of good talk and bad talk on the internet and so on. Students must be slowly introduced to social networking sites. It is not necessary to direct the students to open their accounts. But the students may be asked to take part in discussions on the policy guidelines or terms and conditions that are offered by social networking sites, email service providers and so on, and then create their own accounts in the social networking sites.

4. Students from the age group of 14 to17 may be encouraged to open accounts in the social networking sites and add their parents and teachers in their friend circles. They should be encouraged to create their own safety rules privacy rules and discuss about them with younger students in class debates or awareness sessions. Students should also be encouraged to access informative pages in the social networking sites for gaining more knowledge.

5. It is important to teach students about rational coping mechanisms if and when they accidentally fall victims of cyber crimes. They must be taught how to use the safety tools to protect themselves, when and how to contact the principals, teachers and parents.

6. Schools must arrange for workshops on guiding students for positive usage of internet, which may include sessions on copyright violations. In such workshops, students may be encouraged to express their thoughts. The workshops may be conducted with the police personnel, cyber crime experts, and NGOs as resource persons.

7. Senior students (from the age group of 16 to18) must be encouraged to create their own blog or vlog sites either on their own or as group effort to showcase positive usage of internet.

Similarly, there should be separate set of guidelines for creating awareness among the youth who may be better equipped with devices and have basic knowledge about cyber crimes. In such programmes emphasise must be given to what constitutes offence and why. Further, NGOs as well as DLSAs or NALSA or district police headquarters or National Commission for women may also arrange for sensitisation programmes for police who would deal with cyber crimes targeting women. In such training programmes these authorities can arrange for expert resource persons from NGOs, universities, courts and from the police itself who have experience in dealing with such issues. We have seen that police officers may need to be made more aware about recent developments in laws, the procedure to collect the evidences, victimological aspects of dealing with the victims and therapeutic jurisprudential values of retributive and restorative laws. This can be done by arranging for periodic training sessions.

Development of Laws, Analysis of the Effects of Laws and Guidance to the Victims and Offenders

The second part of combating offences is to consider the policy-making aspects. We understand that there are huge developments that have taken place in India in the late 2000s, but still, existing laws are not fully equipped to deal with the issue; many offences such as revenge porn or grooming still remain unrecognised in India. We propose to bring a new law which should be solely made for dealing with cyber crimes and should not be expanded to cover non-criminal aspects like what the IT Act does. In this relation, mention must be made about earlier proposal for a model charter for preventing online victimisation of women (Halder & Jaishankar, pp 223–228). (See Annexure.) This must be considered for framing a focussed law from the Indian perspective. Further, issues including victim protection and privacy of the victims must also be properly established by law makers. Provisions available for sexual offence victims must be expanded to cyber crime victims as well. This will ensure confidentiality and help the victims to have trust in the law and justice machinery. Along with this, proper consideration must be given for safety of transgender women. Proper recognition of their rights must be extended to cover right against abuse on the internet as well as in the hands of crime and justice machinery since they are often abused by the police when they make complaints regarding online victimisation. Along with it, police officers and lawyers must also be sensitised regarding the ill effects of victim blaming. It needs to be understood that victims may not intentionally invite trouble for themselves. Interrogation and counselling must be carried out with thorough consideration to such points. As has been mentioned in the chapters in this book, each law that are now in use to combat the crimes, have retributive as well as restorative aspects. Lawyers and officers dealing with cyber crimes, victims and offenders must refer to these aspects while preparing case details or communicating with the victims and offenders. Many victims may not want to proceed with court cases. But they need to be made to understand that they have the right to claim compensation for the damage done to them by the offenders. This cannot be availed unless the victim is cooperating with the lawyers, the police, the adjudicating officers or the courts.

For instance, the IT Act under chapter IX lays down provisions for residual penalty which is of civil nature and under chapter XI lays down criminal penalties for several provisions for various offences. While provisions under chapter IX prescribes direct payment of compensation for the damages done to the victim, the latter prescribes jail term as well as payment of fines by the offenders. In case the offender is indicted and fined along with an imprisonment term, the victims may claim compensation for the crimes done to them under various regional victims compensation schemes such as the Tamil Nadu Victim Compensation Scheme, which actually stem out from S.357A of Criminal Procedure Code (CrPC), which provides for creation of victim compensation fund from the fines payable by the offenders and donations by philanthropists. As the cyber civil right campaigners like Professor Danelle Citron in the US have expressed, such compensation may help the victims to regain the monetary loss that may have been caused due to sudden job loss because of the cyber victimisation done to her; it may also help them to regain confidence in the law and justice machinery of the country, which may prevent victims like her from taking up irrational coping mechanisms (Halder & Jaishankar, 2015).

Further, we have noted that there were huge debates regarding government decision on banning porn sites as a safeguard for youth and children. The lead author in her blog 'the great debate on porn ban: my views' (Halder, 2015b) expressed her opinion and concern in this regard[2] It needs to be mentioned that India probably has the world's first civilisation where watching erotica or creating erotica by way of sculptures and documenting about erotica were considered absolutely legal. But neither Kamasutra, the ancient book on erotica, nor any erotic sculpture advocate the abuse of any living being including men, women and children for driving sexual pleasure. With the advent of time and technology, human psychology in regard to consumption of erotica faced a drastic change. With colonial rules, came the period where slaves were used in inhuman ways for deriving sexual pleasure. We have documented some of such incidences (Halder & Jaishankar, 2014). With this, the historians, sociologists, legal researchers and criminologists could frame up how human being were abused for sexual pleasure, which were ethical and legal for some and unethical and illegal for many. Then came the era of cinemas and televisions and the production/distribution of the erotica contents became even easier. There were cinemas with 'A' signs, which were produced only to cater the needs of adults. But in no time these movies found their ways to personal television sets where not only adults, but children also could see such erotica, of course secretly. The point to be noted here is, after several attempts, none could ban the production and distribution of such films. On the other hand, several stakeholders started realising that awareness creation among parents and children may yield better results, to make them understand why such contents should not be consumed for home viewing purpose, especially when there are growing children around. But could this actually stop children from becoming over matured in regard to understanding sex-related issues in the pre-internet era?

Many adolescent children secretly enjoyed book, movies and so on, which were meant for adults, just the way their elders did. This is because children's inquisitiveness regarding sex was suppressed right at the time when they should have been told about this by teachers or elders. Then came the internet era. One of the worst forms of violence against women took place in the cyber space when women were abused to create erotica contents for the porn markets. Children were spared neither. But because children need more care and protection, their cause was highlighted more. Some of the websites did cater to child porn materials with children as actors. The stakeholders who wanted to bring a blanket ban on porn sites not only wanted to emphasise upon the fact that child actors may be abused for creation of such contents, but also that such porn contents may encourage others including adults and children to take up similar measures to abuse other children. Laws were created in both IT Act (S.67B) and as well as Protection of Children from Sexual Offences Act (POCSO) (S.13), whereby such creation and distribution and also consumption were prohibited. These laws actually extended their scopes to the websites hosting such contents. However, the websites are already armed with their own due diligence policies, which stem out from US laws.

Also in India websites were given an advantageous position whereby their own mechanism can detect the illegal contents, remove it from public viewing and block the uploader from uploading any such content again. Only when the websites fail to take note of the reports of the victimisation and the offensive contents as reported by the victims following the reporting/take down policy guidelines, or when in spite of the take down request or request for revealing the identity of the offender made by the police and the courts, the websites fail to take down the contents or cooperate with the police or the courts, that the websites can no longer claim for exemption from the liability (S.79 IT Act). In this regard several rules are also created as intermediary guidelines. But adults were also given consideration while creating laws against porn or obscenity. S.67 of the IT Act 2000 (amended in 2008) prohibits creating, publishing, or distributing obscene materials in the electronic form, and S.67A prohibits publishing and distributing sexually explicit materials in the electronic media. It must be noted that when we speak about adults, no law recognises the term 'pornography' as an offence or part of any offence. There is no legal definition as such of the term. What does it mean then? Is creating, distributing, and producing pornography legal? Are the websites who are created solely for the purpose of catering pornography legal? Is watching pornography legal? No! It may not be legal when pornography is understood in the meaning of sexually explicit object. It is neither legal when the content so created involves other privacy issues including voyeurism, revenge porn, sextortion and so on.

Some of the Indian laws do recognise the earlier mentioned issues, some remain unrecognised. The question is, are consumers/viewers and the websites liable for consuming/catering such contents as adult porn materials? It is interesting to note that if the content is erotica, it does not fall within the category of Ss. 292 IPC (sale of obscene books, pamphlets and so on), 354C IPC (voyeurism), 66E (violation of privacy), 67 and 67A, 67B of the IT Act, 2000 (amended in 2008). As the Supreme Court has observed, the viewers are not responsible when they view these contents in private. But yes, viewers may be liable only when it amounts to sexual harassment within the meaning of various laws in India including Sexual Harassment of Women at Workplace (Prevention, Prohibition and Redressal) Act, 2013; it may also amount to an offence if the viewer forces the partner or spouse to watch the same against his/her wish. Of course, in the latter situation, the burden of proof lies much upon the complainant if he/she wants to establish the fact that such activities were done in a course of mental torture and domestic violence to the spouse. It must be noted that the websites are not responsible if they have observed due diligence.

But then how should we manage the huge growth of porn industry which is largely dependent upon the contributors of home-made porn and consumers? We feel here comes the question of society's and not the court's or the government's lone responsibility. Thousands of porn contents are fed in the websites every minute. These sites include exclusive adult sites, social media such as Facebook, YouTube and so on and also mobile messaging services such as WhatsApp. When we speak about amateur porn contents, we may note that majority of such contents are actually voyeur porn, revenge porn and sexted contents which got leaked due to various reasons. When an adult prefers to watch porn content, he would definitely not know whether the same is a legal content or an illegal content. Just because the content is catered through adult sites, the content may not become offensive. Similarly, just because the content is catered through social media such as Facebook or YouTube, it may not become a legal content.

Consider the gang rape videos. It does not make it legal to watch or circulate such videos just because they are circulated to identify the accused. Even if the victim is not shown, the video harms the privacy of the victim in the same fashion as it may do if it would have shown the victim. In that case, can the government block Facebook or YouTube or WhatsApp because such videos were circulated through them? They cannot. There is a procedure to make the websites take down these contents. Further, what would be the effect of banning if only Indian viewers in India would be barred from viewing some contents but contributors staying abroad can upload revenge porn, voyeur videos from foreign IP addresses? Would that not be more victimising for victims whose privacy has been violated? Such contributors would not be able to show such contents to Indian viewers, but the contents can be visible anywhere else in the world. In such cases, how would the victim be able to prove the case if he/she is provided only with the link and that does not work within Indian jurisdiction? We need to understand that all over the world, police still needs sensitisation to deal with cyber crimes, especially against women and in such cases the victims are bound to face secondary harassment in the hands of police as well. By saying this we argue that websites as organisations must share the social responsibility to stop victimisation of women, men and children.

Websites thrive in the market because of its contributors and consumers. It is only when that the websites take a strong note on contribution of contents which are violative of laws as well as privacy of individuals that the illegal contribution may be brought down. Coming to the consumption, it would be wrong to say that all consumers of porn contents are perverts. Porn contents may be used as sexual stimuli and this factor has been noted by medical researchers especially in sexology, reproduction science and so on. But such stimuli should be used for healthy sexual relationships and purposes, not for violating rights. We completely agree with the view that porn contents do affect youth who get indulged in rape or sexual molestation just to experience direct pleasure from similar situations in real life. Who are responsible for letting the youth consume such contents for unhealthy reasons? Definitely the elders, the teachers who never explained them about sex education and basic guidelines to respect the privacy of women, men and children in schools and homes, and the peers who seek to share the forbidden pleasure. We need to understand that blanket ban on porn sites would never be effective to stop victimisation of women, men and children either in real life or in cyber space. Instead of blanket ban or blocking the traffic for certain websites to all the broadband network consumers, the government should consider taking up policies to detect the rackets that are spreading such contents to the websites, the faulty websites who are failing in practicing due diligence and of course to train the criminal justice organisation to be able to handle reports of victimisation within the shortest time. We need to understand that porn contents are spread not only through adult websites, but also through every day accessible mechanisms such as WhatsApp or even a simple MMS. That is because the contents may be stored in the personal devices and law cannot enable any official to screen every device to detect whether porn contents are stored and what types of contents are stored. This would again bring debates about government surveillance and privacy. Truly, you cannot shoot the messenger, but can declare war against the devils that use the messenger for destructing peace.

Also, we very much support the prospect of bringing 'Right to forget' sort of guidelines/laws for the intermediaries. The victims must be guided properly to approach the available mechanism including the report abuse mechanism of the websites, complaint to the police and also taking up court procedures to erase the unwanted data from the search engines and websites that may be used for victimisation. Further, we strongly suggest that there should be a separate court system to deal with cyber crimes including cyber crimes against women. This court may be created on the similar principles as special courts under POCSO Act are created. We understand that presently the few reported cases are being dealt with by mahila courts. However, we suggest that if special courts with powers to handle cyber offences (within the meaning of IT Act read with provisions from Indian Penal Code, especially those introduced vide Criminal Law Amendment Act, 2013), including those against women may be given this responsibility, the victims could be benefitted more. We hope if such measures are followed for combating offences of online victimisation of women, transgender women and girls, then the victims would be motivated to report and also the rate of crimes against women online may come down.

References

Halder, D. (2015a). Children of internet era: A critical analysis of vulnerability of children in the darker sides of social media and WhatsApp. Published in the Conference Proceedings on Accompanying Social Networking in Teacher Education, (6 March and 27 March). Loyola College of Education, Chennai, pp. 17–24.

———. (2015b). The great debate on porn ban: My views, 12th August 2015. Published in http://debaraticyberspace.blogspot.com

Glossary

Charge sheet	Document prepared by the police on the basis of other relevant documents and evidences including First Information Report and so on, showing name/s of the accused/s and the victim/s, charges of the accused as per the law, victim's statement/s and so on, which is submitted to the court along with other documents and substantial evidences and by the police for enabling the judge to take decision regarding the offence.
Children's court	Special courts constituted under special Acts, like POCSO Act and Juvenile Justice (Care and protection of children) Act, 2000 (amended in 2006 and again in 2016), to deal with crimes against children. Such courts are headed by judicial magistrates of the rank of additional session judges, however, in some cases, session courts may also be designated as children's courts.
Cognizable offence	Offences categorised by the Criminal Procedure Code of India, where police can take-up preliminary investigation and subsequently arrest the accused by taking cognizance of the case themselves.
Cyber bullying	Using harsh, rude, humiliating words through digital communication technology or internet communication technology to insult or annoy other/s.
Cyber child porn	Pornographic materials created using children or pornographic materials produced, distributed for paedophilic purposes.
Cyber crime cells	Particular departments/cell in the police offices which handles cyber crime related cases.

Cyber crime	Crimes committed through or with the help of computer, internet, internet communication technology, digital communication technology targeting the State, Corporate or individual/s or groups of individuals.
Cyber Pornography	Digital materials depicting textual or still or audio–visual images which are sexually arousing contents in nature.
Decryption	Method of converting the encrypted data back to its original textual form.
Encryption	It is a term used in cryptography to denote a specific way of encoding of messages or information which is revealed in its true form and meaning only to the authorised parties who have authorities to access the said data.
Fake avatar	Creating profiles on social media impersonating the victim to give a wrong picture about the victim and to damage the reputation of the victim.
Hacking	Unauthorised access to another person's computer, digital data and so on.
Mahila courts	Courts constituted under special Acts to deal with all sorts of crimes against women speedily in India. Such courts are headed by judicial magistrates of the rank of additional session judges.
No contact order	Orders passed by the courts preventing the accused/harasser/perpetrator from contacting the victim/complainant by any mean, including phone calls, internet communication or physical meeting. However, unlike countries like US, Canada or UK, such orders are not yet available in India in cases related to cyber crime against women in India.
Obscenity	Act which is prurient in nature and corrupts minds.
Online grooming	Criminally motivated communication by perpetrators through internet communication technology/digital communication technology, with naive ICT/DCT users to gain their confidence for paedophilic purposes or for purposes for financial cheating or for online harassment or stalking of adults, especially women.

Online harassment	A combined act of cyber bullying, trolling, defaming online, stalking, threatening, creating fake avatars, infringing digital privacy by way of hacking into personal mails. Cheat messages and so on, or any one or two of the above to harass the victim/s.
Phishing	Mail, message, phone calls and so on, whereby perpetrators attempt to gain information regarding sensitive personal including financial information which may include password, username, date of birth and other banking information of the victim.
Revenge porn	An act of revenge by misusing the personal information of any individual including still/audio-visual images to create fake avatar or profile in social media including adult websites to malign the character of the victim.
Sexting	Sending sexual text messages including nude or half nude self-images through digital communication technology.
Sexually explicit materials	Materials or contents which are created with extreme sexual connotation and which are illegal in nature.
Stalking	Intentionally following someone through digital monitoring which involves persistent contact efforts including repeated phone calls, shadowing or even hacking into the email/social media profile/s, sending threatening mails/messages with intent to harm the victim.
Texting	Sending text messages which may or may not include images through digital communication technology.
Trolling	Posting harsh, insulting opinions in the comment box of any 'poster' in the social media or news media and diverting the main discussion to start verbal fights on related or unrelated issues among other commenters.

Annexure

Model Charter to Prevent Online Victimisation of Women[1]

Contents
Part I: Purpose
Part II: Definition
Part III: Proposal for Cyber Rights for Women
Part IV: Proposal for a Code of Conduct in the Cyber Space
Part V: Proposal for Promotion of Researches on Offensive Cyber Conducts Targeting

Part I: Purpose

This policy guideline may be used to prevent online victimisation of women, define various cyber offences that may happen to women online, prohibit several conducts as unethical and illegal and against the interest of women, spread awareness among men and women about cyber crimes affecting women, and encourage government reporting agencies to understand the nature of the crime and thereby help the women victims etc.

---

[1] Published in Halder, D., & Jaishankar K. (June, 2011). Cyber Crime and the Victimization of Women: Laws, Rights, and Regulations. Hershey, PA, USA: IGI Global.

Part II: Definition

These terms are defined from the female victim's perspective:

1. Hacking: For the purpose of this policy guideline, hacking may mean unauthorised access to the digital contents of another, and also includes blocking the original author of such digital contents from accessing it. The term may also cover modification of such digital contents and/or republishing the modified or altered digital contents for mischievous purposes.

2. Digital contents: For the purpose of this policy guideline, digital contents may mean any content, material, personal information, including personal photograph/images/video clippings etc. of the original owner or her family members, which are used by the original owner as her identity in the web world for the purpose professional as well as personal usage; or are created by the original owner to express her views in the web world.

3. Cyber privacy: For the purpose of this policy guideline, cyber privacy may mean 'right to be left alone' regarding any digital content owned by the original owner; and/or information about the original owner stored either in a government computer or corporate data for health, social security, professional records or monetary data.

4. Online defamation: For the purpose of these policy guidelines, online defamation may mean publication on the internet of information about any individual which the creator of such information knows to be false; and the act is done to harm the reputation of said person.
   Note: Publication in this context may mean spreading the false information about the victim to others, other than the victim.

5. Cyber bullying: For the purpose of this policy guidelines, cyber bullying may mean attacking anyone with harsh or rude words in the cyber space, including public bulletin boards, chat rooms, emails, blogs etc., and such harsh or rude words are particularly made to ridicule one's body shape, gender, physical or mental incapability, race, colour, opinion, educational background, language etc.

6. Cyber grooming: For the purpose of this section, cyber grooming may mean constant interactions/communications with any individual focusing on sexual conducts or other unethical or illegal conducts in a camouflaged manner with a purpose to misuse the

digital presence and/or identity of the respondent herself or personal information provided by her.

7. Cyber stalking: For the purpose of this policy guideline, cyber stalking may mean monitoring the internet activity of any individual, finding out the peers of the victim with whom she interacts the most, mailing or messaging either her or her peers with threatening/abusive/defamatory contents or invading in her personal cyber space and creating a fear factor in her.

8. Cyber harassment: For the purpose of this policy guidelines, cyber harassments may mean and include sending unwanted mails to one's inbox, forcefully including one's id for chatting, sending abusive/harassing/teasing/bullying mails/messages, cyber stalking, invasion of cyber privacy, spreading hate propaganda, defamatory information about the victim to others in the web world, unauthorised using digital identity and digital contents of one individual for the purpose of adult entertaining etc.

9. Cyber blackmailing: Cyber blackmailing may mean and include sending mails/messages to one's inbox with threatening words, asking the recipient to obey the demands of the sender, or otherwise of which the sender promises to reveal her private information/portray her in false manner/do harm to her reputation etc.

10. Forced pornography: For the purpose of this policy guideline, forced pornography may mean and include publishing or using pictures of any individuals which may or may not be modified/voyeured images of one's naked body parts/video clippings of sexual activities of the individual/private residential information etc. of the individual without consent or knowledge of the said individual either in any adult entertainment site or in the open web world through any website or blog etc., with a mischievous intention to portray such individual as porn-model or sex giver; and thereby forcing the said individual against her wishes or knowledge, to be part of the adult entertainment industry or soft core pornography.

11. Cyber hate propaganda: Cyber hate propaganda may mean offensive communication between the sender and multiple recipients with intent to spread hatred against a particular individual for her opinion, race, gender etc.

12. Obscenity: Obscenity may mean any cyber communication or content which is published in the webs world and which contains images, materials, contents etc. which creates 'prurient interests'

and which is against social value system of the 'physical' place where it is downloaded and seen.

13. Offensive communications: Offensive communication may mean and include communications between the sender and the recipient/s which carries offensive contents including threatening/bullying/defamatory/obscene messages.

Part III: Proposal of Cyber Rights for Women

1. **Right to equality**: Right to equality which suggests right against any discrimination of any sort, must be acknowledged as the primary right for women in the cyber space.

2. **Right to live safely with dignity**: This right may include the following:
    (a) Right against 'forced pornography'
    (b) Right against hateful communications including defamations
    (c) Right against hacking for the purpose of sexual as well as non-sexual crimes in the cyber space
    (d) Right against stalking and following harassments
    (e) Right against being abused in all the ways as discussed above on the internet
    (f) Right against blackmailing, threatening and cheating and
    (g) Right to live safely with dignity in the real space along with a clean virtual identity.

3. **Right to speech and expression**: Women must have right to speech and expression of their views about feminism and various other subjects.

4. **Right to information in the cyber space**: This right may include right to access certain windows and right to view other websites.

5. **Right to communicate with others**: This right may mean and include right to free speech and right to choose individuals with whom the woman feels comfortable to communicate. This may also include right to block or remove unwanted individuals who tries to communicate with her against her wish.

6. **Right to make a livelihood from the cyber space and with the assistance of cyber space**: This may include right to express her views and carry on her profession for a livelihood with the aid of cyber space. However this right also includes right to be protected from being used as a trade item for pornographic websites,

obscene contents or even illegal women trafficking through internet without consent of the woman in concern.

7. **Right to have 'own space' on the internet:** This right may include right to access and create a domain, right to create email ids, blogs and also access social networking sites and create profiles etc.

8. **Right to assemble and association:** This right may include right to create any web based association, women-only forums etc.

9. **Right to privacy:** Right to privacy may mean and include right against invasions in her digital contents, private information and also private offline activities which may be published online.

10. **Right to defend self-reputation:** This right may mean right to speech and expression and also right to protect cyber privacy. This right extends to contacting the police or the cyber-crime cells or cyber security experts and or lawyers.

Part IV: Proposal for Code of Conduct in the Cyber Space

Code of conduct for internet users: For the purpose of this policy guideline, we propose a set of code conducts for male and female internet users towards safeguarding women's interest in the cyber space. These are as follows:

1. To respect other's right to privacy;
2. Restraining from indecent conducts in the cyber space;
3. Restraining from using cyber space as a verbal warfare and restraining from using abusive languages;
4. Restraining from using, modifying, republishing others contents without proper permission.

Part V: Proposal for Promotion of Research Works on Offensive Cyber Conducts Targeting Women

To meet the objectives of this policy guideline, international bodies like the United Nations, educational institutes etc. may promote research on offensive cyber conducts targeting women. This will further help to formulate the ideologies and typologies on gender sensitive victimisations in the cyber space.

Index

abusive sexual taunts, 52
adolescent sexual behaviours, 144, 146
adult bullying, 44
aggressiveness, 56, 58
Andaman Jarawa women videos, 22
Anna Mayer case, 49
anti-bullying software creators, 58
anti-sexual content software creators, 58

bad talk, 28, 29, 39, 230
Baazee.com case, 21
Bedi, Pooja, 51
blogs, 37, 49, 103, 161, 230
bullying, 47

camouflaged porn, 135
CCTV surveillance, 112
Centre for Cyber Victim Counselling, 10, 44, 52
Chamberlin, Gethin, 22
chastity, 156
cheating, 82, 162
    personation, 34
child pornography, 6, 136, 139, 148
Citron, Danielle, 11
Common Access Number (CAN), 202
communication conduits, 159, 166
Communication Decency Act, 159, 181

communicative harassment, 50
computer forensic scientists, 209
Computer Forensics Specialist, 207, 210
consensual pornography, 162
Kharak Singh v State of UP, 169
content-agnostic communication network, 158
content hosts, 160
criminal intimidation, 54
cyber bullying, 48, 52
    types, 56
cyber crimes against women
    complaint to local police station, 192
    counter victimisation, 194
    criminal justice machinery, 189
    face victimisation, 190
    hackers role, 194, 195
    online harassments, 191
    police officers experience, 193
    police role, 205
    secondary traumatisation, 190
    victims' responsibilities, 195
cyber harassment, 48
cyber obscenity, 149
cyber space, 158
cyber stalking, 55, 58, 191
    case, 21
    resultant harassment and, 162
    interpersonal privacy infringement, 102

data controllers, 78
  content hosts, 164, 166
  group-1, 164, 165
  group-2, 164
  user, 164
defamation, 38, 41, 54, 55, 67, 110, 168
defamatory speech and expression, 35
demeaning speech and expression, 32
derogatory speech and expression, 32
digital breach of privacy, 91
digital communication technology,
  3, 11
Digital Millennium Copy Right Act,
  161, 167, 181
digital telecommunication system, 157
district legal service authorities
  (DLSA), 228
domestic violence, 47, 105, 163, 234
dual victimisation, 41

ethical hacker, 195
European Union Convention on
  Cybercrime, 2001, 6
eve teasing, 34, 47

Facebook, 160
fake avatars, 16, 102, 153, 156, 170
fantasising killing, 27
First Amendment of US constitution,
  167
Fleischer, Peter, 157, 168
Forensic Science Laboratory, 209
freedom of speech, 157
free speech and expression, 161

GoDaddy.com, 160
Google
  content hosts, 160
  free speech and content policy, 58
  Page Rank, 166
  people finder interchange format
    (PFIF), 163
Goonda's Act, 148

government surveillance, privacy
  infringement, 111
Grievance Officer, 172

hackers, cyber crimes against women,
  194, 195
hard core pornography, 149
hate wave, 68
honour killing, 91
hurling insulting, 49

Idea Cellular advertisement, 5
Indecent Representation of Women
  (Prohibition) Act, 33, 199
Indian laws, liability of intermediaries,
  171
Indian Penal code, 11, 12, 31, 33, 46,
  54, 150, 192, 201
India's first cyber stalking case, 21
Information Technology Act, 2000,
  46, 158, 159, 171, 178, 183
Information Technology
  (intermediary guidelines) Rules,
  2011, 174, 180
information warehouses, 162
internet, 24
  model policy guidelines, 229
  interpersonal conflicts, 55
  interpersonal privacy infringement
    cyberstalking, 102
    fake avatars creation, 102
    revenge pornography, 104
    unauthorised access, 93
ITAA 2008, 184

Juvenile Justice Care and Protection
  Act, 199

labelling and photographing, cyber
  crimes, 210
legal debates, 166
liabilities, 157
  of search engines, 166

protection of privacy, 174
types of, 159

misleading speech and expression, 34
modesty, 156
lowering speech and expression,
32
morality, 37, 38, 66, 152, 155, 156
moral policing group, 53

narcissism, 58
national legal service authorities
(NALSA), 228
nonconsensual pornography, 105
nude photo scandal, 109

obscene speech, 30
offensive behaviour, 55
offensive speech and expressions in
internet
bad talk, 28
criteria, 26
effect on women and girls, 36
online victimisation, 28
patterns of, 29
principles, 27
rights to, 26
offline abuse, 136
OLX.in, 160
online defamation, 191
online gender bullying
adult bullying, 44
causes and effect, 56
computer mediated communication
system, 45
effects, 59
gay relationship and marriage, 45
law makers, 43
nature of, 44
seriousness, 43
trans-women, 60
women and trans-women in India,
profile of, 47

online grooming, 55
anti-stalking law, 76
challenges and regulation, 83
cyber grooming, 76
cyber stalking, 76
data controllers, women and girls,
78
dating sites and, 75
digital communication technology,
79
effects of, 81
job scam cases, 75
parents and children
communication gap, 80
process, 75
psychological condition, 75
sexual exploitation, 80
sexual satisfaction, victims for, 79
victims of, 80
workplace harassment, 80
online harassment, 39, 49, 155, 191
online misogyny, 155
online revenge porn, 135
online sexual gratification, 136
online victimisation, 28, 162
women, 16, 46, 165, 231

paedophilia, 162
Page Rank, 166
people finder interchange format
(PFIF), 163
phishing, 162
POCSO Act, 201, 208, 221
police role, cyber crimes against
women
bail application, 218
cyber crime cells, 208
guidelines and, 212
legal channel, 208
offence nature, 207
POCSO Act, 221
privacy and voyeurism, 208
prosecution, 219

search and seizure of digital
    evidence, 209
  trivial cases, 215
pornography, 151, 152
  child, 6
  consensual, 162
  revenge, 190
power game in online gender
    bullying, 59
power to adjudicate, 222
privacy
  protection laws, 167
  protection of, 175
  US Fourth amendment, 161
privacy infringement, 40
  breach of digital privacy, 91
  cyber crimes, 89
  definition, 90
  digital, 89
  electronic media, 90
  government surveillance, 111
  honour killing, 91
  patterns, 92, 106
  sexual gratification, 90
  unauthorised access, 90
  women and girls, 91
private sessions and gender bullying,
    51
professional designation, 164
prohibited conducts, 61
prosecution of cyber crimes, 219
Protection of Children from Sexual
    Offences Act (POCSO), 46, 199

Reding, Viviane, 168
repetitive, unwelcome and inherently
    coercive acts, 47
revenge porn, 23, 55, 104, 162
  adolescent sexual behaviours, 144
  camouflaged porn, 135
  CBSE notice, 145
  child pornography, 148
  cyber obscenity, 149

Juvenile Justice (Care and
    Protection) Act, 2000, 143
  obscenity in cyber space, 139
  online, 135
  patterns, 135
  self created child pornography, 138
  sex offender and, 139, 146
  sexting, 140
  sexual harassment, 146
  steps, 134
  teen porn, 136
Right to Information Act, 2005, 110,
    184

Safetypin.com, 163
search engines, 165
security verification, 57
seize documentation, 211
seizing agent, 212
self sexual gratification, 144
sensitisation, 228
service providers, 155
  categories of intermediaries, 159
  immunities from liabilities, 180
  Indian laws regarding intermediary
    immunity, 183
  liability, 157
sex offender, 139, 146
sex slaves, 150
sexual gratification, 90
sexual harassment, 50
Sexual Harassment of Women Act
    (2013), 31
Sexual Harassment of Women at
    Workplace (Prevention, Prohibition
    and Redressal) Act (2013), 46, 53,
    199, 234
sexually explicated speech and
    expression, 30
sexual offences, 162
social networking sites, 161, 164
social norms and orthodox values, 9
Subramaniam, Kalki, 22

teen porn, 136
telecommunication service providers, 156
Telecom Regulatory Authority of India (TRAI) website, 108
traditional bullying, 47
transgender women, 40
trans-women and gender bullying, 52
trolling, 44, 46
  targeting women in India
    anti-liberal attitude, 64
    definition, 63
    freedom of speech, 66
    frivolous posts, 63
    impact, 68
    liberal and libertarian views, 65
    personal rights, 67
    privacy settings, 63
    profiling, 62
    status messages, 63
    troll posts, 62
Twitter, 13, 22, 50, 62, 165

Ujala, WhatsApp bullying, 49
unaware criminal justice machinery, 60

victimisation
  fake avatar, creation, 55
  women, 24, 165, 198
victims and offenders
  case details preparation, 231
  child porn materials, 233
  cinemas and televisions, 232
  compensation, 232
  contributors and consumers, 235
  fines, 232
  gang rape videos, 235
  government surveillance and privacy, 236
  intermediary guideline rules, 234
  online victimisation, 231
  porn sites ban, 232
  protection and privacy, 231
  revenge porn, 231
violation of basic human rights, 155
voyeurism, 14, 234

web-hosting service providers, 158
WhatsApp harassment in India, 44
womanly propriety of behaviour, 156
Wordpress.com, 160

YouTube, 22, 140

About the Authors

Dr Debarati Halder is an Advocate and legal scholar. Currently, she is Research Officer, Unitedworld School of Law, Ahmedabad, Gujarat and Managing Director of the Centre for Cyber Victim Counselling (CCVC), India (www.cybervictims.org). She received her LLB from the University of Calcutta and her master's degree in international and constitutional law is from the University of Madras. She holds a PhD degree from the National Law School of India University (NLSIU), Bangalore, India. She has co-authored a book titled *Cyber Crime and the Victimization of Women: Laws, Rights and Regulations* (IGI Global, July 2011). She has published many articles in peer-reviewed journals and chapters in peer-reviewed books. Her work has appeared in scholarly journals, including the *British Journal of Criminology, Journal of Law and Religion, Victims and Offenders*; *Murdoch University E-Journal of Law*; *ERCES Online Quarterly Review*; *TMC Academic Journal (Singapore)*; *Temida and Indian Journal of Criminology & Criminalistics*; and edited volumes, Crimes of the Internet, Trends and Issues of Victimology, Cyber Criminology. She has presented her research works at many international conferences including the Stockholm Criminology Symposium held during 11–13 June 2012 and the International Conference on Social Media for Good, held during 15–16 May 2015 at Istanbul, Turkey. She was a resource person in various programmes conducted by the National Commission for Women, unicef, Facebook, Kerala State Commission for Protection of Child Rights, Rajiv Gandhi National Institute for Youth Development, Women Christian College (Kolkata & Chennai), Loyola College, North Eastern Police Academy, Assam State Commission for Protection of Child Rights and Manonmaniam Sundaranar University, Tirunelveli. Debarati's research interests include constitutional law, international law, victim rights, cyber crimes and laws. Email: debaratihalder@gmail.com URL: http://www.debaratihalder.org

Professor K. Jaishankar is presently the Professor of Criminology and Head of the Department of Criminology at the Raksha Shakti University (Police and Internal Security University), Ahmedabad, Gujarat, India. Prior to this present position, he served as a faculty member at the Department of Criminology and Criminal Justice, Manonmaniam Sundaranar University, Tirunelveli, Tamil Nadu, India. He has published more than hundred publications, including articles, books, book chapters, and editorials. He is the recipient of the prestigious National Academy of Sciences, India (NASI) SCOPUS Young Scientist Award 2012–Social Sciences and ISC – S. S. Srivastava Award for Excellence in Teaching and Research in Criminology. He was a Commonwealth Fellow (2009–2010) at the Centre for Criminal Justice Studies, School of Law, University of Leeds, UK, and has completed a research project on victims of cyber crimes. He is the founding Editor-in-Chief of the *International Journal of Cyber Criminology* (www.cybercrimejournal.com) and Editor-in-Chief of *International Journal of Criminal Justice Sciences* (www.ijcjs.com). He is the founding President of the South Asian Society of Criminology and Victimology (SASCV) (www.sascv.org) and founding Executive Director (Honorary) of the Centre for Cyber Victim Counselling (CCVC) (www.cybervictims.org). He was a member of the UNODC (United Nations Office of Drugs and Crime) Core Group of Experts on Identity-related Crime (2007–08). He is a member of the Membership and Advancement Committee, World Society of Victimology (WSV); International Advisory Board for the Center for the Research and Development of Positive Criminology, Department of Criminology, Bar Illan University, Israel; Advisory Board for the Center for Cybercrime Studies, John Jay College of Criminal Justice, New York, USA; the International Cybercrime Research Centre, Simon Frazer University, Vancouver, Canada; and the Scientific Commission of the International Society of Criminology (ISC). He was a Keynote Speaker at the 15th World Society of Victimology Symposium held in July 2015, at Perth, Australia, and at the 14th World Society of Victimology Symposium held in May 2012 at The Hague, The Netherlands. He was recently appointed as an International Ambassador of the British Society of Criminology (BSC). He is founder of the academic discipline, Cyber Criminology (2007), and is the proponent of the Space Transition Theory of Cyber Crimes (2008). His areas of Academic Competence are victimology, cyber criminology, crime mapping, GIS, communal violence, policing and crime prevention. Email: drjaishankar@gmail.com URL: http://www.jaishankar.org